MW01484927

RESEARCHING FORCED LABOUR
IN THE GLOBAL ECONOMY

PROCEEDINGS OF THE BRITISH ACADEMY • 220

RESEARCHING FORCED LABOUR IN THE GLOBAL ECONOMY

Methodological Challenges and Advances

Edited by
GENEVIEVE LEBARON

Published for THE BRITISH ACADEMY
by OXFORD UNIVERSITY PRESS

Oxford University Press, Great Clarendon Street, Oxford OX2 6DP

First edition published in 2018

British Library Cataloguing in Publication Data
Data available

Library of Congress Cataloging in Publication Data
Data available

Typeset by
Keystroke, Neville Lodge, Tettenhall, Wolverhampton

Printed in Great Britain by
TJ International Ltd, Padstow, Cornwall

ISBN 978-0-19-726647-2

ISSN 0068-1202

Contents

Notes on Contributors

Jean Allain is a Professor in the Faculty of Law, Monash University, Australia, and Professor of International Law at the Wilberforce Institute for the Study of Slavery and Emancipation (WISE), University of Hull, UK. He is Special Adviser to Anti-Slavery International, the world's oldest human rights organisation. His publications include the following books: *The Law and Slavery* (2015), *Slavery in International Law* (2013) and, as editor, *The Legal Understanding of Slavery* (2012).

Robert Caruana is a Professor in Business Ethics at the International Centre for Corporate Social Responsibility (ICCSR) of Nottingham University Business School. His research interests include corporate and consumer responsibility, labour exploitation, power relations and critical discourse analysis. He has published in journals such as *Organization Studies*, *Journal of Business Ethics*, *Marketing Theory*, *European Journal of Marketing* and *Annals of Tourism Research*. His most recent work explores the emergence of modern slavery as a legal category, and his current research project specifically examines corporate-public discourse around the UK Modern Slavery Act 2015.

Andrew Crane is a Professor of Business and Society and Director of the Centre for Business, Organisations and Society in the School of Management at the University of Bath. His recent work has focused on understanding the business of modern slavery and helping public, private and civil organisations develop evidence-based solutions to the problem. His books include the award-winning textbook *Business Ethics* and the *Oxford Handbook of Corporate Social Responsibility*. He has published in some of the world's leading scholarly management journals, including the *Academy of Management Review* and *Journal of Management Studies*.

Jenny Chan is Assistant Professor of Sociology at the Hong Kong Polytechnic University. Prior to joining the university, she was a Lecturer of Sociology and Contemporary China Studies at the School of Interdisciplinary Area Studies and a Junior Research Fellow at Kellogg College, University of Oxford. She serves as the Vice President (Communications) of the International Sociological Association's Research Committee on Labor Movements, as Editor of the *Global Labour Journal* and as Contributing Editor of *the Asia-Pacific Journal*.

Neil Howard is the Prize Fellow in International Development at the University of Bath. His research combines political economy and political anthropology to examine the political, economic and ideological construction of 'human trafficking', 'forced labour' and 'modern slavery'. It has been published widely, including in the *ANNALS of the American Academy of Political and Social Science*, *Development in Practice* and *International Migration*. His first book is entitled *Child Trafficking, Youth Labour Mobility and the Politics of Protection* (Palgrave Macmillan, 2016).

Genevieve LeBaron is Professor of Politics and Co-Director of the Sheffield Political Economy Research Institute (SPERI) at the University of Sheffield. She is also Co-Chair of Yale University's Modern Slavery Working Group and a UK ESRC Future Research Leaders Fellow (2016–19). Her current research focuses on the global business of forced labour and the politics and effectiveness of governance initiatives to combat it. She has held visiting positions at Yale University, the International Labour Organization, the University of California, Berkeley, and Sciences Po, Paris, and has published in some of the world's leading political science journals, including *Regulation & Governance*, *Review of International Studies* and *Review of International Political Economy*. She was ranked number 1 academic (and 38th overall) on the 2017 global Top 100 Human Trafficking and Slavery Influence Leaders List.

Samuel Okyere is an Assistant Professor of Sociology and Criminology at the University of Nottingham in the United Kingdom. His work critically interrogates policy and popular perspectives on child labour, forced labour, human trafficking, prostitution and other phenomena described by some actors as modern slavery. These and a preoccupation with the interplay between dominant liberal human/child rights discourses and social justice, power, precarity, inequality, exploitation, (un)freedom and domination under conditions of globalisation underpin his research of children's and young people's labour mobility and their involvement in artisanal mining, prostitution, commercial farming, fishing and other precarious forms of work.

Nicola Phillips is Vice President and Vice Principal (Education), and Professor of Political Economy, at King's College London. She is a former Chair of the British International Studies Association (BISA) and a past editor of the journals *New Political Economy* and *Review of International Political Economy*. She works in the field of global political economy, with interests focusing on global economic governance, inequality, and labour in global production. Between 2010 and 2013, she held a prestigious Major Research Fellowship from the Leverhulme Trust for research on forced labour and human trafficking for labour exploitation in the global economy.

Jessica R. Pliley is an Associate Professor of Women's, Gender and Sexuality History at Texas State University. She is the author of *Policing Sexuality: The Mann Act and the Making of the FBI* (Harvard University Press, 2014) and co-editor of *Global Anti-vice Activism, 1890–1950: Fighting Drink, Drugs, and 'Immorality'* (Cambridge University Press, 2016). Her articles have appeared in the *Journal of Women's History*, the *Journal of the Gilded Age and Progressive Era* and the *Journal of the History of Sexuality*. From 2017 to 2018, she has been the co-organiser of the Gilder Lehrman Center for the Study of Slavery, Resistance, and Abolition's Working Group on Modern Slavery and Trafficking at Yale University.

Joel Quirk is a Professor of Politics at the University of the Witwatersrand. His research focuses on slavery and abolition, human mobility and human rights, global governance and social movements, repairing historical wrongs, and the history and politics of sub-Saharan Africa. Recent works include *The Anti-Slavery Project* (2011), *Mobility Makes States* (2015) and *Contemporary Slavery* (2017).

Andreas Rühmkorf is a Lecturer in Commercial Law at the University of Sheffield, UK. He is the author of the monograph *Corporate Social Responsibility, Private Law and Global Supply Chains* (Edward Elgar Publishing, 2015). His recent publications include G. LeBaron and A. Rühmkorf, 'The Domestic Politics of Corporate Accountability Legislation: Struggles over the 2015 UK Modern Slavery Act', in *Socio-Economic Review* (2017) and G. LeBaron and A. Rühmkorf, 'Steering CSR through Home State Regulation: A Comparison of the Impact of the UK Bribery Act and Modern Slavery Act on Global Supply Chain Governance', *Global Policy*, 2017).

Acknowledgements

In 2015, I was fortunate to receive a British Academy Rising Star Engagement Award (BARSEA) from the British Academy for the Humanities and Social Sciences. Using funding from my award, I hosted a two-day symposium at the University of Sheffield in October 2015 titled 'Challenges in Researching the Shadow Economy: A Methods Symposium on Forced Labour'. This symposium gathered together an interdisciplinary group of scholars at the forefront of empirical research on forced labour as well as experts from the International Labour Organization and Anti-Slavery International to tackle the methodological challenges that stand in the way of building a reliable, robust and ethically sound knowledge base on the business of forced labour. The idea for this volume surfaced from these discussions, after which I held a second workshop at the British Academy in London in October 2016 to harmonise and finalise the book.

A host of friends and colleagues encouraged and supported me during the BARSEA project and this book's development. Andrew Gamble served as Fellow of the British Academy Champion for my BARSEA and my mentor for its duration; his faith in my abilities and advice on the early development of this volume were crucial for getting it off the ground. I am grateful to Nicola Phillips, Andrew Crane, Jean Allain, Tony Payne, Stephen Farrall, Jane Lister and Peter Dauvergne for their expert advice and helpful conversations. I am grateful to the Special Action Programme to Combat Forced Labour at the International Labour Organization in Geneva – particularly Beate Andrees, Jean-Marie Kagabo, Michaëlle de Cock and Caroline O'Reilly – for their involvement in my BARSEA project.

Several colleagues gave feedback on draft chapters and the volume as a whole: Amanda Berlan, Luc Fransen, Judy Fudge, James Harrison, Chun-Yi Lee, Hannah Lewis, Aidan McQuade, Jeroen Merk, Siobhan McGrath, Sverre Molland, Ben Rogaly, Zoe Trodd and Peer Zumbansen. Collectively, this project benefited from their insights and critiques.

I am indebted to the administrative staff at the University of Sheffield who supported my BARSEA workshops: Laure Astill, Gemma Bennett, Sarah Cooke, Jason Freeman, Charlotte Harden, Tom Hunt and Ann-Marie Smart. Penelope Kyritsis expertly edited each chapter in this volume and provided invaluable assistance and good cheer in drawing the final manuscript together.

As an editor, I am grateful to Yale University's Gilder Lehrman Center for the Study of Slavery, Resistance, and Abolition (GLC) for hosting me as their Human Trafficking and Modern Day Slavery Fellow in 2015–16. I conceptualised and wrote the proposal for this volume during my fellowship. Special thanks to GLC Director David Blight, who has been an inspiring mentor and offered incisive advice and encouragement throughout the project. Appreciation must also go to GLC staff David Spatz, Melissa McGrath, Tom Thurston, Michelle Zacks and visiting fellows Sophie White, Susanna Ashton and Joshua Rothman for creating such a fun and encouraging academic home during my time at Yale.

At the British Academy, I am grateful to Brigid Hamilton-Jones, Geetha Nair and James Rivington for their help and advice in assembling this volume, as well as to Christine Trieu, Jonathan Matthews, Ken Emond and Harriet Barnes for their support and encouragement throughout my BARSEA.

1

Understanding the Global Business of Forced Labour: An Introduction

GENEVIEVE LEBARON

Introduction

BY MOST ACCOUNTS, FORCED labour, human trafficking and modern slavery are proliferating rapidly in the global economy. Recent media reports – including the discovery of widespread trafficking and forced labour in Thailand's shrimp industry (Hodal *et al.* 2014), bonded labour at one of Apple's major Chinese electronics suppliers (BBC 2015), and the devastating deaths of workers constructing stadiums for Qatar's World Cup (Smith 2016) – have brought businesses' use of exploitative and illegal labour practices into the global spotlight. Amid public and consumer calls to address forced labour and hold businesses accountable, governments around the world have begun to enact legislation to combat and prevent forced labour and human trafficking in supply chains.

Yet, in spite of soaring media and policy attention, reliable research on the business of forced labour remains difficult to come by. Forced labour is notoriously challenging to investigate given that it is illegal, and powerful corporations and governments are reluctant to grant academics access to their workers and supply chains. Forced labour research is also fraught with ethical challenges, including the possibility that involving highly vulnerable workers in research could further endanger them if detected by managers. Given the risks associated with researching the business of forced labour, until very recently few scholars even attempted to collect hard or systematic data. Instead, researchers have often had little choice but to rely on poor quality second-hand data, frequently generated by civil society or industry actors with vested interests in portraying the problem in a certain light.

As a result, the evidence base on contemporary forced labour is both dangerously thin and riddled with bias. The most often-cited national-level statistics on forced labour – the Global Slavery Index produced by the advocacy group the Walk Free Foundation, widely referenced in policy initiatives to combat forced labour – were recently given a high 'Pinocchio' ranking by the *Washington Post's*

Fact Checker column, which noted that 'these guestimates remain too shaky to be cited without a healthy dose of skepticism' (Kessler 2015).[1] The credibility of large swathes of qualitative information on forced labour produced by journalists and advocacy groups has also recently been subject to criticism by scholars and commentators concerned that the scope, nature and solutions to the problem are being misrepresented as media outlets publish shock headlines to draw readers and advocacy groups compete to attract funding (O'Connell Davidson 2015; Weitzer 2014, 2015; Chuang 2014).

This knowledge deficit about forced labour has had negative consequences for both academic enquiry and policy efforts to combat severe labour exploitation in the global economy, especially with regard to the following three gaps. First, although forced labour is widely understood as a thriving phenomenon, little is known about the political economic dynamics that cause it to proliferate within countries and industries. Too often, the root causes of contemporary forced labour are attributed to the past, such as to histories of 'traditional' or 'primitive' social structures, thus obfuscating the causal role of contemporary political economic actors – from states to private companies – in facilitating the resilience and re-emergence of forced labour today.[2] Second, and relatedly, while extensive attention has been drawn towards the moral shortcomings and greed of individual perpetrators of forced labour, the question of why, when and how businesses are able to enact forced labour with impunity, and the circumstances under which it arises in contemporary markets, has been far less explored. The persistent tendency to see forced labour as a randomly occurring phenomenon enacted by a few 'bad apples' or 'unscrupulous employers' (ILO 2012) – as opposed to a coherent management strategy rooted in core features of the global political economy – means that we still know very little about the patterns of how, when and where money is made from forced labour and the circumstances under which businesses are able to profit from it, despite it being illegal in most jurisdictions. Third, the lack of hard baseline data about forced labour means that it is not currently possible to evaluate the effectiveness of public and private governance initiatives to combat the business of forced labour within countries or supply chains. This is troubling, given the immense human suffering and exploitation at stake, as well as the resources being channelled into anti-slavery measures; according to one estimate, US$1.23 billion was spent by 12 national governments on anti-slavery policy between 2003 and 2012 alone (Ucnikova 2014). Governments around the world, civil society groups and growing numbers of multinational corporations (MNCs) are enacting

---

[1] At the time of writing, the latest version of the Global Slavery Index was published in 2016; the new global estimates announced by Walk Free and the International Labour Organization for release in 2017 have not yet been published.

[2] For an overview of the problematic relation posited between past and present in scholarship on slavery, see Quirk and LeBaron (2015).

'anti-slavery' initiatives to prevent and address forced labour in supply chains. Yet, without reliable country and sector-level estimates of forced labour, and an in-depth understanding of the patterns and root causes that give rise to forced labour within industry, we have no way of knowing whether such efforts are working towards eliminating forced labour.

Some experts and human rights defenders have raised the point that the problem goes far beyond being unable to accurately assess the effectiveness of current initiatives, arguing that the poor quality of knowledge underpinning initiatives to combat severe labour exploitation means that anti-slavery and anti-trafficking initiatives are having perverse effects – sometimes causing harm to the victims they are purportedly designed to protect. Nearly a decade ago, the Global Alliance Against Traffic in Women warned that government anti-slavery and anti-trafficking measures in eight countries, including the United States and United Kingdom, were causing 'collateral damage' and were 'counter-productive for some of the very people they are supposed to benefit most directly' (Dottridge 2007: 2). Scholars have echoed these concerns, including researchers who have found that workers that have been 'liberated' from slavery and trafficking by civil society groups are likely to end up in exploitative labour conditions (Shih 2015). There is clearly an urgent need for better and independently generated information on the causes and patterns of forced labour in the global economy, as well as the effectiveness of reigning solutions.

A cutting-edge literature is making progress in responding to these gaps in knowledge by investigating how and why forced labour emerges in the contemporary global economy, as well as its business dynamics (Crane 2013; Phillips 2013; Barrientos *et al.* 2013; Fudge & Strauss 2013; Mezzadri 2016). Rather than focusing on technical questions or measures of prevalence, this body of work is focused on an in-depth investigation of the political economic dynamics of forced labour, as well as evaluating the effectiveness of existing anti-slavery and anti-trafficking interventions. This research is corroborating and adding empirical strength to some existing claims in the literature, such as that vulnerability to severe labour exploitation is fundamentally shaped by poverty, the lack of labour protections and rights, and social discrimination (Phillips 2011; O'Connell Davidson & Howard 2015). It is also challenging conventional narratives, revealing severe labour exploitation is a coherent and predictable feature of many sectors and regions of the global political economy (Crane *et al.* 2017; LeBaron *et al.* 2018; Anderson & Rogaly 2007; McGrath 2013), as opposed to an individualised and randomly occurring human rights issue perpetrated by a few wicked and greedy employers. This literature is important because it takes the political economic root causes of forced labour seriously, exploring the global relations of power, profit and poverty that both shape and give rise to severe exploitation. It is advancing theory by showing that – contrary to the expectations of many economists – the expansion of markets and globalisation appears to be fuelling forced labour rather than leading to its demise (Phillips 2011; Barrientos *et al.* 2013). However, the literature is also significant for its methodological contribution. Scholars are beginning to generate rare and robust empirical data that sheds light on the factors that create vulnerability to severe labour exploitation as well as businesses' demand for it, as they creatively navigate the obstacles inherent in researching forced labour and develop innovative methodologies.

This volume draws together contributors to this emerging wave of scholarship to tackle the core challenge of researching forced labour. It aims to push forward the study of forced labour in three key ways. First, it contributes to strengthening research methods for investigating contemporary forced labour, human trafficking and slavery. The volume includes reflections on best practices for a full range of qualitative methodologies used to study forced labour – including ethnography, discourse analysis, supply-chain mapping, interviews, participant observation and archival research – as well as on possibilities for bridging qualitative and quantitative methods. The volume seeks to benchmark recent methodological advances, chart the conceptual and practical challenges faced by researchers of forced labour in the global economy, and present reflections on how these challenges can be overcome to build a more accurate, transparent, ethical and comparable evidence base on forced labour. Second, the volume bridges distinct streams of scholarship from across the humanities and social sciences to consolidate the emerging empirical evidence base on forced labour. Because scholarship on the political economy of forced labour has tended to be fragmented across diverse academic disciplines – from management studies to anthropology – and has equally eclectic theoretical and epistemological foundations, this body of scholarship has rarely been viewed as a coherent whole. However, the scholars in this volume are united in their contention that the best pathway towards understanding the role and value of forced labour in the global economy lies in robust, in-depth and accurate research, rather than in debating abstract and outdated theoretical propositions about capitalism's purported incompatibility with unfree labour or producing catchy statistics to fuel sensationalist newspaper headlines. By drawing together this otherwise splintered body of scholarship, the volume seeks to join up empirically overlapping but hitherto disparate literatures. Finally, the volume seeks to make an empirical contribution. The chapters present rare empirical evidence that sheds light on forced labour's resilience amid the deepening and expansion of capitalist markets, presenting and discussing data from studies of forced labour within the mining, agricultural, electronics, construction, garment and other industries, across several regions of the world. These empirical contributions are both urgent and important, given the serious paucity of detailed empirical scholarship on forced labour in the global economy. Overall, the aim of the volume is to further strengthen research in this rapidly developing field.

Our effort here is guided by the belief that how forced labour is studied dramatically shapes how it is understood and combated in the real world. As the field matures and a variety of new methodologies are pioneered to study forced labour, there is considerable value in reflecting openly on the methodological challenges inherent in research on forced labour in the global economy, and on the methods that are working to produce better quality data. Rather than being focused on methods for their own sake, this volume takes a problem-focused approach, considering the advantages and limitations of different methods in terms of the light they shed on the dynamics of contemporary forced labour. The chapters in Part I reflect on the political, analytical and methodological issues that researchers of forced labour confront, contending that the very choices they make about how to frame and define the problem are inherently political. They also provide an overview of key gaps in data and propose future research in the field. In Part II, authors reflect on how specific methodological tools are concretely used to investigate forced labour, drawing on their own experiences of research in this area. Throughout both parts of the book, authors explore possibilities for better research on forced labour, demonstrating that, despite the inevitable challenges to conducting sound primary research on forced labour, these obstacles are not insurmountable.

In the remainder of this introductory chapter, I provide an overview of the overarching political, analytical and practical challenges of researching forced labour in the global economy and our efforts to tackle them in the scholarship contributing to this volume. Before doing so, I provide the context for our volume by briefly explaining the emergence and evolution of the literature on forced labour in the global economy.

The emergence and evolution of forced labour research

Academic research on forced labour in the global economy has diverse and complex roots that can be traced back to distinct debates across diverse academic disciplines. To name just a few, these include: theoretical Marxist and feminist political economy debates about the nature of the capitalist mode of production and its relationship to unfree and unwaged labour (Banaji 1977; Brass 2011; Mies 1999); historiographical debates about capitalism, slavery and their evolution in the wake of legal emancipation from slavery during the nineteenth and early twentieth centuries (Foner 1995; Nakano Glenn 2004); legal literatures on workers' exploitation, rights and protection (Vosko 2000; Fudge 2005); anthropological debates about bonded and child labour, and how understandings of such practices are shaped by cultural and ideological differences (Qureshi & Khan 2016; Berlan 2013); and development studies debates about migration and the role of mobility regimes in constraining workers' freedom and movement (Kempadoo & Doezema 1998; Anderson 2013). Many of these debates stretch back to the 1970s or long before. Indeed, questions about how slavery would be impacted by the rise of capitalism and the spread and deepening of markets was a central concern of eighteenth-century political economist Adam Smith, whose thinking influenced early liberal, neoclassical and Marxist streams of economics and political economy. The key point is that it's difficult, if not impossible, to identify a single origin for research on contemporary forced labour because of the wide-ranging nature of the theoretical and disciplinary foundations of contemporary scholarship and because scholars have long applied varied lenses to the problem.

However, in the 1990s, alongside rising concerns about human trafficking in global governance circles, emerged a body of scholarship that cut across and blurred many of these disciplinary boundaries. Specifically dedicated to documenting a 'modern' form of twenty-first century 'slavery', this literature differed from previous research through its assumption that the worst forms of exploitation could be isolated from the labour market, labour exploitation, migration systems and workers' rights more broadly. Scholarship in this vein framed 'new slavery' as a discrete problem that required new and targeted forms of action (Bales 1999). The voluminous literature on modern slavery that has appeared since that time (Kara 2009; Skinner 2009; Craig 2010) is an influential predecessor and reference point for contemporary literature on forced labour in the global economy and so is worth briefly exploring here.

Scholarship within the new slavery literature is interdisciplinary and varies with respect to theoretical emphasis and how the problem of modern slavery is defined. However, this body of work is united around two central contentions: first, that a new form of slavery is playing an alarming, significant and growing role in the economy today (Skinner 2009; Kara 2009); and, second, that modern slavery differs in marked ways from historic forms of slavery, which are usually defined with reference to nineteenth-century plantation slavery in the United States (Bales 2004: 15). Kevin Bales' book *Disposable People: New Slavery in the Global Economy* (1999) has significantly shaped how the problem of modern slavery is conceptualised and defined within this literature. Bales argued that Western societies are confronting a new and rapidly expanding problem of modern slavery, which 'is like a new disease for which no vaccine exists . . . And this disease is spreading. As the new slavery increases, the number of people enslaved grows every day. We're facing an epidemic of slavery that is tied through the global economy to our own lives' (2012: 32). Bales and his contemporaries have popularised the notion that there are 'more slaves today than at any time in human history' and that modern slaves are both cheaper and more heavily exploited than those in the Atlantic Slave Trade were (Bales & Soodalter 2010; Bales 1999).

Many scholars writing within this tradition identify with a civil society movement they refer to as new abolitionism, and their writings about modern slavery have catalysed the contemporary abolitionist movement dedicated to combating modern slavery around the world. In the 2004 preface to the revised edition of *Disposable People*, for instance, Bales notes that 'of all the outcomes of the publication of *Disposable People*, the most exciting is the establishment of Free the Slaves, the first broad-based anti-slavery organisation in modern America' (2004: xii), an organisation which Bales served as president of for many years. This chapter is less interested in debating the successes or pitfalls of the abolitionist movement, as this has already been vigorously done elsewhere (for recent critiques, see: Shih & Quirk 2017; O'Connell Davidson 2015; Chuang 2014; Kotiswaran 2017). Instead, the point here is to note that, from the outset, knowledge production within the new slavery tradition has been oriented towards sparking action, consequently shaping the approach taken to scholarship.

No doubt, early scholars in this tradition faced immense challenges in securing accurate and comprehensive data, given how costly and time-consuming studies on illicit economic practices can be. Nevertheless, this lack of data did not stop scholars from making sweeping pronouncements about the character, scope and profitability of modern slavery – or from striving to publish the types of stories and statistics that would get policymakers' attention. As Nicola Phillips' chapter in this volume describes, there has been a tendency to make inflated claims on the basis of sparse research in an effort to underscore the importance of the problem and urgency of action. Bales confirmed this when he acknowledged that his influential estimate in *Disposable People* that there were 27 million modern slaves in the world – a number relentlessly cited in the media as well as by politicians from Hilary Clinton to Ban Ki-Moon – was an 'educated guess' rather than an estimate based on reliable empirical data or produced through accepted statistical methodology (Bales 2012: 295). While the new slavery literature's claims have often had shaky empirical foundations, they have nevertheless been influential in shaping the ways that policymakers and the public have understood the problem.

To name just two of many possible examples, it is commonly asserted within the new slavery literature that modern slavery is accelerating rapidly and producing immense profits for businesses. As Bales put it in *Disposable People*: 'Slavery is a booming business and the number of slaves is increasing. People get rich by using slaves. And when they've finished with their slaves, they just throw these people away. This is the new slavery, which focuses on big profits and cheap lives' (2004: 4). These are bold pronouncements, and at the time of their publication they were an important corrective to a widespread theory in the social sciences that coerced labour would be eradicated and replaced by free labour as capitalist globalisation swept across the planet (Rao 1970; see also Miles 1987). Indeed, scholars of political economy have long tended to assume *a priori* that fully functional capitalist enterprise cannot operate efficiently or profitably without workers who are juridically free, and that forced labour is incompatible with advanced productive forces, economic efficiency and market expansion. The new slavery literature challenged this theorisation, drawing attention to the ways forced labour continued to flourish. However, the literature's claims were not well supported by evidence. Without reliable baseline data on forced labour by country or sector, or time-series data demonstrating that such practices and profits are expanding – none of which exists as of yet, and therefore was certainly unavailable when *Disposable People* was first written – it is actually impossible to confirm the true scale of forced labour, or whether it is growing. Further, the notion that slavery produces 'big profits' is a largely untested hypothesis, as we have yet to collect and analyse information on the businesses that perpetrate forced labour in any systematic way (see LeBaron & Crane, this volume). Nevertheless, despite lacking data to support these claims, this literature has been influential in shaping popular representations and perceptions of the problem. For instance, a recent *New York Times* editorial, 'Modern Slavery Grows', noted 'global slavery has become a profitable growth industry' without offering evidence to support the claim that slavery is growing in statistical terms (New York Times Editorial Board 2014). Again, while the point here is not to debate the merits of the new slavery literature or movement, it is critical to observe that, in the rush to generate knowledge that would spark action to combat severe labour exploitation, commentators have often given the impression that more is known about the scope, character and business dynamics of forced labour than *is* actually known, or has been convincingly demonstrated through rigorous research, where rigour is defined with respect to the traditions and standards of a scholar's discipline.

This disregard for sound empirical data and methods has led to three limiting tendencies for the state of knowledge and action on forced labour in the global economy. In the first case, the certainty with which unfounded information was and continues to be presented has led to a tendency for gaps in knowledge and data to be covered up rather than illuminated. A good example here is the Global Slavery Index produced by the Walk Free Foundation, an organisation founded in 2012 by mining industry billionaire Andrew Forrest with a pledge to end slavery and human trafficking worldwide within a generation. According to the *Wall Street Journal*, the impetus for the Global Slavery Index was Bill Gates' advice to Forrest to find a way to quantify modern slavery so that the issue would be taken more seriously. Thus, 'Mr. Forrest decided to rank countries based on the prevalence of slavery' (Wolfe 2016). The lack of reliable data to inform such rankings didn't hinder or delay the initiative. As Anne Gallagher has described, the first Index claimed to provide national measurements of the prevalence of slavery for over 160 countries on the basis of 'random sample surveys in seven countries and derived data involving three others, supplemented by existing survey data of highly variable quality from a further nine' (2014). As she notes, 'even the well-informed reader will struggle to understand how the fragile data from 19 countries . . . was so confidently extrapolated across to the remaining 148' (2014; see also: Gallagher 2016; Weitzer 2014, 2015; Guth *et al.* 2014). Capturing the sentiments of many scholars and commentators, Gallagher has claimed that these statistics are 'at best unverifiable and at worst demonstrably false' (2017; see also Quirk & Broome 2015).

Now, it is perhaps not surprising that an anti-slavery NGO seeking to raise awareness about and spark action against modern slavery has produced metrics that represent the problem with greater certainty than is scientifically warranted, and at a larger scale than is estimated by other actors – the Global Slavery Index estimates 45.8 million victims of modern slavery globally, while the International Labour Organization's estimate of victims of forced labour is closer to 21 million. It is similarly unsurprising that an NGO that relies on corporate funding prioritised a 'big data' approach that does little to fundamentally challenge the status quo in order to present modern slavery as an 'exceptional' problem in an otherwise well-functioning global economy. Politically, this is a safe choice for an NGO, since digging into the root causes of forced labour could unearth the role of, say, the unfettered power and profits of MNCs or the role of globally unequal production processes; drawing attention to those could be bad for business. However, the traction that the abolitionist movement's shaky statistics and unsupported claims have received within the academic literature is confounding. Countless books and articles make reference to 'facts' put forward by the new slavery literature that have not been convincingly or credibly demonstrated through research. One damaging consequence of this overall situation is the widespread perception that we know a great deal about forced labour in the global economy, when in reality there has been very little in-depth research. Efforts to raise awareness about the problem of forced labour have thus often involved covering up gaps in our knowledge instead of bringing them to light.

Secondly, and relatedly, the framing of the problem in ways that makes it 'solvable' within a generation – essentially, the portrayal of modern slavery as something that can be neatly isolated from broader structural dynamics within the global economy and eradicated without the fundamental transformation of said dynamics – has hampered understandings of the causes of severe labour exploitation. Accounts of modern slavery's causes in the global economy frequently centre around the greed and moral shortcomings of individual perpetrators, criminality and corruption, or vague and nebulous notions of poverty and globalisation – with solutions that tend to focus on awareness raising, criminal justice approaches, and passing legislation. These accounts tend to avoid politically contentious questions about corporate power and profitability, the role of states and their lacking enforcement of labour protections, or national and international political economic policies. Shockingly little research has been conducted on the political economic root causes of severe labour exploitation (LeBaron *et al.* 2018; chapters by Phillips; Quirk; LeBaron & Crane, this volume). Conveniently, the portrayal of modern slavery as an exceptional problem within the otherwise free market has helped garner bipartisan political support for the cause, and has created a broad and inclusive anti-slavery movement comprised of religious organisations, college students, celebrities, billionaires, powerful governments and many of the world's largest corporations. But in overlooking the political economic causes of forced labour, the anti-slavery movement – and the scholarship it is informed by – merely target symptoms rather than the underlying causes. This strategic gap in knowledge production allows actors who are complicit in forced labour to present themselves as part of the solution to exploitation rather than the problem. The long-standing avoidance of politically contentious questions has meant that there is still only sparse and early-stage research about the root causes of forced labour, and, as Joel Quirk's chapter makes clear, when available research calls into question dominant policy approaches to combating forced labour, it tends to be cast aside.

Finally, in the race to generate evidence to spur action, there has been insufficient attention directed towards the politics and real-world impacts of the information being produced. As Nicola Phillips puts it in her chapter in this volume, there has been a tendency to overlook the politics of how data on forced labour are used. A number of scholars and organisations have raised compelling concerns that, however well intentioned the recent production and use of inaccurate and misleading information about modern slavery has been, they have led to ineffective responses. As Jessie Brunner documented in her study *Inaccurate Numbers, Inadequate Policies*, policies and programmes based on poor data will be equally poor in their effectiveness (2015). Misinformation also has the potential to negatively impact and endanger the populations whose lives are targeted for improvement by projects, policies and interventions (United Nations 2002; Dottridge 2014). This needs to be taken seriously, given the possibility that vast amounts of energy and hundreds of millions of dollars are being invested in anti-slavery policy and initiatives that actually hurt rather than help some of the world's most vulnerable people.

To summarise, mainstream scholarship has tended to depict modern slavery in misleading ways, including through 'facts' and 'statistics' that simply do not add up from a methodological or evidentiary standpoint. Yet, such depictions have nevertheless informed recent government policies, civil society initiatives and business efforts to combat severe labour exploitation, and have led to concerns about the accuracy of key actors' conceptualisation of the problem and the ineffectiveness of prevailing solutions. This situation has also led to a widespread impression that much is known about forced labour in the global economy when in fact research remains in its early stages. Further, it has popularised approaches to studying and 'solving' the problem that do little to investigate or challenge its political, economic and social root causes. There is therefore an urgent need for independent academic analysis and reliable research on the global business of forced labour.

In recognition of this, in recent years, scholars have taken a fresh approach anchored in strong and accurate empirical research. As is well reflected in the scholarship assembled within this volume, scholars are increasingly conducting in-depth ethnographic studies among populations classified as victims of modern slavery and human trafficking across many sectors and countries (Shih 2015; Okyere 2017). They are studying the business models of forced labour and seek to understand how they generate profits in many settings and industries (Allain *et al.* 2013; Phillips 2011; McGrath 2013; Mezzadri 2016; Chan & Selden 2017). This volume draws together an interdisciplinary group of scholars to reflect on the obstacles they have encountered – and their experiences in navigating them – when researching forced labour. In the following section, I provide an overview of key challenges of research on contemporary forced labour and our efforts to tackle them in this volume.

Advancing scholarship on forced labour

In the chapters that follow, this volume considers the core and overlapping challenges inherent in researching forced labour – namely, that it is politically sensitive, logistically and practically challenging, expensive, ethically and analytically complex and can require collaboration with stakeholders who have competing interests. We focus particularly on two sets of challenges: political and methodological.

Political challenges

Researching forced labour is beset by political challenges. While politics is not an unusual dimension of research in the social sciences and humanities, the political challenges of forced labour research are particularly acute given the intense demand for primary data to inform policy. The ongoing lack of hard data on forced labour is widely lamented, and there is a widespread assumption among policy and advocacy circles that hard empirical data on forced labour is necessary to objectively inform policy. Essentially, the idea is that acquiring a higher quantity of scientifically produced data would de-politicise and neutralise the problem of forced labour, which would in turn ease the efficacy of governance responses in the global economy.

However, as contributors to this volume demonstrate (see especially chapters by Phillips; Quirk; Okyere; Pliley; Howard), there is no such thing as apolitical data on forced labour. The way that the problem of forced labour is framed and understood – who or what is demonstrated to bear responsibility, the way that data is collected and presented, and especially whether and how its causes are foregrounded or obscured – is shaped by researchers' choices, whether they are aware of it or not. As Sam Okyere argues in Chapter 6, 'subjectivity and politically grounded positions inevitably shape all research and analysis', and that is particularly true of research on forced labour.

Furthermore, the data that researchers do create on forced labour is of intense interest to the real-world actors engaged in efforts to address the problem as they understand it – including workers' rights organisations, policymakers, religious groups and NGOs. These actors have differing ideological orientations and contrasting (and often competing) economic and political interests and agendas. Given the likelihood that research will be used to inform policy and practice and its potential to bring about social change, there is a critical need for researchers to be accountable for the information they produce. As Joel Quirk's chapter argues, there is a need for researchers to contemplate the politics of 'what happens next' once they have collected information on forced labour. While it is true that what happens is often out of the researcher's control, there is nevertheless a need for researchers to be conscious of the potential impacts of their research on political activism, policymaking and civil society responses to forced labour.

Methodological challenges

The methodological challenges associated with researching forced labour are numerous and complex. These include: ensuring the credibility, quality and representativeness of data; gaining access to research participants; the ethics of conducting research among participants, who may vary from highly vulnerable children and adults to criminal perpetrators of illegal practices; the need to ensure researchers' and research participants' safety; practical considerations such as language skills and logistics; the difficulty of accurately representing those whose lives are brought into focus by the research; tensions that may arise with local research partners, funders or civil society organisations; balancing methodological transparency with ethics and anonymity; and the need to carefully safeguard and anonymise sensitive data.

This volume seeks to shed light on these methodological challenges, focusing on qualitative research on forced labour in the global economy. The book contains reflections on how data on forced labour could be strengthened, including by exploring new avenues to generate data (see especially chapters by LeBaron & Crane; Rühmkorf; and Caruana), by modifying field research practices (see chapters by Chan; Okyere; and Howard), and by improving data analysis. In Part II of the volume, experienced researchers of forced labour reflect on the methodologies they have used in their own research – especially on challenges around ethics, access, logistics, representation and collaboration – with the hope of helping future researchers to become better equipped to navigate these obstacles.

The chapters in Part 1 also seek to chart and shed light on methodological challenges, focusing on the wider analytical and definitional problems confronted by researchers of forced labour. One of the most important questions tackled in Part I is how to define forced labour in a consistent, measurable and practical way, given the wide variety of types of forced labour and variegated settings in which it thrives. Definitional challenges around forced, unfree, precarious and slave labour are contentious and have been extensively documented in the literature by scholars and practitioners (see, for instance, ILO 2012; ILO 2009; Lerche 2007; Lewis *et al.* 2015; Guérin 2013); they will not be settled in this volume, but it is worthwhile to briefly set out and distinguish our approach.

The authors in this book are guided by the international legal definition of forced labour (see chapter by Allain), as determined by the ILO's 1930 Forced Labour Convention: 'All work or service which is exacted from any person under the menace of any penalty and for which the said person has not offered himself voluntarily.' Yet, we also recognise the difficulties and limitations of mobilising this definition in practice, and are conscious of the differences between common uses of this definition and the reality of the exploitation uncovered in our field research. Three limits stand out as especially important, and while the authors within the volume seek to overcome these limits in varied ways, some general trends emerge. First, the threshold of whether a worker's experience fits into the category of 'forced' or exploitative labour can be challenging to determine, and empirical research increasingly points to the reality that many workers move between these categories in relatively short periods of time. This book recognises that the boundaries between categories of 'forced' labour and regular labour exploitation are porous. Rather than focusing on the binary of whether a particular situation constitutes forced labour or not, the authors in this volume foreground the various aspects leading to situations of involuntariness, coercion and exploitation. Second, although the ILO has made it clear that it does not consider the threat of economic coercion – such as the threat of starvation or destitution – to be sufficiently coercive to render labour 'forced', the reality is that there is increasing evidence that many victims of severe exploitation demonstrate agency when entering into and remaining in forced labour situations if they lack alternative means of obtaining subsistence. That said, this book foregrounds the relevance and role of economic coercion in shaping the dynamics of labour exploitation, and raises questions about the need to pay better attention to the role of economic coercion within the literature. Finally, the standard legal definition of forced labour understands involuntariness and coercion in individualised terms. Yet, the analysis in this volume recognises that individual relationships of coercion and domination are shaped by structural relations, including: legacies of historic injustice; systemically unequal social relations, such as those along lines of gender, citizenship, sexuality and race; and unequal global and national political economic systems. Briefly put, while authors within this volume are cognisant of the importance of a specific, consistent definition demarcating the worst forms of abuse and unfreedom from broader relations of exploitation, they also recognise that forced labour is not an easily isolatable and discreet category, but is rather an extreme within a broader landscape of abuse and exploitation (see also LeBaron & Phillips 2018; LeBaron *et al.* 2018).

The book seeks to advance the methodological conversation about definitions in three main ways. First, it cautions against the tendency to define and study severe labour exploitation in an isolated way, echoing critiques that viewing forced labour through a narrow lens encourages a focus on the 'tip of the iceberg' while distracting from and normalising poor working conditions more broadly. Indeed, as many chapters in this volume make clear, as soon as a researcher sets out to study forced labour as a distinct relation – one that can be isolated and studied in exclusion from other forms of exploitation – she has already made an analytical choice with important methodological implications. While contributors to the volume have navigated this issue in different ways, overall the analysis presented here suggests that it is possible and desirable for researchers to cast their definitional nets narrowly and accurately on 'the tip of the iceberg' (the worst, most exploitative forms of labour abuse typically described as forced labour), at the same time as they maintain a broad understanding of 'the iceberg' (the broader conditions of abuse and exploitation that workers may confront, for instance unfair wage deductions or compulsory overtime, which are often much more widespread but may not meet the threshold of forced labour). Further, both are necessary if we are to understand the full complexity of actually lived and existing labour relations. As Jean Allain's chapter makes clear, harmonisation around the international legal definition of forced labour would go a long way towards achieving consistency and comparability across research in the humanities and social sciences; however, as researchers coalesce around this narrow definition, they should aim to situate their study of forced labour within the broader relations of exploitation, vulnerability and marginalisation that anchor these extreme cases.

Second, the volume highlights the difficulties of identifying key elements of the legal definition of forced labour – such as 'involuntariness' or 'coercion' – in practice, and the need to revisit concepts, definitions and categories during the research process if they are discovered not to accurately reflect realities on the ground. Neil Howard's and Sam Okyere's chapters argue that greater reflexivity is needed to ensure that the complex realities uncovered through research are fully and accurately represented by researchers, and highlight the role of researcher positionality and bias in shaping the categories that are used.

Finally, the volume seeks to advance the conversation about definitions by demonstrating the importance of critically reflecting on the origins and omissions of various concepts, both in our own research and in the real world. As chapters by Robert Caruana and Jessica Pliley discuss, the very ways that definitions of concepts like modern slavery come about, how and why they become accepted or rejected, and the ways in which definitions shape studies of severe labour exploitation need to be analysed. For instance, in Pliley's study of the history of sex trafficking in the United States, she discovered that the Federal Bureau of Investigation's categorisation of victims through the concept of 'white slavery' reflected prevailing race and gender biases, and served to deepen and exacerbate discriminatory practices by lending justification for state criminal justice responses. The importance of precision and reflexivity in definitions used in forced labour research is therefore not limited to our own work, but also encompasses the need to critically analyse the various definitions that are used by policy and advocacy organisations and how these link to and further their political projects.

In convening experienced researchers to share reflections on how they have navigated methodological challenges of forced labour research, it is hoped that this volume will catalyse and further inspire the commitment to strong empirical research in the field, as well as prompt researchers to reflect on the political foundations and impact of their research. Indeed, in developing methods for forced labour research, the volume is intended to offer a resource for scholars from across the social sciences and humanities and for researchers outside of the academy who set out to study these problems. However, as new research is undertaken, the primacy of vigorous ethics procedures and protocols – and of safeguarding these at every stage of research – cannot be overemphasised. As several chapters in the volume highlight, forced labour is a different lived experience – depending on age, gender, local context, among many other factors – and the experience of forced labour has different consequences on people's life trajectories. Research ethics and recognition of researcher positionality are critical – particularly when working with vulnerable populations. When using methodologies that involve direct contact with these populations, researchers need to be extremely careful about how, when and where research participants are recruited, approached and interviewed; how data is collected and stored; and the implications of research findings and recommendations for policy and advocacy interventions. While a comprehensive review of the ethical challenges inherent in researching forced labour lies outside the scope of this volume, it underscores the importance for researchers to prioritise worker and researcher safety; to represent workers' experiences in ways that are accurate; and to be reflexive about how their perceptions of such experiences are shaped by their own positionality, as well as how their research may affect policymaking.

Limitations and what this book is not

As could be expected, given the volume's focus on the expansive and multifarious topic of forced labour in the global economy, this volume does not intend to provide a comprehensive guide to researching forced labour. In addition to the intentions and advantages described above, the approach taken to the volume inevitably comes with limitations. These are worth briefly reflecting on here.

This volume does not offer a one-size-fits-all method for studying forced labour. Nor does it offer a standardised interpretation of what constitutes 'rigour', 'reliability' or 'transparency' in forced labour research. Standards and accepted characteristics of these criteria vary by discipline, and it would be impossible to generalise across all of the social science and humanities disciplines represented in this volume, which include law, management studies, politics, geography, global health, development studies, gender studies and sociology.

In addition, the volume does not coalesce around a single epistemological or ontological approach for researching forced labour. Indeed, scholars in this volume differ with respect to their epistemological approach to forced labour research, ranging from post-positivist to constructivist and encompassing many viewpoints in between. The diversity of approaches assembled within the volume is intentional, recognising that forced labour is a multi-faceted and complex problem that can be fruitfully explored through many complementary research strategies and forms of enquiry.

The breadth of methods covered in the volume, as well as the decision to not discuss methods in isolation but alongside the presentation of original research, unfortunately entails occasional trade-offs in relation to depth of exploration. The chapters are not intended to offer fully developed 'how to guides' to the methods they discuss but, rather, seek to shed light on some of the key prospects and limits for each method and to show how approaches to enquiry work in practice. The approach taken to methods in this volume is straightforward and practical. Contributors are not interested here in methodological innovation or discussion for its own sake; rather, they are trying to get at deeper and better understandings of the problem.

The volume encompasses a wide range of qualitative methodologies, including ethnography, discourse analysis, archival research, interviews, participant observation, legal analysis, and business and supply-chain mapping. It engages only very lightly with the methodological challenges in quantitative research on forced labour, since these are already being widely discussed by a number of scholars and organisations, including the International Labour Organization. There are of course many other methods that could have been fruitfully included in this volume, and should be explored in future works. Our approach has sought to shed light on a varied and inclusive range of methods from across the social sciences and humanities.

Finally, this book primarily draws together contributors from the English-language literature. It features discussion of several types of labour exploitation – ranging from child labour to forced labour to human trafficking – used by businesses in multiple sectors and regions of the world. But this approach creates several blind spots, particularly in terms of forced labour taking place in the 'private realm', such as in the context of domestic labour and social reproduction. We hope that future work will take up the complete range of regions, sectors, models of exploitation and methodological challenges that we were not able to fully address in this volume.

Chapter overviews

Part I of this volume considers the political, theoretical, definitional and empirical limitations that currently constrain research on forced labour in the global economy and offers reflections on how these can be overcome. It comprises five chapters. In Chapter 2, Genevieve LeBaron and Andrew Crane argue that the business of forced labour needs to be taken much more seriously in the literature.

They survey the gaps in knowledge and data on the business of forced labour and, drawing from the management studies literature on modern slavery, reflect on how business methodologies can be strengthened to deepen understandings of forced labour's business and organisational dynamics. In doing so, LeBaron and Crane discuss and offer reflections from their previous research on forced labour's business models and supply chains in the UK and India.

In Chapter 3, Nicola Phillips considers the political challenges that surround forced labour research, particularly in relation to how high-level quantitative data and metrics on forced labour are produced and used. Phillips argues that there has been a tendency to manipulate data on forced labour towards political ends, including both to inflate and to understate prevalence numbers and evidence, and that such manipulations have been crucial in justifying the action or inaction of advocacy groups and policymakers. Discussing governments' uses of large-scale quantitative data efforts, including the Global Slavery Index and US Trafficking in Persons Report, Phillips cautions against the drive towards quantification in forced labour research, highlighting how the resulting numbers are used towards particular ends. She reflects on how future research on forced labour at the global level can be advanced in light of these challenges.

Joel Quirk extends the discussion on political challenges in Chapter 4, inviting researchers to reflect on the links between research and political activism, and especially on 'what happens next' once data and information on forced labour have been collected. Discussing the politics of recent NGO, activist and government initiatives to combat forced labour, Quirk analyses the dominant tendency to frame research on modern slavery and human trafficking as a singular and exceptional problem, and argues that although the policy changes this research has helped yield have been celebrated as a 'success', they have yielded very little by way of concrete improvements for vulnerable, marginalised and exploited populations. He argues that there is an urgent need for stronger research on forced labour, which can in turn inform better activism to bring about more systematic and meaningful change that addresses the root causes of exploitation in the global economy.

Part I closes with two chapters focused on the challenge of defining forced labour in empirical research. Jean Allain argues in Chapter 5 that researchers' adoption of a consistent definition for the concept of forced labour would considerably strengthen the evidence base of forced labour research. At the same time, he demonstrates that the threshold for what states and international organisations consider 'forced' labour and 'acceptable' forms of exploitation is historically contingent and unstable. Allain offers a detailed breakdown of the international legal definition of forced labour that can be used by researchers and explains how this differs from definitions of slavery and legal exploitation. Rather than suggest that all researchers focus on one category of labour relations over others, Allain stresses the importance of transparency and consistency with regard to concepts and terminology. This, he argues, will promote comparability across various types and degrees of labour exploitation and ensure that researchers are 'speaking the same language' in forced labour research.

In Chapter 6, Samuel Okyere offers a complementary perspective on definitions. Discussing how researcher bias shapes data collection and analysis, Okyere argues that although labour practices on the ground frequently do not reflect dominant concepts used by researchers – including 'child slavery' and 'forced labour' – those concepts continue to be mobilised for moral and political reasons, to the detriment of research quality, validity and reliability. He critically analyses the definitions used in an NGO study of child labour within the Ghanaian artisanal gold mining sector and argues that NGOs privileged *a priori* definitions reflecting their own political goals and biases over the local realities they encountered in their research. He cautions that while the use of concepts like 'forced child labour' or 'child mining slaves' can help to attract funding and attention to research, researchers need to critically reflect on whether or not these accurately capture workers' agency in the setting under study.

In Part II, contributors present research conducted on forced labour in various sectors and parts of the world, and reflect on the methodologies used to generate it. It opens with Chapter 7 by Neil Howard, who argues for the need for researchers to conduct in-depth research among victims of forced labour, in order to correct the damaging tendency for research on modern slavery and human trafficking to be speculative and inaccurate. Reflecting on ethnographic methods, interviews and focus group research he conducted with over 150 Beninese youth working in artisanal quarries in Nigeria, Howard explains how this can be done in an ethical, respectful and empowering way. He underscores the importance for research on the business of forced labour to incorporate the voices and perspectives of vulnerable workers at the base of supply chains.

Chapter 8 by Jenny Chan also reflects on ethnographic and interview methods, drawing on her experience conducting research among student interns in China's electronics industry, including undercover research at a major electronics factory that supplies to Apple. She highlights the importance of triangulating between various data sources – including between interviews with workers and experts and documentary evidence such as employment contracts and wage statements – for understanding the forms of exploitation that student interns were facing. In her discussion of how employers in the industry circumnavigate labour regulations, Chan highlights the importance of understanding the business models of forced labour in the context of supply chains.

In Chapter 9, Andreas Rühmkorf discusses legal research strategies to understand forced labour in global supply chains. He evaluates the practical challenges that private commercial relationships present for researchers of forced labour in supply chains, such as the fact that many sources of data are proprietary and not covered under freedom of information protections. Offering reflections from his own research on MNC policies to combat and prevent forced labour in supply chains, he discusses how researchers can navigate access and data scarcity issues to conduct research on how forced labour practices are shaped by business policies along the supply chain.

In Chapter 10, Robert Caruana illuminates the potential of discourse analysis as a method for research on severe labour exploitation. Drawing on a case study of media, government and civil society discourses surrounding the 2015 UK Modern Slavery Act, he argues that discourse analysis holds considerable value in illuminating how different actors with vested interests – including companies, NGOs and the media – construct concepts such as 'modern slavery' towards variegated ends. Caruana's analysis complements the discussion of research on forced labour practices within the volume by describing how severe labour exploitation is itself socially constructed as an object of knowledge.

Jessica Pliley's concluding chapter argues that just as generating reliable data about forced labour and trafficking is a challenge for scholars of contemporary practices, so too is it for historians. Reflecting on the archival methods used in her study of the United States' first anti-sex trafficking law, encompassing over 1,000 investigative case files housed at the United States National Archives, Pliley documents the definitional, political and practical challenges inherent in quantifying sex trafficking in the early twentieth century. She argues that there are striking continuities between the challenges inherent in researching the business of forced labour in the past and in the present, as well as in the complex linkages between research on forced labour and trafficking and real-world action to combat it.

Overall, the volume seeks to map the latest theoretical and empirical research in this growing and important field. It captures methodological insights that will advance future research into the business dynamics of forced labour in the global economy, and provides crucial insights into how those dynamics might best be addressed.

References

Allain, J., Crane, A., LeBaron, G. & Behbahani, L. (2013), *Forced Labour's Business Models and Supply Chains* (York, UK, Joseph Rowntree Foundation).

Anderson, B. (2013), *Us and Them? The Dangerous Politics of Immigration Control* (Oxford, Oxford University Press).

Anderson, B. & Rogaly, B. (2007), 'Forced Labour and Migration to the UK', COMPAS and the Trades Union Congress, accessed 1 August 2017, https://www.compas.ox.ac.uk/media/PR-2007-Forced_Labour_TUC.pdf

Bales, K. (1999), *Disposable People: New Slavery in the Global Economy* (Berkeley, University of California Press).

Bales, K. (2004), *Disposable People: New Slavery in the Global Economy*, rev. edn (Berkeley, University of California Press).

Bales, K. (2012), *Disposable People: New Slavery in the Global Economy*, 3rd edn (Berkeley, University of California Press).

Bales, K. & Soodalter, R. (2010), *The Slave Next Door: Human Trafficking and Slavery in America Today* (Berkeley, University of California Press).

Banaji, J. (1977), 'Modes of Production in a Materialist Conception of History', *Capital & Class*, 3: 1–41.

Barrientos, S., Kothari, U. & Phillips, N. (2013), 'Dynamics of Unfree Labour in the Contemporary Global Economy,' *Journal of Development Studies*, 49, 8: 1037–41. DOI 10.1080/00220388.2013.780043

BBC (2015), 'Apple Bans "Bonded Servitude" for Factory Workers', *BBC News* (12 February 2015), accessed 1 August 2017, http://www.bbc.co.uk/news/technology-31438699

Berlan, A. (2013), 'Social Sustainability in Agriculture: An Anthropological Perspective on Child Labour,' *Journal of Development Studies*, 49, 8: 1088–100. DOI 10.1080/00220388.2013.780041

Brass, T. (2011), *Labor Regime Change in the Twenty-First Century: Unfreedom, Capitalism and Primitive Accumulation* (Chicago, IL, Haymarket).

Brunner, J. (2015), *Inaccurate Numbers, Inadequate Policies: Enhancing Data to Evaluate the Prevalence of Human Trafficking in ASEAN* (Honolulu, East-West Center).

Chan, J. & Selden, M. (2017), 'The Labour Politics of China's Rural Migrant Workers', *Globalizations*, 14, 2: 259–71. DOI 10.1080/14747731.2016.1200263

Chuang, J. (2014), 'Exploitation Creep and the Unmaking of Human Trafficking Law', *American Journal of International Law*, 108, 4: 609–49. DOI 10.5305/amerjintelaw. 108.4.0609

Craig, G. (ed.) (2010), *Child Slavery Now: A Contemporary Reader* (Bristol, Policy Press).

Crane, A. (2013), 'Modern Slavery as a Management Practice: Exploring the Capabilities and Conditions for Human Exploitation', *Academy of Management Review*, 38, 1: 49–69. DOI 10.5465/amr.2011.0145

Crane, A., LeBaron, G., Allain, J. & Behbahani, L. (2017), 'Governance Gaps in Eradicating Forced Labour: From Global to Domestic Supply Chains', *Regulation & Governance*. DOI 10.1111/rego.12162

Dottridge, M. (ed.) (2007), *Collateral Damage: The Impact of Anti-trafficking Measures on Human Rights around the World* (Bangkok, Global Alliance against Traffic in Women).

Dottridge, M. (2014), 'Editorial: How Is the Money to Combat Human Trafficking Spent?', *Anti-Trafficking Review*, 3: 3–14. DOI 10.14197/atr.20121431

Foner, E. (1995), *Free Soil, Free Labor, Free Men: The Ideology of the Republican Party before the Civil War* (Oxford, Oxford University Press).

Fudge, J. (2005), 'Beyond Vulnerable Workers: Towards a New Standard Employment Relationship,' *Canadian Labour and Employment Law Journal*, 12: 151–76.

Fudge, J. & Strauss, K. (eds) (2013), *Temporary Work, Agencies, and Unfree Labor: Insecurity in the New World of Work* (New York, Routledge), 143–63.

Gallagher, A. (2014), 'The Global Slavery Index Is Based on Flawed Data: Why Does No One Say So?', *The Guardian* (28 November 2014).

Gallagher, A. (2016), 'Unravelling the 2016 Global Slavery Index: Part One', *openDemocracy: 50.50* (28 June 2016).

Gallagher, A. (2017), 'Four Dangerous Assumptions about Human Trafficking', World Economic Forum, accessed 19 July 2018, https://www.weforum.org/agenda/2017/08/4-fallacies-slowing-the-fight-against-human-trafficking/

Guérin, I. (2013), 'Bonded Labour, Agrarian Changes and Capitalism: Emerging Patterns in South India', *Journal of Agrarian Change*, 13, 1: 405–23.

Guth, A., Anderson, R., Kinnard, K. & Tran, H. (2014), 'Proper Methodology and Methods of Collecting and Analyzing Slavery Data: An Examination of the Global Slavery Index', *Social Inclusion*, 2, 4: 14–22. DOI 10.17645/si.v2i4.195

Hodal, K., Kelly, C. & Lawrence, F. (2014), 'Revealed: Asian Slave Labour Producing Prawns for Supermarkets in US, UK', *The Guardian* (10 June 2014), https://www.theguardian.com/global-development/2014/jun/10/supermarket-prawns-thailand-produced-slave-labour

ILO (2009), *Operational Indicators of Trafficking in Human Beings* (Geneva, ILO).

ILO (2012), *Hard to See, Harder to Count: Survey Guidelines to Estimate Forced Labour of Adults and Children* (Geneva, ILO).

Kara, S. (2009), *Sex Trafficking: Inside the Business of Modern Slavery* (New York, Columbia University Press).

Kempadoo, K. & Doezema, J. (eds) (1998), *Global Sex Workers: Rights, Resistance and Redefinitions* (New York, Routledge).

Kessler, G. (2015), 'Why You Should Be Wary of Statistics on "Modern Slavery" and "Trafficking"', *Washington Post* (24 April 2015), https://www.washingtonpost.com/news/fact-checker/wp/2015/04/24/why-you-should-be-wary-of-statistics-on-modern-slavery-and-trafficking/?utm_term=.4962e3a9fe82

Kotiswaran, P. (ed.) (2017), *Revisiting the Law and Governance of Trafficking, Forced Labour and Modern Slavery* (Cambridge, Cambridge University Press).

LeBaron, G. & Phillips, N. (2018), 'States and the Political Economy of Unfree Labour', *New Political Economy*. DOI 10.1080/13563467.2017.1420642

LeBaron, G., Howard, N., Thibos, C. & Kyritsis, P. (2018), *Confronting Root Causes: Forced Labour in Global Supply Chains* (London and Sheffield, openDemocracy and SPERI).

Lerche, J. (2007), 'A Global Alliance against Forced Labour? Unfree Labour, Neo-liberal Globalization and the International Labour Organization', *Journal of Agrarian Change*, 7: 425–52.

Lewis, H., Dwyer, P., Hodkinson, S. & Waite, L. (eds) (2015), *Precarious Lives: Forced Labour, Exploitation and Asylum* (London: Policy Press).

McGrath, S. (2013), 'Many Chains to Break: The Multi-dimensional Concept of Slave Labour in Brazil', *Antipode*, 45: 1005–28.

Mezzadri, A. (2016), *The Sweatshop Regime: Labouring Bodies, Exploitation and Garments Made in India* (Cambridge, Cambridge University Press).

Mies, M. (1999), *Patriarchy and Accumulation on a World Scale: Women in the International Division of Labour* (London, Zed Books).

Miles, R. (1987), *Capitalism and Unfree Labour: Anomaly or Necessity?* (London, Tavistock Books).

Nakano Glenn, E. (2004), *Unequal Freedom: How Race and Gender Shaped American Citizenship and Labor* (Cambridge, MA, Harvard University Press).

New York Times Editorial Board (2014), 'Modern Slavery Grows', *New York Times* (2 December 2014), https://www.nytimes.com/2014/12/03/opinion/modern-slavery-grows.html?mcubz=0

O'Connell Davidson, J. (2015), *Modern Slavery: The Margins of Freedom* (London, Palgrave).

O'Connell Davidson, J. & Howard, N. (eds) (2015), *Migration and Mobility* (London, openDemocracy).

Okyere, S. (2017), 'Moral Economies and Child Labour in Artisanal Gold Mining', in L. Brace & J. O'Connell Davidson (eds), *Slaveries Old and New: The Meanings of Freedom* (Oxford, Oxford University Press).

Phillips, N. (2011), 'Informality, Global Production Networks and the Dynamics of "Adverse Incorporation"', *Global Networks*, 11, 3: 380–97. DOI 10.1111/j.1471-0374.2011.00331.x

Phillips, N. (2013), 'Unfree Labour and Adverse Incorporation in the Global Economy: Comparative Perspectives on Brazil and India', *Economy and Society*, 42, 2: 171–96. DOI 10.1080/03085147.2012.718630

Quirk, J. & Broome, A. (2015), 'The Politics of Numbers: The Global Slavery Index and the Marketplace of Activism', *openDemocracy: Beyond Trafficking and Slavery* (10 March 2015).

Quirk, J. & LeBaron, G. (2015), 'The Use and Abuse of History: Slavery and Its Contemporary Legacies', *openDemocracy: Beyond Trafficking and Slavery* (21 April 2015), https://www.opendemocracy.net/beyondslavery/joel-quirk-genevieve-lebaron/use-and-abuse-of-history-slavery-and-its-contemporary-leg

Qureshi, A. & Khan, A. (eds) (2016), *Bonded Labour in Pakistan* (Oxford, Oxford University Press).

Rao, R. (1970), 'In Search of the Capitalist Farmer: A Comment', *Economic and Political Weekly*, 5, 51: 2055–6.

Shih, E. (2015), 'The Price of Freedom: Moral and Political Economies of the Global Anti-trafficking Movement', unpublished doctoral dissertation, University of California Los Angeles.

Shih, E. & Quirk, J. (2017), 'Introduction: Do the Hidden Costs Outweigh the Practical Benefits of Human Trafficking Awareness Campaigns?', *openDemocracy: Beyond Trafficking and Slavery* (11 January 2017).

Skinner, B. (2009), *A Crime So Monstrous: Face-to-Face with Modern Day Slavery* (New York, Free Press).

Smith, G. (2016), 'Another Report Damns Qatar's Treatment of World Cup Workers', *Fortune* (31 March 2016), http://fortune.com/2016/03/31/qatar-world-cup-workers/

Ucnikova, M. (2014), 'OECD and Modern Slavery: How Much Aid Money Is Spent to Tackle the Issue?', *Anti-Trafficking Review*, 3: 133–50. DOI 10.14197/atr.20121437

United Nations (2002), *Recommended Principles and Guidelines on Human Rights and Human Trafficking* (New York, United Nations Economic and Social Council).

Vosko, L. (2000), *Temporary Work: The Gendered Rise of a Precarious Employment Relationship* (Toronto, Toronto University Press).

Weitzer, R. (2014), 'Miscounting Human Trafficking and Slavery', *open Democracy: Beyond Trafficking and Slavery* (8 October 2014), accessed 8 October 2016, https://www.opendemocracy.net/beyondslavery/ronald-weitzer/miscounting-human-trafficking-and-slavery

Weitzer, R. (2015), 'Researching Prostitution and Sex Trafficking Comparatively', *Sexuality Research and Social Policy*, 12, 2: 81–91. DOI 10.1007/s13178-014-0168-3

Wolfe, A. (2016), 'Andrew Forrest's Mission to End Modern Slavery', *Wall Street Journal* (24 June 2016), https://www.wsj.com/articles/andrew-forrests-mission-to-end-modern-slavery-1466800377

Part I

Surveying the Gaps: Analytical and Methodological Challenges

2

Methodological Challenges in the Business of Forced Labour

GENEVIEVE LEBARON AND ANDREW CRANE

Introduction

MOST MODERN FORMS OF slavery, trafficking and forced labour either involve business or affect it in some way. From illegal mica mined by vulnerable children in Andhra Pradesh (Bhalla *et al.* 2016) to vegetables harvested by forced workers within the United Kingdom (Scott *et al.* 2012), the worst forms of labour exploitation are frequently linked to industry. Yet, while these incidents of exploitation have received ample attention, the business actors behind them have remained hidden.

That is not to suggest that businesses are entirely overlooked in the context of forced labour. Indeed, businesses – and especially multinational corporations (MNCs) – are often the subject of extensive attention in discussions about forced labour in public, policy and academic conversations. Victims of forced labour are suing MNCs in high-profile lawsuits, such as in the ongoing case against Canadian mining company Nevsun for alleged slave labour in Eritrea (Laanela & Merali 2016). NGOs, trade unions and workers' advocacy groups, too, expend considerable energy linking incidents of forced and child labour to the powerful and wealthy MNCs steering global supply chains (Wilshaw *et al.* 2013; ITUC 2016).

Connecting MNCs that have carefully cultivated reputations to forced labour no doubt attracts attention to the issue, far more than could be garnered by exposing its use by business actors without brands well known by consumers. But the overwhelming emphasis on MNCs as the key business actor with responsibility for forced labour has obscured the role of the smaller and often more informal organisations that actually perpetrate forced labour. The singular emphasis on MNCs at the top of the supply chain has also prevented us from grasping the patterns surrounding forced labour in supply chains, such as why forced labour seems to be used by some business actors and not others; why it tends to appear in some portions of supply chains rather than others; how businesses profit from forced labour; and the circumstances under which they are caught or get away with it. Too often,

Proceedings of the British Academy, **220**, 25–43. © The British Academy 2018.

the businesses that exploit forced labour are simply written off by the media and government as 'unscrupulous employers' (Warrell 2015) or individual criminals. This has given rise to the perception that forced labour occurs randomly within modern industry, rather than in accordance with coherent, economically rational patterns that make it possible to anticipate its occurrence or understand how businesses systematically profit from it.

Scholars, too, have insufficiently focused on the business dynamics and pressures that facilitate the use of forced labour. While there has been extensive work on the business drivers behind and response to poor labour conditions in global supply chains (Egels-Zandén 2014; Locke *et al.* 2009; Roberts 2003), there has been far less attention afforded to more extreme and illegal forms of exploitation. These practices, and the business actors engaged in them, at the outer edges of the exploitation continuum might be expected to differ in some important ways, but it is an empirical question as to the degree or nature of any such deviation from what we already know about the business of poor working conditions. However, where the business of forced labour has been investigated, scholars have tended to focus on the role, power and regulation of MNCs; the evolving nature of global production and trade practices; and the dynamics of global corporate supply chains that deliver 'slavery-tainted' goods to wealthy Western consumers (van den Anker 2004; Bowe 2007; Fifka & Frangen-Zeitinger 2014; Bales 2000; Phillips 2013). No doubt, these structural political economic dynamics and high-level business relations are important. But they cannot substitute for an understanding of how the business of forced labour actually operates on the ground; nor could they determine *a priori* the patterns of forced labour found in practice.

As such, in spite of the close and persistent links between contemporary forced labour and modern industry, we know remarkably little about the business and organisational dynamics of forced labour, including how and why it is deployed as part of a business model; how forced labour is managed; how forced labour operates within and between organisations, including the supply chain; the impacts and interrelationships between forced labour and consumers, workers and other stakeholders of business; and the role of multi-stakeholder initiatives and other mechanisms in combating forced labour. These kinds of questions are rich with opportunity for extending our understanding of the phenomenon of forced labour in unique and important ways. After all, most forms of forced labour take place in a business context and are driven by business imperatives.

We argue in this chapter that it is necessary take the business of forced labour seriously if we are to understand and address it in a meaningful way. In the first section, we survey the gaps in knowledge and data surrounding business and forced labour. The second section provides an overview of analytical tools that can be used to understand the business and organisational dynamics of forced labour. In section three, we reflect on how business methodologies can be strengthened to overcome the substantive gaps that exist in our knowledge about how forced labour works as a business. We conclude that both stronger conceptual paradigms and more robust empirical methods and data are necessary to advance the literature.

Gaps in the data

Unsurprisingly, there are notable gaps in data on the business of forced labour, perhaps even more so than in other areas of research on the phenomenon. This is partly due to the lack of researchers in the field of forced labour research with specific expertise in business and management, and partly because there are particular empirical challenges when researching the business dynamics of forced labour (see also chapters by LeBaron and Rühmkorf in this volume). Also, because forced labour circumscribes some quite specific labour practices and experiences of workers, caution must be exercised in extrapolating from our extant understanding of the business dynamics surrounding less extreme forms of exploitation. Moreover, the field of forced labour encompasses a range of empirical contexts (such as domestic workers, agency workers, sex workers, agricultural and mining workers, among others) that are beyond the purview of the mainstream corporate social responsibility (CSR) and working conditions debate. So, the business of forced labour is sufficiently distinctive to require new empirical insight in order to build new theories as well as to develop boundary conditions for our existing theoretical accounts.

Unfortunately, existing accounts of the business of forced labour tend to lack the empirical rigour of much of the broader research on CSR, private governance and working conditions. Siddharth Kara's book *Sex Trafficking: Inside the Business of Modern Slavery* (2009) provides a good example of some of these limitations. Not only is there only half of one chapter devoted to any type of business analysis in the entire book (despite the promise of the book's subtitle), but much of this analysis relies on scant data and poor execution. In one particularly notable passage, Kara estimates the elasticity of demand for sex acts (how much demand for a particular act changes with the price) compared with other products by interviewing four sex-worker clients and eighteen of his friends. Though he acknowledges that this analysis is 'highly rudimentary' (36) and the sample is 'not nearly enough for a statistically defensible curve' (35), this severely underplays the essential futility of such analysis. Even in Kara's follow-up books, most notably *Modern Slavery: A Global Perspective* (2017), which presents a more data-driven view of the business of forced labour, the same problems reappear. For example, the elasticity calculation is extended to a survey of 60 sex-work consumers which Kara claims (34) 'affirms that demand-side interventions have the most potential to reduce sex-trafficking in the near term', despite the fact that, as an economic estimation, it is highly questionable and bears little relation to the type of sophisticated analyses of sex-work economics that have been published on large-scale datasets of directly reported behavioural data (see, for example, Ahlburg & Jensen 1998; Arunachalam & Shah 2013; Gertler *et al.* 2005). These barriers are not insurmountable, but they do require more and better-quality data. They might also demand a different set of methodologies from those we have been using so far.

So what data do we need in order to inform a better understanding of the business of forced labour? The key gaps are in the detail of how forced labour works as a business. For example, there is a common presumption in the popular and academic discourse around forced labour and slavery that perpetrators make huge profits and become rich from their use of the practice. Kevin Bales, for instance, identifies 'very high profits' as a defining characteristic of modern forms of slavery compared with historical forms in his book *Disposable People* (2012). This, however, is a largely untested hypothesis, in large part because we have yet to collect and fully analyse the financial details of perpetrators in any systematic way. Kara (2017) at least provides an initial estimation in a series of slavery enterprise profit and loss statements which indeed suggest that slavery is overwhelmingly profitable. However, he provides few details as to the sources of his data on enterprise-level revenues and costs, although he does detail a large swathe of victim interviews and provides his research instrument, which does not include any questions on such revenues and costs beyond the amounts that workers pay and are paid. Thus, we are left to conclude that these estimates are based largely on speculation rather than hard data, especially given that Kara is honest in detailing various unsuccessful attempts to interview recruiters linked to debt bondage (188), or to get any detailed cost and revenue data from Thai shipping trawler captains (237). Essentially, then, we still do not know the true costs of forced labour for perpetrators – in terms of recruiting workers, employing enforcers and paying bribes – as well as the perceived risks of prosecution.

Similarly, we need to know the margins associated with specific stages of the value chains involved in forced labour. This would allow us to determine how value is distributed through the chain and, subsequently, to uncover which exact actors are able to extract rents and make abnormal profits. What size cut do intermediaries take, for example, and how are recruiting agents' fees structured in the case of forced labour? Different types of value chains, with different institutional structures, are likely to give rise to different economic complexions.

Another major gap in our data relates to the costs and revenues associated with various ancillary services – such as accommodation, food, travel and visa services – that are sold to forced labourers in order to escalate and sustain their indebtedness. While we know that these can be used to develop a different form of business model based more on revenue generation than cost reduction (Allain *et al.* 2013), we do not know with any precision how these transactions work, how prices are set, or what the costs are in various industries. Given that business models of forced labour often rely on exploitative practices in relation to workers' wages – including unauthorised deductions, predatory credit and loan arrangements, under-calculation of work performed (such as in relation to daily quotas for tea picked or shirts sewed), and the withholding and underpayment of wages – the precise financial arrangements between workers and employers and intermediaries are important to understand in detail.

In addition to collecting better information on the actors involved in the business of forced labour and the financial details that shape their relationship to one another, more precise information is needed about the supply chains in which the businesses of forced labour operate. This data can be difficult to obtain, given that commercial contracts between businesses along the supply chain are private and often closely guarded, particularly by consumer-facing firms. Complicating the problem further, following official paper trails will not always lead researchers to perpetrators of forced labour because these businesses tend to operate within informal, remote or illegal portions of supply chains. Forced labour has been documented, for instance, to occur in home-based work, among unauthorised subcontractors, and on remote and illegal sites (e.g. illegal mining or logging in protected rainforests), as well as at the hands of unregistered labour providers who move forced workers between worksites (Mezzadri 2016; Phillips 2013; Verité 2017). Given that the contractual dynamics between businesses along the supply chain – including price, lead time for orders and fluctuations in demand – are well documented to create pressures towards labour exploitation, it is important to understand how businesses along the supply chain relate to each other.

Table 2.1 summarises the data that is required to advance and deepen our understanding of the business of forced labour.

In the next section, we describe an analytical framework that can be used to understand this data. We then offer reflections on how this data can be obtained based on our own research experience.

Taking business seriously

An emerging body of literature within management studies gives us some useful analytical tools with which to tackle serious study of business and forced labour (Crane 2013; Crane et al. 2017; Choi-Fitzpatrick 2017; Gold *et al.* 2015; New 2015). It is outside of the scope of our chapter to comprehensively review this burgeoning literature, so we focus on two key concepts that are essential to deepening understandings of the business of forced labour: business models and supply chains.

Understanding business models

Scholars and activists often assume that businesses use forced labour because it is cheaper than the alternative of using legal labour practices. From this perspective,

Table 2.1 The business of forced labour: key gaps in data

	Patterns of forced labour	Supply chain	Business actors	Workers	Perpetrators
Quantitative	Prevalence and distribution of forced labour in sectors and supply chains.	Total value of product or service; distribution of value along the chain; timing and geography of export, import and sale.	Size, profitability and geographic distribution of actors within business and supply chain.	Financial details, including: wages (promised and actual); deductions from pay; credit and loan relations with recruiters, transporters and managers; demographic information.	Financial details, including cost and revenue structures; demographic information.
Qualitative	Why, when, where and how forced labour is recruited, deployed and released; relation of forced labour to 'regular exploitation'.	Distribution of power, risk and reward along the chain, including cost, time and business pressures; structure and enforcement of labour standards initiatives and laws along the chain.	Role of each actor within business model; relation of business actors deploying forced labour to other actors in the supply chain; relation of informal business activity to formal.	When, why and how workers become vulnerable to forced labour; how formal and informal actors seek to profit from and exploit vulnerability; what prevents their exit from exploitation; how and when they are able to exit.	How, why and when forced labour is deployed as part of a business model; how forced labour is managed; how perpetrators manage risk and escape prosecution by authorities.

businesses use forced labour as one of a range of cost-cutting strategies to generate higher profits. As a recent ITUC report put it, 'slavery, informal work, precarious short-term contracts, low wages, unsafe work and dangerous chemicals, forced overtime, attacks by government on labour laws and social protection, inequality—it's all part of a great global scandal that is today driven by corporate greed with an eternal quest for profit and shareholder value' (2016: 3).

Recent empirical work has demonstrated that this set of assumptions about how and why businesses use forced labour is somewhat too simplistic. In our 2013 study (with Jean Allain and Laya Behbahani) of the business models of forced labour within the UK food, construction and cannabis industries, we demonstrate that it is not always the case that the money made from forced labour comes from cutting down labour costs (Allain *et al.* 2013). And even where it is the case, businesses use forced labour to cut costs in different ways and for different reasons. Some businesses use forced labour to stay afloat as a low-margin business in a competitive industry, while for others forced labour is a strategy to minimise risk. For instance, in the UK cannabis industry, a key benefit of forced labour for perpetrators is that because victims are vulnerable and often have irregular immigration status, they are less likely to inform the police about the illegal enterprises of their exploiters. For other businesses, forced labour is not about straightforward labour cost reduction, but involves revenue generation, such as when organisations sell overpriced transportation or accommodation to workers on remote worksites with no other means of obtaining those services. In short, businesses make money from forced labour in different ways and are driven to do so by different types of business pressures. These variations need to be taken seriously if we hope to achieve an understanding of the circumstances under which business organisations experience a 'demand' for forced labour.

Systematically analysing business models can help to elucidate when, why and how businesses exploit forced labour, as well as how they make money from it. A business model 'describes the rationale of how an organisation creates, delivers, and captures value' (Osterwalder & Pigneur 2010: 14). In other words, the concept explains the economic logic of a business organisation, how it functions, and where its profits come from. While in earlier eras of production, business models were relatively straightforward – businesses made money simply by making a product or selling a service at a price that exceeded the cost of production – business models have become more complicated in the contemporary global economy. Organisations seek to deliver and capture value in a variety of ways, such as by charging advertisers rather than the users of their services, or by outsourcing lower value-adding activities to third parties while focusing on activities that are more profitable. Business models also vary depending on the industry, the performance of competitors, and socio-economic dynamics like the strength of enforcement of labour laws. They can also evolve over time as enterprises experiment with innovations in their business models (Amit & Zott 2012).

Just as with other components, where forced labour is part of a business model, it is possible to understand the role it plays within an organisation's cost and revenue structures. For instance, the costs of forced labour might include recruiting, smuggling and concealing vulnerable workers or precluding their exit from the workplace through violence or other means. The risks might include the possibility of arrest, being fined or losing clients if the use of forced labour is detected by ethical auditors or the police. In short, forced labour will only be used when it makes business sense to do so. Thus, rather than being seen as abnormal, forced labour can be understood in terms of rational economic calculation on the part of perpetrators given particular market opportunities, constraints and preferences (Schloenhardt 1999). We do not mean to suggest that forced labour will be used in every instance in which it would be profitable, just that where it is used it is feasible to understand its business rationale in a systematic way. There are advantages to following the law and many business models do not depend on illegal labour practices.

To evaluate the role of forced labour within a business model, there are three key issues to consider (Allain *et al.* 2013: 26). First, who is employing forced labour? Is it an intermediary organisation (e.g. a labour agency supplying workers to a farmer or manufacturer) or is it the producer organisation directly involved in the production of goods or services (e.g. a farmer, manufacturer or miner)? Second, how is the employer making money from forced labour and how does this practice impact the organisation's overall costs and revenue structures? Finally, what business models does forced labour give rise to within the organisation? By distinguishing between the organisations that perpetrate forced labour, specifying how forced labour fits into cost and revenue structures, and the business models that result from these dynamics, researchers can shed light on the patterns of when, why and how various types of businesses use forced labour across industries and sectors.

Understanding supply chains

Just as detailing business models helps to deepen our understanding of the perpetrators of forced labour, mapping supply chains can help us to understand how the businesses perpetrating forced labour relate to and interact with other business actors. Many scholars within development studies, geography, politics, sociology and management, among other disciplines, already use the concept of supply chains (which are also referred to as global production networks, global value chains and global commodity chains) to frame studies of labour exploitation. But, as mentioned earlier, this interdisciplinary literature has tended to focus primarily on labour standards in global product supply chains led by MNCs, and especially on workers geographically located in developing countries. While the literature has helpfully begun to illuminate some of the dynamics of forced labour within individual supply chains – for example, the cattle industry in Brazil (Phillips 2013) or garments in India (Mezzadri 2016) – empirical work has barely scratched the surface of understanding the overall patterns of forced labour in supply chains. A broader and more systematic approach to understanding forced labour in supply chains is needed if we are going to generate the comparative data necessary to understand the business of forced labour.

Previous studies of global value chains have stressed four key dimensions for understanding the operation of these chains: structure, geography, governance and institutional context (Gereffi *et al.* 2005). These four dimensions serve as a useful starting place for understanding the presence of forced labour within these chains. In the first case, examining the structure of product and labour supply chains linked to forced labour can elucidate how – and at which point along the supply chain – the perpetrators of forced labour intersect with legal industry. A product supply chain describes the various stages that a product goes through as it is transformed from a raw material (e.g. coltan, copper) into a finished product (e.g. mobile phone). Each link of the product supply chain consists of activities that add value to the inputs associated with that stage (e.g. manufacture or distribution). For instance, the materials that go into a mobile phone move across several countries and through the hands of many companies as they journey through the stages of production from raw material extraction to retail. In addition to a product supply chain, the production of many goods also involves labour supply chains, which may give rise to forced labour; though they are frequently overlooked in the forced labour literature, understanding the structure of these chains is just as important. A labour supply chain consists of the employment relationships that a worker goes through to arrive at the worksite. Labour supply chains can be quite short where workers have direct employment relationships with producers; however, these chains can involve multiple layers of contracting and intermediaries, where intermediaries, including labour agencies or recruiters, are involved in supplying workers to producers. Sometimes, intermediaries even employ workers directly, moving them around from worksite to worksite week on week to fill temporary labour shortages.

Systematically mapping the structures of product and labour supply chains is critical if we are to understand the business dynamics that give rise to forced labour. Existing research suggests that long and complex product supply chains are most closely associated with forced labour, and that forced labour is especially likely to occur at the bottom sub-tiers of outsourced production (Phillips 2013; Verité 2014; ITUC 2016). However, empirical research is at its very early stages, and recent studies have demonstrated that forced labour also occurs within relatively short and simple supply chains (Crane *et al.* 2017). There is a need to better understand the structure of the supply chains that businesses configured around forced labour are part of.

Second and relatedly, examining a supply chain's geographic configuration – the geography of its flows of products and people – can shed light on the spatial dimensions of businesses that perpetrate forced labour. At present, it is not clear whether forced labour tends to be more heavily concentrated within supply chains geared towards export or within supply chains producing goods for domestic consumption. Additionally, it is not clear which geographic flows of labour are most commonly associated with forced labour. Carefully mapping the geographic configuration of product and labour supply chains will help to shed light on a number of open empirical questions about how, why and when forced labour is used in domestic and global businesses. In particular, there is a need to consider the global, regional or intra-national flows of people and products involved in a supply chain, and how these might promote or mitigate the business of forced labour.

Third, systematically exploring the internal governance dynamics of supply chains can illuminate the pressures towards forced labour caused by power dynamics and business-to-business relationships along the chain. Research on labour standards in the apparel and electronics industries has documented the role of power asymmetries and uneven value distribution among firms in giving rise to labour exploitation (Locke 2013; Anner *et al.* 2013). This has often been identified within chains with hierarchical governance dynamics, where suppliers can become economically 'captive' to lead firms insofar as switching clients is prohibitively costly for them (Gereffi *et al.* 2005). These supply chains frequently involve heavy monitoring of suppliers through social audits, certification and other means, which can shape the presence and patterns of forced labour (New 2015; Gold *et al.* 2015). Examining the governance structures of supply chains can shed light on how businesses interact with each other and, in particular, the pressures faced by business actors along the chain. Understanding these pressures is critical to understanding why businesses experience a 'demand' for forced labour.

Finally, investigating the institutional context surrounding forced labour in supply chains can help to illuminate the governance gaps that currently stand in the way of its effective detection and elimination. Studies have demonstrated how deficits in the state protection of vulnerable workers, as well as deficiencies in private industry-led social audit and certification systems, can lead to forced labour in both developing (Barrientos *et al.* 2011) and developed (Crane *et al.* 2017) country settings. Examining these institutional contexts can help shed light on why, when and how perpetrators of forced labour are able to operate with impunity.

In short, two key concepts from the management literature – business models and supply chains – can serve as useful analytical tools to researchers interested in understanding the business dynamics of forced labour. As we have argued, business models of forced labour have been frequently overlooked in favour of a focus on the MNCs at the helm of supply chains. However, understanding the various ways that perpetrators profit from forced labour deepens our understanding of its operation on the ground. Furthermore, a more systematic investigation of supply chains would be helpful for analysing the business pressures and structures that give rise to forced labour. These concepts can be valuable theoretical tools in steering research on the business of forced labour and, in particular, taking it beyond descriptive accounts to better understand and compare the factors driving the business of forced labour in various sectors and contexts.

New data: accessing that which is hidden

Thus far, we have argued that better data is required to deepen our understanding of the business of forced labour, and have introduced concepts to help guide and focus data collection. We now turn to the question of where researchers can look for stronger data. Because so much forced labour arises through informal and often illegal business, it should come as little surprise that we face significant obstacles when trying to access reliable data – more so than when researching business in the formal economy. This section of the chapter draws lessons from successful studies within literatures on other difficult to research subjects, including drug selling and sex work, as well as our own collaborative and individual research on the business of forced labour, to offer suggestions for how reliable information can be obtained.

Primary data: direct and indirect sources

One solution to the gaps in data we have identified is to explore the specific role of formal economy organisations in forced labour. For instance, empirical studies of value chains, labour exploitation and social auditing can be refined to take account of the business dynamics of forced labour. Niklas Egels-Zandén's (2014) research on suppliers' compliance with multinationals' codes of conduct, for example, is based on unofficial interviews with employees of suppliers. This allowed him to identify techniques used to deceive monitoring organisations that might very well be replicated in forced labour-type situations. We might also explore the accounting technologies used to prevent forced labour from coming within the purview of regulators, rendering the illegitimate legitimate. A good example of the latter is Dean Neu's (2012) qualitative study of the accounting strategies used by employers and undocumented workers to influence how and where economic transactions with illegal workers are recorded.

A potential direct source of data, then, is victims themselves, as discussed in the example below. But, as Crane's research has shown (2013), the opaque accounting used by perpetrators to prevent forced labour victims from understanding their own debts could make them unreliable informants in many instances. In this respect, there is no real substitute for getting data directly from perpetrators on the details of their businesses, such as their cost and revenue structures.

This approach was utilised by Steven Levitt and Sudhir Venkatesh (2000) in their empirical analysis of a drug dealing street gang in Chicago. Using a unique dataset of detailed financial information on the gang's activities obtained from a former gang member, the authors demonstrated considerably lower returns to drug selling than had been reported in the literature to date (based primarily on self-reports from drug dealers), a highly skewed wage distribution, and clear evidence of decision-making impossible to reconcile with economic optimisation. As Levitt and his co-author Stephen Dubner describe in their well-known book *Freakonomics* (2009), Venkatesh acquired access to the data following a period of immersive ethnographic research where he 'practically lived' in the housing project that was home to the gang, watching the gang members 'up close, at work, and at home'.

Ethnography is not the obvious way to acquire detailed quantitative data, but it has a long history of use in research on crime (Ferrell *et al.* 1998) and has increasingly been used in studies of forced and child labour (see chapter by Howard in this volume). Certainly, the need to develop trust with research subjects in (or with experience in) criminal enterprises necessitates a period of deep, long-term engagement with the field. This holds true for ethnography or any other methodology. Such an approach has considerable challenges – especially given the time pressures of academic publishing – but holds great potential for unlocking new insights into the business of forced labour. Very few of the researchers who have used ethnographic methods to study forced or child labour have been interested in its business dimensions; however, the quality and depth of information generated on the experiences of exploitation in these studies are indicative of their potential to draw out important data for deepening our understandings of both victims and perpetrators of forced labour. Conducting ethnography among vulnerable workers and perpetrators of exploitation entails a number of crucial ethical considerations (see chapters by Howard, Chan and LeBaron in this volume) for researchers need to seek direct information through this approach. As Stringer and Simmons (2015) report in relation to their research on forced labour in the New Zealand fishing industry, participants (and their families), researchers and translators were all subjected to considerable risks as a result of their involvement in the research – including intimidation, direct physical threats, stalking and restrictions on movement and communication. The need to acknowledge and prepare for such methodological risks is clear.

In addition to methodologies that involve direct contact with the people who have first-hand experience as either victims or perpetrators of forced labour, collecting data from indirect sources can be a way to secure reliable information on the business of forced labour. Interviewing experts who regularly interact with these business actors and workers can give researchers reliable data on how they operate. For instance, in a recent major study of the underground commercial sex economy, researchers spoke to pimps, traffickers and sex workers to estimate industry profits and understand cost and revenue flows, but also interviewed law enforcement personnel and prosecutors to gain insights into the structure of the sex market and how it differed across various cities, as well as the organisational dynamics of perpetrators (Dank *et al.* 2014). In our 2013 study of forced labour in the UK, we found key informants (e.g. social auditors and police officers with experience detecting forced labour) to be invaluable sources of information about the patterns of forced labour in the cannabis, construction and food industries, and how these had evolved over time.

Because all data sources on the business of forced labour will be imperfect, combining and triangulating between several types of information can strengthen primary data collection. Using both direct and indirect sources of information, and triangulating information collected from different actors along the supply chain, helps to ensure that information is sufficiently detailed, reliable and robust.

Example: business of forced labour in global tea supply chains

In 2015, LeBaron received a grant from the UK Economic and Social Research Council to investigate the business models of forced labour in global agricultural supply chains, focusing on tea and cocoa. Although the methods cannot be fully documented here, a brief overview of the sources of information used to understand forced labour in the tea industry in two regions of India (Kerala and Assam) helps illustrate the avenues we mentioned for researchers seeking to collect stronger data.

The project combined and triangulated four sources of direct and indirect information to decipher the business models of forced labour in the tea industry. First, a pilot study and scoping interviews were conducted with experts who had first-hand knowledge of labour exploitation within the tea industry, which included workers' rights and empowerment organisations, trade unions, certifiers and ethical auditors. These interviews generated insights into the overall patterns of forced labour and exploitation in the industry – including sources of workers' vulnerability to forced labour and the strategies businesses used to exploit them – which informed interview guides and survey questionnaires used in the main study. Second, following a period of participant observation and immersion, ethnographic interviews were conducted with tea workers (N=60). These interviews generated quantitative information about financial details, including wages, productivity quotas, deductions made from pay, credit and loan dynamics with managers and moneylenders, and costs of living, as well as qualitative information about working and living conditions and the role and prevalence of forced labour within the tea industry. Third, a survey with tea workers (N=500) was conducted using random sampling, which incorporated plantations of different sizes, ethical certification status, ownership structures (MNCs vs domestic companies) and geographical locations. This survey allowed us to triangulate and ensure the soundness of the interview data; it also provided more detailed information about the role and prevalence of forced

labour and exploitation within the tea industry. Finally, after a period of participant observation and immersion, interviews were conducted with tea plantation
managers and local tea industry associations (N=10) to collect financial details on
tea plantation business models as a whole, including cost and revenue structures,
information about the supply chains that the tea was being sold into, data on other
business actors including intermediaries, as well as on how business models were
impacted by state and private labour standards enforcement. Collecting and triangulating data from these four sources shed light on the patterns of when, why and
how forced labour was being used by tea producers.

This original dataset was then combined with another original dataset we com-
piled on the tea supply chain, which also incorporated direct and indirect accounts.
The tea supply chain dataset drew together three main sources of information.
First, it gathered data about the structure, geography, institutional dynamics and
governance structures of the global tea supply chains led by the ten largest tea
companies from industry databases and export data covering tea shipments from
India to the UK in 2015 and 2016. Second, interviews were conducted with tea
packagers, exporters, investors and government officials with responsibility for
the tea industry in India (N=10) to collect qualitative and quantitative information
about the supply chain, including business pressures, the enforcement of labour
standards and the value of the various activities along the supply chain. Finally,
interviews were conducted with tea companies and ethical certifiers (N=10),
focused on supply chain governance and efforts to prevent and address forced
labour in supply chains.

This dataset was difficult to collect given the complex and variegated logistical, ethical and linguistic challenges of accessing and interviewing vulnerable and
elite populations. It took an eight-person research team over one year to collect the
data, additional time to transcribe, clean, anonymise and code, and extensive effort
and training to manage the data in a way that ensured the protection of vulnerable
research participants.

As a whole, this primary dataset sheds light on the risks of labour exploitation,
including forced labour, in the tea industry and provides leverage to explore the
demographic features of workers – such as migration status, age and gender –
which have been identified in the literature to be risk factors for who is likely to be
subjected to forced labour. In addition, it sheds light on how, when and why forced
labour is deployed as part of a business model; how forced labour is managed; and
the supply chain pressures that trigger businesses' 'demand' for forced labour.
Finally, it allowed the researcher to compare business models across tea plantations
of various sizes, ownership structures, destinations of product (domestic vs export
consumption) and geographies (districts and regions).

Using secondary data

Not everyone will have the resources or time to collect primary data on the business of forced labour. Fortunately, there is a sizable and growing pool of high-quality secondary data that researchers could analyse to advance our understandings of the business of forced labour.

Researchers interested in analysing patterns surrounding the business of forced labour could turn to country and sector-based data. Some governments make data about the business of forced labour available to researchers. For instance, as part of their recently launched Decent Work SMARTLAB, the Federal Labor Prosecution Office in Brazil and the International Labour Organization in Brazil have published a database called Slave Labour in Brazil Digital Observatory documenting thousands of incidents of slavery that occurred within Brazil's private sector between 2003 and 2017 (Government of Brazil & ILO 2017). Similarly, the United States Department of Labor's Office of Child Labor, Forced Labor and Human Trafficking has commissioned and made public research on child and forced labour in many industries and countries. The United States Department of Labor has also funded independent research organisations such as Verité to conduct primary studies of forced labour, which are sometimes available for free online. For instance, Verité's major study *Forced Labor in the Production of Electronic Goods in Malaysia* is rich with detail that would interest researchers (Verité 2014). Like all sources of data on forced labour, government data has its drawbacks and limits; however, they can still lead to important and interesting insights. There is ample work to be done to analyse the patterns of forced labour across sectors. Researchers could also build out from these studies and combine them with other datasets (e.g. country-level data from the World Bank Enterprise Survey, which covers over 127,000 firms in 139 countries, or the International Organization for Migration's Global Migration Data Analysis Centre) to deepen understandings of the industry, country and regional contexts in which the business of forced labour operates.

There are a number of other key research questions about the business of forced labour that can be explored through secondary data. For instance, although the literature on business responses to labour exploitation in global supply chains (Fransen 2011; Anner *et al.* 2013) has not typically focused on forced labour, many of the same data sources could be analysed to explore what MNCs are doing to address the problem of forced labour, human trafficking and slavery in global supply chains. These sources include audit reports, company annual reports, terms and conditions for suppliers, and policy documents and reports related to ethical certification programmes like Fairtrade. In addition, as the current wave of transparency legislation compels companies to publish disclosures on their efforts to prevent and address forced labour in global supply chains, these statements provide an interesting lens into company policies and action. Several databases now gather together these statements, such as tiscreport.org, which at the time of writing included statements from nearly 150,000 organisations. A possible drawback of working with industry data is that these documents may introduce a bias, since companies want to portray themselves as leaders in addressing forced labour for reputational reasons and sales. All data will have limits, but can be combined and triangulated to yield important insights.

Conclusion

We have argued in this chapter that, in spite of the growing interest among scholars, policymakers and the public in the business of forced labour, we still know very little about the kinds of enterprises that are involved. To the extent that there is a focus on business, the attention is on large MNCs rather than on those harder to find, local and small-scale operators that are perpetrating forced labour on the ground. Understanding the business of forced labour – and informing policy measures to detect, address and increase business accountability for exploitation in supply chains – requires us to take business much more seriously than has been typical of the literature to date. There is a need to look at the business models and dynamics of forced labour in greater detail.

To that end, we have outlined two management concepts that can be used to theorise the business of forced labour – business models and supply chains – and reflected on how these concepts could be systematically deployed to focus and deepen empirical research in this area. We have provided an overview of the key gaps in data as well as suggestions for direct and indirect sources of information through which researchers could access that data, drawing lessons from our own research on the business of forced labour as well as inspiration from studies on other illegal business practices for how this research could happen. Such research is not easy to conduct – it is fraught with logistical and ethical challenges. However, it is possible and necessary to study the business of forced labour in a rigorous way that promotes comparability across sectors, supply chains and regions of the world. This research plays a crucial role in understanding the role and value of forced labour in the global economy, and in informing efforts to eradicate it.

References

Ahlburg, D. A. & Jensen, E. R. (1998), 'The Economics of the Commercial Sex Industry', in M. Ainsworth, L. Fransen & M. Over (eds), *Confronting AIDS: Evidence from the Developing World*) (Brussels, European Commission), 147–73.

Allain, J., Crane, A., LeBaron, G. & Behbahani, L. (2013), *Forced Labour's Business Models and Supply Chains* (York, UK, Joseph Rowntree Foundation).

Amit, R. & Zott, C. (2012), 'Creating Value through Business Model Innovation', *MIT Sloan Management Review*, 53, 3: 41–9.

Anner, M., Bair, J. & Blasi, J. (2013), 'Towards Joint Liability in Global Supply Chains: Addressing the Root Causes of Labor Violations in International Subcontracting Networks', *Comparative Labor Law and Policy Journal*, 35, 1: 1–43.

Arunachalam, R. & Shah, M. (2013), 'Compensated for Life Sex Work and Disease Risk', *Journal of Human Resources*, 48, 2: 345–69.

Bales, K. (2000), 'Expendable People: Slavery in the Age of Globalization', *Journal of International Affairs*, 53, 2: 461–84.

Bales, K. (2012), *Disposable People: New Slavery in the Global Economy* (Berkeley, University of California Press).

Barrientos, S., Mayer, F., Pickles, J. & Posthuma, A. (2011), 'Decent Work in Global Production Networks: Framing the Policy Debate', *International Labour Review*, 150, 3/4: 297–317.

Bhalla, N., Chandran, R. & Nagaraj, A. (2016), 'Blood Mica: Deaths of Child Workers in India's Mica "Ghost" Mines Covered up to Keep Industry Alive', accessed 20 July 2017, http://uk.reuters.com/article/us-india-mica-children-idUKKCN10D2NA

Bowe, J. (2007), *Nobodies: Modern American Slave Labor and the Dark Side of the New Global Economy* (New York, Random House).

Choi-Fitzpatrick, A. (2017), *What Slaveholders Think: How Contemporary Perpetrators Rationalize What They Do* (New York, Columbia University Press).

Crane, A. (2013), 'Modern Slavery as a Management Practice: Exploring the Conditions and Capabilities for Human Exploitation', *Academy of Management Review*, 38, 1: 49–69.

Crane, A., LeBaron, G., Allain, J. & Behbahani, L. (2017), 'Governance Gaps in Eradicating Forced Labor: From Global to Domestic Supply Chains', *Regulation & Governance*. DOI 10.1111/rego.12162

Dank, M., Khan, B., Downey, P. M., Kotonias, C., Mayer, D., Owens, C., Pacifici, L. & Yu, L. (2014), *Estimating the Size and Structure of the Underground Commercial Sex Economy in Eight Major US Cities*, accessed 25 July 2017, http://www.urban.org/sites/default/files/alfresco/publication-pdfs/413047-Estimating-the-Size-and-Structure-of-the-Underground-Commercial-Sex-Economy-in-Eight-Major-US-Cities.PDF

Egels-Zandén, N. J. (2014), 'Revisiting Supplier Compliance with MNC Codes of Conduct: Recoupling Policy and Practice at Chinese Toy Suppliers', *Journal of Business Ethics*, 119, 1: 59–75.

Ferrell, J., Hamm, M., Adler, P. & Adler, P. A. (1998), *Ethnography at the Edge: Crime, Deviance, and Field Research* (Boston, MA, Northeastern University Press).

Fifka, M. & Frangen-Zeitinger, A. (2015), 'Multinational Corporations in Developing Countries: Bringers of Working Standards or Modern Slaveholders', in S. O. Idowu, C. S. Frederiksen, A. Y. Mermod & M. E. Nielsen (eds), *Corporate Social Responsibility and Governance: Theory and Practice* (Berlin, Springer International Publishing).

Fransen, L. (2011), *Corporate Social Responsibility and Global Labor Standards: Firms and Activists in the Making of Private Regulation* (London, Routledge).

Gereffi, G., Humphrey, J. & Sturgeon, T. (2005), 'The Governance of Global Value Chains', *Review of International Political Economy*, 12, 1: 78–104.

Gertler, P., Shah, M. & Bertozzi, S. M. (2005), 'Risky Business: The Market for Unprotected Commercial Sex', *Journal of Political Economy*, 113, 3: 518–50.

Gold, S., Trautrims, A. & Trodd, Z. (2015), 'Modern Slavery Challenges to Supply Chain Management', *Supply Chain Management: An International Journal*, 20, 5: 485–94.

Government of Brazil and International Labour Organization (2017), *The Decent Work SMARTLAB*, accessed 27 July 2017, https://smartlab.mpt.mp.br/?language=en_US

ITUC (2016), *Scandal: Inside the Global Supply Chains of 50 Top Companies*, accessed 27 July 2017, https://www.ituc-csi.org/IMG/pdf/pdffrontlines_scandal_en-2.pdf

Kara, S. (2009), *Sex Trafficking: Inside the Business of Modern Slavery* (New York, Columbia University Press).

Kara, S. (2017), *Modern Slavery: A Global Perspective* (New York: Columbia University Press).

Laanela, M. & Merali, F. (2016), 'Forced Labour Lawsuit against Vancouver Mining Company Can Proceed', accessed 13 October 2016, http://www.cbc.ca/news/canada/british-columbia/nevsun-eritrean-lawsuit-1.3795687

Levitt, S. & Dubner, S. (2009), *Freakonomics: A Rogue Economist Explores the Hidden Side of Everything* (New York, William Morrow Publishing).

Levitt, S. & Venkatesh, S. (2000), 'An Economic Analysis of a Drug-Selling Gang's Finances', *Quarterly Journal of Economics*, 115, 3: 755–89.

Locke, R. (2013), *The Promise and Limits of Private Power: Promoting Labor Standards in a Global Economy* (New York, Cambridge University Press).

Locke, R., Amengual, M. & Mangla, A. (2009), 'Virtue out of Necessity? Compliance, Commitment, and the Improvement of Labor Conditions in Global Supply Chains', *Politics & Society*, 37, 3: 319–51.

Mezzadri, A. (2016), *The Sweatshop Regime: Labouring Bodies, Exploitation and Garments Made in India* (Cambridge, Cambridge University Press).

Neu, D. (2012), 'Accounting and Undocumented Work', *Contemporary Accounting Research*, 29, 1: 13–37.

New, S. J. (2015), 'Modern Slavery and the Supply Chain: The Limits of Corporate Social Responsibility?', *Supply Chain Management: An International Journal*, 20, 6: 697–707.

Osterwalder, A. & Pigneur, Y. (2010), *Business Model Generation: A Handbook for Visionaries, Game Changers, and Challengers* (London, Wiley).

Phillips, N. (2013), 'Unfree Labour and Adverse Incorporation in the Global Economy: Comparative Perspectives on Brazil and India', *Economy and Society*, 42, 2: 171–96. DOI 10.1080/03085147.2012.718630

Roberts, S. (2003), 'Supply Chain Specific? Understanding the Patchy Success of Ethical Sourcing Initiatives', *Journal of Business Ethics*, 44, 2/3: 159–70.

Schloenhardt, A. (1999), 'Organized Crime and the Business of Migrant Trafficking', *Crime, Law and Social Change*, 32, 3: 203–33.

Scott, S., Craig, G. & Geddes, A. (2012), *Forced Labour in the UK Food Industry* (York, UK, Joseph Rowntree Foundation).

Stringer, C. & Simmons, G. (2015), 'Stepping through the Looking Glass', *Journal of Management Inquiry*, 24, 3: 253–63.

van den Anker, C. (ed.) (2004), *The Political Economy of New Slavery* (London, Palgrave).

Verité (2014), *Forced Labor in the Production of Electronic Goods in Malaysia: A Comprehensive Study of Scope and Characteristics*, accessed 1 July 2017, https://www.verite.org/wp-content/uploads/2016/11/VeriteForcedLaborMalaysianElectronics2014.pdf

Verité (2017), *Strengthening Protections against Trafficking in Persons in Federal and Corporate Supply Chains: Research on Risk in 43 Commodities Worldwide*, accessed 1 August 2017, https://www.verite.org/wp-content/uploads/2017/04/EO-and-Commodity-Reports-Combined-FINAL-2017.pdf

Warrell, H. (2015), 'Ruthless UK Employers Trap Migrants in "Modern-Day Slavery"', *Financial Times*, accessed 15 July 2017, https://www.ft.com/content/43daccd0-410d-11e5-9abe-5b335da3a90e

Wilshaw, R., Liesbeth, U., Chi, D. Q. & Thuy, P. T. (2013), *Labour Rights in Unilever's Supply Chain: From Compliance towards Good Practice*, accessed 20 July 2017, https://www.ituc-csi.org/IMG/pdf/rr-unilever-supply-chain-labour-rights-vietnam-310113-en.pdf

3

The Politics of Numbers:
Beyond Methodological Challenges
in Research on Forced Labour

NICOLA PHILLIPS[1]

Introduction

IT IS, BY NOW, stating the entirely obvious to say that researching forced labour is beset by methodological challenges. Other chapters in this volume have offered eloquent discussions of the nature of these challenges, many of which also apply to research on other forms of illicit and criminal activity in the global economy. The barriers to effective data collection are myriad, challenging both the researcher and the 'consumer' of the research in their efforts to understand the extent, nature and, importantly, causes of this resilient global problem. This chapter aims to further that discussion by developing the argument that these problems are not simply methodological or practical, but also intrinsically and intensely *political*.

The notion that there is a politics to the collection and presentation of evidence and data – a politics of numbers – is far from new. But it is, I suggest, too often overlooked in the area of research on forced labour. Indeed, this arena has been no exception to the drive across the public policy world towards 'a hyper-numeric world preoccupied with quantification' (Andreas & Greenhill 2010: 1), which is reflected in the trend in academia to privilege quantitative methods as holding a superior 'scientific' status (Phillips & Weaver 2010). The provision of 'hard data' has become a prerequisite and precursor to not only political recognition of forced labour, but also serious policy debate or action around the issue. In the absence

[1] This chapter benefited immensely from the book workshop convened by the editor of this volume at the British Academy in October 2016. I am grateful to project colleagues for their insightful suggestions, which they will find to have been readily taken up in what follows. I also acknowledge the generous support of the Leverhulme Trust (Major Research Fellowship F00120BW) in facilitating the research on which this chapter draws.

of data that are deemed to be 'hard' enough, the reticence to engage meaningfully in political action remains pronounced, whether as a convenient mechanism for avoidance or as an impediment to obtaining sufficient leverage to secure real political attention. Furthermore, this drive towards quantification has opened up a new form of competition – between and among academics, actors and organisations in an emerging industry of 'information' – to deliver the gold-standard set of forced labour estimates that will inform global policy debate. Indeed, it has become hard to escape the impression that the numbers themselves have disproportionately become the focus of attention, with the ultimate aim being to quantify, rather than to better understand the nature and causes of the problem itself.

In common with all other areas of transnational crime, the illicit character of forced labour leads to 'a politics of numbers that is particularly susceptible to speculation, distortion, and sometimes even outright fabrication that is rarely questioned or challenged in policy debates and media reporting' (Andreas 2010: 23). Significantly, data on the incidence of forced labour have been pulled in opposite directions: towards both an inflation of the numbers and evidence, and an understatement of data and evidence. The dynamics of data manipulation are driven by various forms of politics and by the political uses to which the data are put, leading to significant distortion of both the nature and the underlying causes of the problem. Understanding the political nature of the challenges to researching forced labour, as well as the politics surrounding the collection and use of data and evidence, is in this sense vital to a consideration of the business of forced labour and the challenges for achieving the much-needed 'scaling up' of our research in this area.

In this chapter, I reflect on the politics of numbers in the area of forced labour, attempting to capture some of the complexity of how evidence is generated and used politically. I first consider the politics of quantification – that is, the process of generating estimates of the scale and incidence of forced labour – with a focus on the twin issues of 'what is counted' and 'where you look'. The second part of this chapter considers the politics of how data on forced labour are used, exploring political uses of data both in abstract terms and in concrete domestic and international contexts. While the politics of quantification and the political uses of data often overlap, I advance with a slightly artificial separation in order to draw attention to two specific issues: in the first instance, the politics of counting – given the importance of the 'cottage industry' that has sprung up in the arena of global quantification – and in the second, how the resulting numbers are used by actors in the field of forced labour to serve particular ends. The third and final section reflects on the challenges thereby posed for future research on forced labour at the global level, with the aim of substantiating the contention that the politics of research in this area are just as central to these challenges as methodological or practical concerns.

The politics of quantification

The drive for 'hard data' in the area of forced labour stems first and foremost from a demand – mostly from policymakers – for evidence of the scale of the problem. In a sense, this is hardly unreasonable, as it is difficult to consider appropriate responses to a particular problem unless the dimensions of the problem in question are clear. However, in this particular policy area, as in many others, the lack of reliable data has often served as a pretext for inaction. Decisions to commit scarce resources are made conditional on the provision of unequivocal evidence that the scale of problem x is manifestly greater than the scale of problem y. Without such evidence, it is difficult to politically justify – or essentially 'sell' – the dedication of resources; likewise, it is difficult to lobby effectively for the provision of resources. Australian billionaire Andrew Forrest famously quoted Bill Gates' advice during the establishment of his charity Walk Free: 'if you can't measure it, it doesn't exist'. This mantra led to the initiation of the Global Slavery Index (GSI) as the latest high-profile attempt at producing global statistics (Behrman 2013).[2] The problem, as we see at length in this volume, is that unequivocal quantification of forced labour simply cannot be produced. This has led many to worry about attaching a quantitative indicator for trafficking to the UN Sustainable Development Goals, referring to the 'number of victims of human trafficking per 100,000 population, by sex, age group and form of exploitation', and to argue that, given the existing limits of data collection in this arena, it is at best premature to attempt to do so (Gallagher 2016). Nevertheless, the drive towards quantification shows no sign of abating.

To the extent that political action is dependent on the identification of a quantifiable problem, the dangers of data manipulation become very real in the area of forced labour. There is a tendency to inflate estimates of the incidence of forced labour to exert political pressure on those who control resources or set political agendas – in most cases, national governments and international organisations. Alternatively, national governments or international organisations themselves may – unwittingly or purposefully – inflate certain figures in service of particular political ends. It has been shown repeatedly how this works. Given the paucity of accurate and reliable data on the scale of forced labour, academic and other analysts frequently resort to publishing speculative estimates, using the known numbers but, not unreasonably, issuing caveats that the real figures might be much higher. These much higher figures are then taken to be the 'known' figures, and corresponding further assumptions are made that, given the grey areas of calculation, the real figures may be much higher still. Nick Davies documented how this phenomenon manifested in the UK context at the end of the 2000s, when the Home

---

[2] The Global Slavery Index can be accessed here: https://www.globalslaveryindex.org/

Office selected the highest possible speculative estimates from academic research it commissioned on sex trafficking into the United Kingdom, and then used these figures as factual in evidence to a House of Commons joint committee on human rights, without flagging any of the careful caveats issued by the researchers. Other organisations and media outlets picked up these figures and followed suit, using the 'official' Home Office estimate as the new baseline, but going on to declare that this estimate was likely to have been conservative – thus furthering the trend towards data inflation (Davies 2009). The attempt to cater for the unavailability of comprehensive data on trafficking or forced labour, accompanied by further manipulation, led to the data becoming even less reliable. As a result, the hyperinflation of data is perpetuated in a cycle, and attention to the underlying problem of forced labour becomes diverted by continual arguments about the veracity of the circulating data.

Similarly, the GSI, first published in 2013, proffered significantly increased estimates of the incidence of slavery in comparison to the existing benchmark data published as the International Labour Organization's (ILO) Global Estimates. To simplify a massively complex methodology (GSI 2016), the key to the GSI's calculation is extrapolation from new and existing random sample data from 19 countries to estimate the incidence of slavery across 148 countries. Perhaps unsurprisingly, the resulting data have attracted compelling criticism. What is more surprising is actually how little critical scrutiny has been forthcoming, amid a generalised glowing reception from the global elite of governments, international organisations, philanthropists and others (Gallagher 2013). It has been observed that the reasons are at least in part political: Walk Free, the charity that initiated and has funded the GSI, has emerged as a major philanthropic donor in the field of forced labour at a time when funding for anti-slavery initiatives is either in decline or remains negligible (Gallagher 2013). Thus, the GSI's estimates of the incidence of forced labour, which are much higher than the previous ILO data, are insulated from scrutiny for political reasons, accepted as 'fact' and deployed as the new consensus underpinning global policy. The production of higher estimates was, of course, an almost inevitable outcome of the GSI process, given competition for headline status which we noted at the start of the chapter.

Conversely, there is an opposite and equally strong tendency to deflate estimates of the incidence of forced labour, when the priority is to maintain the status quo and avoid additional scrutiny. This tendency is particularly pronounced in the international arena, where the international politics of trafficking and forced labour are dominated by the United States and particular international organisations' efforts to rank and 'certify' countries according to their efforts to combat the problem, or to expose the extent to which trafficking and forced labour are occurring in particular settings – an example of a growing phenomenon of 'scorecard diplomacy' (Kelley 2017). We will consider this issue in more detail in the following section, but here it is sufficient to note that – particularly where there is a possibility of trade sanctions, consumer boycotts, actions by transnational firms and investors, or other political action aimed at countries demonstrating high levels of forced labour – there are clear political incentives for certain governments to understate the extent of the problem in their country.

Likewise, political difficulty arises in situations where the estimated incidence of forced labour or trafficking is high, but levels of successful prosecution or assistance to victims are relatively low. It was speculated, for instance, that the United States Department of Justice was motivated to lower its estimates progressively between 2002 and 2005, from 50,000 new victims of trafficking per year to 17,500, in order to compensate for the fact that records showed only 1,000 victims receiving government assistance, a very limited number of prosecutions, and the approval of very few T-visas (those granted to victims of trafficking) (Haynes 2007). The Department of Justice gave no reason for its revised estimates, nor for the inadequate levels of assistance to victims.

Beyond basic political incentives for manipulating data, well-intentioned or otherwise, an enduring underpinning challenge is defining the parameters of forced labour. In this context, there are two main competing positions. The first argues that, for a definition of forced labour to have any meaning, it must necessarily be understood in specific and fairly narrow terms, that is, as a phenomenon that is separate from other forms of exploitation. The second position contends that the first approach is too narrow and consequently misses the enormous 'grey areas' in which so many thousands and millions of people are suffering exploitation and abuse. For the first group, casting the net into those grey areas constitutes an unacceptable distortion of the problem and a dilution of the necessary focus on the worst forms of exploitation; for the second group, the failure to employ a more nuanced understanding contributes to 'ring-fencing' the problem of forced labour, permitting only the most extreme forms of exploitation to receive any political or policy airspace (Lerche 2007; Skrivankova 2010; McGrath 2013; Phillips & Mieres 2014; Phillips 2015). For proponents of the second group, the complexity of the problem is thereby underestimated, its 'political sanitisation' (Lerche 2007) is enabled, and human responsibility towards those affected by the problem is abrogated.

The issue of human trafficking for sexual exploitation has been a key battleground in this respect, reflecting ongoing and intensely passionate debate about where – if at all – the dividing lines can be said to exist between forced sexual labour, sexual exploitation and sex work. An interesting account documents how the politics surrounding sex work and prostitution in the United States may have distorted the trafficking agenda: the conflation of prostitution with trafficking for sexual exploitation in quantitative estimates – a political move reflecting longstanding political and cultural agendas – has led to considerable inflation of the incidence of trafficking (Feingold 2010). Elsewhere, the separation of trafficking/forced labour and sex work is held to be very much clearer, although again the political underpinnings of this distinction are intensely contested. At the same time, the deployment of encompassing definitions of trafficking – including, for instance, mail-order brides or women working for escort agencies (Haynes 2007; Davies 2009) – incurs criticism for inappropriately inflating estimates of the problem in ways that deprive the issue of its political or moral force.

The politics of definition manifest similarly in the arena of forced labour, including in the context of the 'business' of forced labour. In this case, the tendency has if anything been more towards adopting distinctly restrictive definitions of forced labour, and the political impetus has consistently been towards isolating forced labour from the broader issue of labour exploitation in national and global economies. The tremendously diverse manifestations of labour exploitation are politically sensitive, and governments and international organisations across the world are cautious when it comes to the politics of business relations. Ring-fencing forced labour to the extent that the problem is presented as being 'exceptional' is a considerably safer political approach, and one that lends more easily to political consensus. The quantitative estimates, corresponding with a high definitional threshold, paint the scale of the problem as being less challenging to business and less demanding of significant change to core business models and practices. Roger Plant, formerly of the ILO, makes the surely correct point that action on forced labour specifically may serve as a practical way of getting things done on issues like migration policy or wider forms of labour market governance, all while bypassing some of the political landmines that otherwise accompany political and public debates in these arenas (Plant 2007: 16). In other words, workaround solutions may well be better than stalemate. Nevertheless, there is a danger that when forced labour is presented as separate from other kinds of labour exploitation, quantitative estimates are depressed, and the debate is further distanced from the underlying economic causes of the problem, making the possibility of effective policy action even more remote (Phillips & Mieres 2014).

An exception to this generalised tendency towards definitional narrowing has been the Brazilian campaign against what is in that country termed, somewhat controversially, 'slave labour' (Gomes 2009). This phenomenon is defined in Brazilian law as '[r]educing someone to a condition analogous to slavery, whether by subjecting them to forced labour or exhaustive working hours, *or* by subjecting him or her to degrading working conditions or restricting their movement by any means, due to debts to the employer or its representative' (cited in Gomes 2009: 1, emphasis added). The inclusion of 'degrading working conditions' as a *sufficient* indicator offers a much more encompassing criterion than that which is customarily used in definitions of 'forced labour'. In practice, much has hinged on how 'degrading' has been defined and interpreted by the key actors involved in Brazil's national campaign against slavery. While the Brazilian government of the 2000s positioned itself at the forefront of the global effort against slavery and forced labour, in what was an unprecedented policy effort (Sakamoto 2007), this more inclusive definition was nevertheless unable to gain traction outside Brazil. This is perhaps not surprising, given the significant political challenges that it posed for national governments and international organisations, particularly in terms of their relations with domestic and transnational business interests. Significantly, the landmark National Pact for the Eradication of Slave Labor of 2005 in Brazil, which invited the commitment of firms and employers to the anti-slavery effort, was the subject of a Direct Unconstitutionality Lawsuit brought to the Supreme Court by the National Farming Confederation (Phillips & Sakamoto 2012).

Evidently, 'what is counted' as forced labour therefore shapes the resulting estimates of its incidence, and has very real consequences for human beings. If 'what is counted' makes a world of difference, then so too does its counterpart, 'where you look', which similarly is conditioned by an underpinning politics. A familiar argument addresses the historically greater attention that has been paid to sexual exploitation as opposed to labour exploitation, or the greater attention that international organisations and interested governments have given to forced labour in the developing world rather than in 'richer' countries of the Global 'North'. More recently, the same could be said about the focus on forced labour in global supply chains that has emerged over the 2000s, as opposed to forced labour in the domestic work industry, where advocates draw attention to an ongoing neglect (e.g. Mantouvalou 2015). Yet, the issue of 'where you look' can also be manipulated to present a partial profile of the problem in a particular location or sector. An example relates to forced child labour in the Indian garment industry, where the government has famously claimed that garment factories have now become 'child-labour-free'. However, the data on this sector do not indicate a diminishing incidence of child labour nor a decline in the numbers of children working in such conditions; rather, the problem has been displaced to the household sector and is now, through complex, informal subcontracting arrangements, largely curtained off from the view of factory auditors and labour inspectors (Bhaskaran *et al.* 2014; Phillips *et al.* 2014). Garment production has therefore not become 'child-labour-free', but instead the problem has been displaced to arenas which lie outside those conventionally counted in government or firm-level quantification efforts.

From a slightly different angle, the issue of 'where you look' extends to the political considerations that underpin the deployment of resources for the interests of identification and quantification of forced labour. A pertinent example is again Brazil, where official statistics have been used to draw a sectoral picture of the incidence of slavery (Sakamoto 2007; Phillips & Sakamoto 2012). The problem is recorded as being concentrated in the agricultural economy, and the statistics show that a preponderance of identified cases of slavery exists in the sugar cane sector. In this case, quantification efforts are driven by the work of the federal labour inspection system to document instances in which slavery-like conditions are present. The system works with finite resources, and active political decisions dictate resource allocation as well as the priorities for expenditure. The sugar cane sector was identified as a particular focus in the 2000s, when the Brazilian government was pursuing a national development strategy to position Brazil as the world's most important producer of sugar cane-based ethanol and biofuels and, as such, was concerned about the global reputational integrity of that sector in terms of labour standards and slavery. What the statistics reflect, in this sense, is the purposeful dedication of resources to labour inspection in the sugar cane sector, and consequently a greater level of identification of slavery. We do not know whether the incidence of slavery in the sugar sector is *in reality* greater than in, say, the cattle ranching sector, or whether the greater incidence is simply a product of the politics of 'where you look' (Phillips & Sakamoto 2012).

The political uses of data

There is now a voluminous literature in the social sciences, business and management sciences and beyond concerning the political drivers and uses of quantification. From arguments concerning the use of quantification as a way of generating political trust (Porter 1996; Fligstein 1998) to studies of quantification as the basis for decision-making and governance processes (Erkkilä *et al.* 2016) and discussions of the relationship between quantification and outcomes in particular issue areas (Andreas & Greenhill 2010), the literature unequivocally demonstrates that numbers are at least as political as they are scientific, rarely 'objective' and never politically neutral.

For the purposes of this chapter, and due to the constraints imposed by space on such an expansive subject matter, two dimensions of the political uses of data are most relevant. The first concerns the narrative power of numbers and data. Simply put, establishing a narrative is key to the foundations of political action, be it to justify government legislation or to exert political pressure on governments, organisations or firms to act in this policy area. Numbers are invariably the key headline for generating political interest and help establish the significance of the problem in a more accessible way. Equally importantly, data depicting trends are key to political narratives as the foundation for action. For example, the commonly heard but as yet unsubstantiated view that forced labour is increasing globally carries immense power in making the case for urgent action, going beyond the notion that forced labour is an aberration affecting few people and that it is in the process of being eradicated. The use of numbers to establish that government action or firm-level action is working is equally powerful; in the case of firms, data which show a decreased incidence of forced labour are key to managing reputational dynamics and relationships with consumers.

The second dimension of the political use of data that is of particular relevance is how quantification is deployed as an instrument of political control. The focus in the ample literature tends to fall on the governance mechanisms associated with target setting (e.g. Matthews 2016), and the arena of forced labour is no exception to this set of dynamics. It is particularly evident in the context of law enforcement, in terms of government oversight of both policing and the judicial process. Conversations and interviews with police forces in the United Kingdom have indicated an increasing drive towards quantification in relation to setting target numbers for identifying victims, arrests and prosecutions, and parallel concerns about the implications of an expanding remit for scarce resources. This is particularly so in relation to forced labour and trafficking for labour exploitation, where it is widely accepted that the scale of the problem is considerable, and anxieties persist about how it could be appropriately addressed within severe budgetary and resource constraints.[3]

Parallel processes can be observed in recent attempts by government to use numbers to ratchet up the rhetoric in relations with business, notably in the legislation passed in the state of California on Transparency in Supply Chains, federal legislation in the United States on trafficking in arenas such as procurement, and the UK Modern Slavery Act. It has been argued that the political pressure brought to bear through these kinds of 'disclosure' legislation is more ostensible than real in terms of the relationship between government and business, inasmuch as the legislation lacks meaningful provision for enforcement and, in reality, demands little of firms.[4] But it does have more bite in terms of political relationships between business and consumers (Phillips 2015; Phillips *et al.* 2018). The legislation itself does not demand of firms that they quantify the incidence of forced labour in supply chains, nor that they offer quantitative evidence of their progress in this area. Nevertheless, a huge amount of energy was expended on establishing quantitative 'headlines' in advance of the introduction of the legislation, as a key part of winning over a traditionally sceptical business community to the political case for regulation of this kind (LeBaron & Rühmkorf 2017).

It is also relevant that fears concerning the political uses of data have led to reticence in cooperating with data collection efforts. A prominent example is the UK's National Referral Mechanism (NRM), envisaged as an important element of the government's data collection effort, which relies on non-governmental organisations (NGOs) to refer suspected victims of trafficking to law enforcement agencies (specifically the National Crime Agency) for further investigation. The consultation surrounding the review of the NRM in 2014 threw up ample evidence of difficulties concerning the political uses of referral data, in particular in relation to the role of the Home Office. Put simply, the fear for some NGOs was that immigration authorities would have direct access to referrals under the NRM, such

---

[3] Confidential interviews conducted in connection with research for my Leverhulme Major Research Fellowship on 'Forced Labour and Trafficking for Labour Exploitation in the Global Economy', 2010–13 (F00120BW).

[4] Disclosure legislation relies on the requirement of publicity, obliging companies to provide publicly available information on specified dimensions of their operations. In the present context, these dimensions relate to the nature and implications of their activities throughout the global supply chain, specifically in relation to labour standards. See Phillips *et al.* (2018).

that the immigration status of potential victims would receive undue attention, and their vulnerability would be increased by referral to the authorities. The conflation of asylum claims and trafficking claims of people subject to immigration control has been an ongoing criticism of the NRM process (see Law Centre NI 2014). As such, in the early 2000s, the data collection effort was hampered by the reticence of some NGOs to engage in the NRM process, because of concerns about the political purposes for which data will be employed.[5]

The use of quantification as a mechanism of political leverage is strikingly evident in the realm of international politics. Perhaps the most obvious example is the US Department of State's Trafficking in Persons (TIP) Report, established as part of the Trafficking Victims Protection Act of 2000. The annual TIP Report analyses foreign governments' compliance with minimum standards in their anti-trafficking efforts, and ranks them in tiers accordingly. Apart from its agenda-setting power, the TIP Report process holds out the threat of sanctions against governments that are failing to comply with these standards. The TIP Report process has been complemented by the aforementioned GSI process, which relies heavily on TIP Reports in order to release into the public domain assessments of the scale of the problem across 148 countries, and by the US Department of Labor's annual reports identifying goods produced by forced or child labour across the world.

The TIP Report attracted considerable criticism early on in its existence, even from within the United States. The General Accounting Office (GAO) took the State Department to task for incomplete and unreliable data, as well as its failures to justify its ranking of countries (both those appearing in the top tier for full compliance, and those in tiers two and three indicating non-compliance). In the view of the GAO, the credibility of the TIP process was thereby undermined, as was its utility as a diplomatic tool to achieve its desired outcomes (US GAO 2006). There was also a strong sense of déjà vu in relation to US drug certification policy in the 1980s, as governments chafed against the presumption of the US government in appointing itself the judge of global anti-trafficking efforts, its focus on the developing world and its much less punitive approach to its own status and that of other 'developed-country' governments, and – perhaps most compellingly – the ways in which the rankings were highly politicised. Countries of key political or economic strategic importance to the United States were perceived to have been given a much easier ride than those that were not. The 2015 TIP Report attracted particularly heavy criticism for being 'watered down' by strategic considerations, such that Malaysia, Cuba, China, India, Uzbekistan and Mexico all received better scores than those recommended by the State Department's human-rights experts, and more generally for the ways in which deference to the State Department's expertise had been undermined by other state agencies (*The Guardian* 2015; Carney 2015).

---

[5] Confidential interviews with UK NGOs and law enforcement agencies, in connection with Leverhulme Major Research Fellowship, 2010–13.

In these necessarily brief examples, we see clearly the complex political nexus between narrative and control in how data on forced labour are used. Data are key to establishing a compelling narrative about the importance and urgency of forced labour – in ways which most of us would accept as highly desirable. Yet we have seen that this narrative is rarely straightforward, inasmuch as it is key to how the issue is framed and approached in policy terms. Highly political and politicised sets of choices inform which narratives are produced by which kinds of data – reflecting and furthering political agendas about which forms of forced labour or trafficking matter – which agencies are responsible for governing the issue on the basis of these political agendas, and, importantly, which actors wield the financial and philanthropic power to shape the narrative. On the basis of the power that particular actors and agencies wield in the world of quantification, particular narratives become powerful instruments of political control, shaping and disciplining governance practices, controlling which actors in the field achieve political influence, and deciding, in effect, who is and is not to be counted as a victim of exploitation. Narrative power and political control thus go hand in hand, underscoring how quantification and data are never politically neutral in this or any other field of social and political action.

Conclusion: the challenges for research on forced labour

Our illustrative discussion of the politics of quantification and the political uses of data demonstrates that the challenges for future work on forced labour are not simply methodological, but rather are intrinsically political. By way of conclusion, I wish to focus on three particular challenges for the task of 'scaling up' research on forced labour, and offer some observations on how researchers might go about responding to them.

The first challenge relates to the task of scaling up from the national level to the global level. By this I refer, essentially, to the challenge of generating quantitative and qualitative data that better capture the global scale and profile of the problem of forced labour. To date, estimation methodologies have generally concentrated on the use of new or existing national data on forced labour, and taken those data as the basis for extrapolation to the global level. To an extent, such a method is as good as any other, in an issue area in which no method is ever going to fully capture the detail of an essentially hidden problem that by its nature makes accurate quantification impossible. It is nevertheless, as we have seen, a problematic method, which carries real political consequences. The task of extrapolation is always fraught with difficulty, inasmuch as it necessarily involves heroic assumptions about the generalisability of data from one country to another, and indeed to the global level. Some such assumptions might be reasonably safe, but we have no means yet of knowing whether empirical extrapolation adequately captures the scale and, more importantly, profile of forced labour across the world.

This concern is particularly pertinent given that the major GSI estimates, as noted earlier, rely on extrapolation from such a small number of countries, based on an essentially small-scale random sampling exercise. However, it afflicts other estimates in different ways. The ILO Global Estimates are based in large part on national data provided by national governments. This is defended inasmuch as national governments are the obvious actors on which to rely for data collection. However, two immediate problems present themselves. The first is the massive variation in the quality of data collection, some of it the result of institutional capacity but some also the result of variation in 'what is counted' and 'where you look'. Given the scale of differences between national legislative and legal definitions and frameworks in the area of forced labour, and the significant politicisation of data collection and enforcement efforts, relying on national data immediately becomes a questionable basis for accurate quantification. The second problem relates to all of the issues we have identified here concerning the manipulation and distortion of data for political purposes, particularly where, in a world of TIP rankings and corresponding political and economic sanctions, most governments have a strong incentive to downplay the scale of problems in their countries. Again, extrapolation from national statistics, most of them provided by governments themselves, is inherently unsatisfactory. *Faute de mieux*, it has become the standard basis for quantification attempts, but cannot unproblematically be accepted or assumed to yield reliable data. The task for future research is to develop better methodologies that overcome some of these technical *and political* limitations.

A way forward is to accept an extrapolation method, but to ensure that it is based on very serious, extensive and methodologically robust comparative research. This will not overcome all of the technical and political problems we have identified, but at least it will heighten the credibility of the resulting extrapolated global estimates. A more controversial alternative is to abandon the seemingly heroic task of producing global estimates for now, despite their political usefulness in establishing a narrative, and concentrate our academic and policy efforts on national and/ or regional estimates – the latter, I suggest, being the most compelling alternative. On such a basis, we could then collectively return to the global ambition, having scaled up first from national to regional, and then from regional to global. Again, this does not overcome many of the political problems, but these are inherent to the enterprise, and the task becomes one of carefully, candidly acknowledging these political limitations and reflecting on their significance for the research that is produced. Some regional-level analysis does exist and is very useful, but it seems fair to say that the game is increasingly driven by the political prestige that attaches to the heroic (and very competitive) global estimation challenge, often to the detriment of the rigour and quality of the statistical base on which such estimates are forced to rest. Given the nature of the problem and the challenges posed by its 'illicitness', there can be few alternatives to painstaking, slow, methodologically rigorous and politically reflective research into the incidence and profile of forced labour on the ground, eschewing the temptation to indulge in grandiose extrapolation, and finding more imaginative ways to shape the narrative about forced labour and its relationship with policy.

The second challenge intersects closely with the first: it is the challenge of moving beyond the production of snapshot ecological data (notably on the incidence of forced labour) towards data that tell us something meaningful about underlying causes. At present, the overriding preoccupation with numbers and global estimates has generated data that tell us next to nothing about the root causes of forced labour, how and why it occurs, and why it is so resilient. In other words, there is little connection as of yet between research seeking to uncover the causal dynamics underpinning the global problem of forced labour – with which many of the scholars collected together in this volume are associated – and the work that focuses its attention on quantitative estimation.

Needless to say, this represents a considerable problem. To an extent, it is true that quantitative estimation is necessary as a platform for further research and policy. But the difficulty in the present situation is that efforts towards quantification have displaced the key questions of the root causes of forced labour, and this displacement is politically expedient, allowing governments and other actors to shift the focus from the politically difficult questions about how forced labour is connected to the functioning of the economy (national and global) to a less challenging causal narrative of criminal activity, government corruption, inadequate regulation, and so on. The global elite is able to applaud high-profile efforts at quantitative estimation, but it is hard to imagine them responding enthusiastically to quantitative and qualitative data that challenge governments, organisations, firms and societies to look hard at the structural dynamics associated with causation, particularly in relation to underpinning economic models.

The challenge for research, however, is to do precisely this – to move from ecological data to quantitative and qualitative data that allow us to say something meaningful about causation. Such an enterprise is fraught with difficulty. One can construct a general, theoretical perspective on the root causes of forced labour connected to, say, global production and global value chains (Phillips 2013; Barrientos *et al.* 2013) or domestic value chains (Crane *et al.* 2017), but this cannot answer the question of, for example, why some workers find themselves in situations of forced labour and others do not. The challenge is therefore to move not only beyond the specific to the generalisable, but also from the generalisable to the specific, in an attempt to account for contingency and variation while providing much needed 'big-picture' perspectives on the causal dynamics which produce forced labour. Once again, it returns to the need for a concerted research effort, resisting the temptations of the grandiose in favour of careful, detailed research, which can then form the basis of careful and appropriate policy. By now, it should be clear that this is not just a question of method, but also one of the politics of how research and policy intersect, what kinds of research are taken up and deemed politically acceptable, and how the political ramifications of causal data could be managed.

The final challenge draws us back to a passing comment made in the introduction, which concerns the academic politics surrounding research on forced labour. In parallel with the drive towards quantification in public and policy life, the academic disciplines of the social sciences have drifted towards a culture in which quantitative research methods are increasingly deemed in some parts of the academic world to be methodologically superior to qualitative methods (e.g. Phillips & Weaver 2010). Increasingly rigid assumptions about what constitute 'proper' methods and evidence in social science act to set and police the parameters of what is and can be studied in our field. One of the reasons why the issues of forced labour, child labour and human trafficking have received so little attention may well relate to their inevitable defiance of systematic qualitative and quantitative study, leaving them outside the parameters of the sorts of research favoured or considered sufficiently 'rigorous' or 'scientific' by particular constituencies within our disciplines. This is lamentable not simply in intellectual terms, but also for the ways in which it closes down incentives for work on problems of such immediate importance in the contemporary world, where a better understanding of what we are dealing with is critical to the elaboration of effective strategies for addressing these most extreme forms of human exploitation.

The challenge of scaling up forced labour research is therefore political in this sense as well, involving a need to engage with the politics of academic culture and a willingness, in essence, to work against the current to ensure that this kind of research retains its importance. Methodological rigour is paramount, but so too is a defence of the importance of research where, for all the reasons we have documented, data cannot be considered reliable, large-N datasets are not available, and sophisticated data analysis techniques are consequently not always viable. The enterprise of generating better quantitative data is vital to our field and the kinds of policy action that might address the global problems of forced labour, but cannot displace the types of qualitative research that are also needed, particularly in understanding their underpinning causes. The political challenges are in all these ways formidable, but sensitivity to them and the development of imaginative responses are indispensable to the collective task of addressing the issues at stake.

References

Andreas, P. (2010), 'The Politics of Measuring Illicit Flows and Policy Effectiveness', in P. Andreas & K. M. Greenhill (eds), *Sex, Drugs, and Body Counts: The Politics of Numbers in Global Crime and Conflict* (Ithaca, NY, Cornell University Press), 23–45.

Andreas, P. & Greenhill, K. M. (eds) (2010), *Sex, Drugs and Body Counts: The Politics of Numbers in Global Crime and Conflict* (Ithaca, NY, Cornell University Press).

Barrientos, S., Kothari, U. & Phillips, N. (2013), 'Dynamics of Unfree Labour in the Contemporary Global Economy,' *Journal of Development Studies*, 49, 8: 1037–41. DOI 10.1080/00220388.2013.780043

Behrman, E. (2013), 'Gates Helps Australia's Richest Man in Bid to End Slavery', *Bloomberg Technology* (14 April 2013).

Bhaskaran, R., Nathan, D., Phillips, N. & Upendranadh, C. (2014), 'Vulnerable Workers and Labour Standards (Non-)Compliance in Global Production Networks: Home-Based Child Labour in Delhi's Garment Sector', in A. Rossi, A. Luinstra & J. Pickles (eds), *Toward Better Work: Understanding Labour in Apparel Global Value Chains* (Basingstoke, ILO and Palgrave Macmillan), 172–90.

Carney, J. (2015), 'Sen. Menendez Slams "Politicization" of Human Trafficking Report', *The Hill* (27 July 2015).

Crane, A., LeBaron, G., Allain, J. & Behbahani, L. (2017), 'Governance Gaps in Eradicating Forced Labour: From Global to Domestic Supply Chains', *Regulation & Governance*. DOI 10.1111/rego.12162

Davies, N. (2009), 'Victims Who Never Existed', *Guardian Weekly Review* (6 November 2009).

Erkkilä, T., Peters, B. G. & Piironen, O. (2016), 'The Politics of Comparative Quantification: The Case of Governance Metrics', *Journal of Comparative Policy Analysis: Research and Practice*, 18: 319–28.

Feingold, D. A. (2010), 'Trafficking in Numbers: The Social Construction of Human Trafficking Data', in P. Andreas & K. M. Greenhill (eds), *Sex, Drugs, and Body Counts: The Politics of Numbers in Global Crime and Conflict* (Ithaca, NY, Cornell University Press), 46–74.

Fligstein, N. (1998), 'The Politics of Quantification', *Accounting, Organizations and Society*, 23: 325–31.

Gallagher, A. (2013), 'The Global Slavery Index Is Based on Flawed Data: Why Does No One Say So?', *Guardian* (28 November 2013).

Gallagher, A. (2016), 'Unravelling the 2016 Global Slavery Index: Part One', *openDemocracy: 50:50* (28 June 2016).

Gomes, A. de Castro (2009), 'Trabalho Análogo a de Escravo: Construindo um Problema', Rio de Janeiro.

GSI (Global Slavery Index) (2016), 'Detailed Methodology', accessed 17 July 2016, http://downloads.globalslaveryindex.org/GSI-2016-Detailed-Methodology-1500310181.pdf

Guardian Modern-Day Slavery in Focus (2015), 'US State Department Watered down Annual Report on Human Trafficking', *The Guardian* (4 August 2015).

Haynes, D. F. (2007), '(Not) Found Chained to a Bed in a Brothel: Conceptual, Legal and Procedural Failures to Fulfill the Promise of the Trafficking Victims Protection Act', *Georgetown Immigration Law Journal*, 21: 337–81.

Kelley, J. (2017), *Scorecard Diplomacy: Grading States to Influence Their Reputation and Behavior* (Cambridge, Cambridge University Press).

Law Centre NI (Northern Ireland) (2014), 'Response to the NRM review, September 2014', accessed 30 October 2016, http://www.lawcentreni.org/Publications/Policy-Responses/Home_Office_NRM_Review_FULL.pdf

LeBaron, G. & Rühmkorf, A. (2017), 'The Domestic Politics of Corporate Accountability Legislation: Struggles Over the 2015 UK Modern Slavery Act', *Socio-Economic Review*, https://doi.org/10.1093/ser/mwx047.

Lerche, J. (2007), 'A Global Alliance against Forced Labour? Unfree Labour, Neo-liberal Globalization and the International Labour Organization', *Journal of Agrarian Change*, 7: 425–52.

McGrath, S. (2013), 'Many Chains to Break: The Multi-dimensional Concept of Slave Labour in Brazil', *Antipode*, 45: 1005–28.

Mantouvalou, V. (2015), '"Am I Free Now?" Overseas Domestic Workers in Slavery', *Journal of Law and Society*, 42: 329–57.

Matthews, F. (2016), 'Letting Go and Holding on: The Politics of Performance Management in the United Kingdom', *Public Policy and Administration*, 31: 303–23.

Phillips, N. (2013), 'Unfree Labour and Adverse Incorporation in the Global Economy: Comparative Perspectives on Brazil and India', *Economy and Society*, 42, 2: 171–96. DOI 10.1080/03085147.2012.718630

Phillips, N. (2015), 'Private Governance and the Problem of Trafficking and Slavery in Global Supply Chains', in L. Waite, H. Lewis, G. Craig & K. Skrivankova (eds), *Vulnerability, Exploitation and Migrants: Insecure Work in a Globalised Economy* (Basingstoke, Palgrave), 15–27.

Phillips, N. & Mieres, F. (2014), 'The Governance of Forced Labour in the Global Economy', *Globalizations*, 1–17. DOI 10.1080/14747731.2014.932507

Phillips, N. & Sakamoto, L. (2012), 'Global Production Networks, Chronic Poverty and "Slave Labor" in Brazil', *Studies in Comparative International Development*, 47: 287–315.

Phillips, N. & Weaver, C. E. (eds) (2010), *International Political Economy: Debating the Past, Present and Future* (London, Routledge).

Phillips, N., Bhaskaran, R., Nathan, D. & Upendranadh, C. (2014), 'The Social Foundations of Global Production Networks: Towards a Global Political Economy of Child Labour', *Third World Quarterly*, 35: 428–46.

Phillips, N., LeBaron, G. & Wallin, S. (2018), *Mapping and Measuring the Effectiveness of Labour-Related Disclosure Requirements for Global Supply Chains*, International Labour Organization Working Paper No. 32. Available online: http://www.ilo.org/global/research/publications/working-papers/WCMS_632120/lang--en/index.htm.

Plant, R. (2007), 'Forced Labour, Slavery and Poverty Reduction: Challenges for Development Agencies', presentation to UK High-Level Conference to Examine the Links between Poverty, Slavery and Social Exclusion, FCO and DfID, London, 30 October.

Porter, T. M. (1996), *Trust in Numbers: The Pursuit of Objectivity in Science and Public Life* (Princeton, NJ, Princeton University Press).

Sakamoto, L. (2007), 'Os Acionistas da Casa-grande: A Reinvenção Capitalista do Trabalho Escravo no Brasil Contemporâneo', unpublished PhD dissertation, Universidade de São Paulo, São Paulo.

Skrivankova, K. (2010), *Between Decent Work and Forced Labour: Examining the Continuum of Exploitation*, report for the Joseph Rowntreee Foundation.

US GAO (US Government Accountability Office) (2006), *Human Trafficking: Better Data, Strategy, and Reporting Needed to Enhance U.S. Anti-Trafficking Efforts Abroad*, report to the Chairman, Committee on the Judiciary, and the Chairman, Committee on International Relations, House of Representatives, Report GAO-06-825, Washington, DC.

4

Evaluating the Political Effects of Anti-slavery and Anti-trafficking Activism

JOEL QUIRK

Introduction

CHANGING THE WORLD FOR the better has never been easy. As a now extensive literature on social movements and transnational advocacy networks has demonstrated,
there are numerous obstacles that need to be overcome before any kind of meaningful change can take place. These obstacles include ideological opposition,
institutional inertia and strategic self-interest, along with further complications
associated with questions of leadership, strategy, organisation and mobilisation
(Tarrow 2011; Carpenter 2014; Wong 2012). It has also become clear, moreover,
that even landmark political campaigns routinely fall short of their ultimate goals,
and therefore routinely end up with partial or qualified gains. Even high-profile
campaigns that have been widely celebrated as successful milestones, such as
historical campaigns against legal slave systems or European colonial rule, have
been challenged in relation to the unfinished business of both the racial afterlives
of historical slave systems and the enduring coloniality of power (Sharpe 2016;
Mignolo 2012). Much the same story applies to self-identified 'modern-day abo-
litionists', who similarly highlight the limitations of the legal abolition of slavery
as part of their larger case regarding the need for ongoing action against extreme
forms of exploitation and abuse in the world today.

The mechanics and effects of political activism have all kinds of implications
for both research and researchers. Most researchers not only seek to better understand the world, they also aspire to make a useful contribution to broader efforts
to change the world for the better. This is especially true of researchers working on questions relating to slavery, human trafficking and forced labour, since
their choice of topics frequently arises out of an underlying personal commitment
to help combat the types of abuses which they study. Research is therefore frequently conceived as making a contribution within the context of a larger division
of labour, wherein research generates useful information or evidence, which is then

Proceedings of the British Academy, **220**, 60–78. © The British Academy 2018.

in turn – potentially or hopefully – harnessed by others on the 'front line' for the purposes of activism, mobilisation or reform. While this rough division of labour between information and activism sounds good in theory, it frequently ends up being messy, under-theorised and/or inefficient in practice (Jacobsen & Landau 2003; Shaw 2003).

This chapter starts with the premise that one of the core goals of research should be to enable relevant campaigners, activists and institutions to 'fight better' within the context of larger efforts to combat abuses of human rights. By speaking in these terms, I want to focus attention upon the potential role of researchers in generating tools, insights, information and arguments that will help to improve the prospects, proposals and strategies associated with forms of political activism and mobilisation. This focus on activism marks a departure from other chapters in this collection, which are chiefly concerned with different ways in which information regarding patterns and effects of severe labour exploitation can be collected and interpreted. The goal of the chapter is instead to extend the remit of the collection to include a further analysis of 'what happens next' once information has been collected.

Drawing upon ideas and insights from existing works on social movements and transnational advocacy networks, I consider some of the main ways in which 'success' or 'progress' have been – and, I would argue, should be – evaluated when it comes to ongoing forms of political activism and institutional policy specifically targeting slavery, trafficking and forced labour. In pursuit of this overall goal, I briefly analyse two widely celebrated examples of 'successful' responses to modern slavery and trafficking: the Modern Slavery Act (UK) and the Trafficking in Persons Reports (US). The principal argument that emerges from this analysis is that anti-slavery/anti-trafficking needs to be nested within a broader portfolio of practices, interests and ideologies, rather than treated as a singular topic that is assumed to enjoy a separate and elevated humanitarian or bipartisan political status. As we shall see below, much of the popular appeal and recent political 'success' of anti-slavery and anti-trafficking can be largely attributed to the degree to which 'modern slavery' has been constructed as a singular and exceptional problem that rarely threatens major political and economic interests, particularly in the Global North. In this political environment, fighting better must be understood in terms of carefully analysing and strategically targeting the systematic sources of forced labour, vulnerability and marginalisation.

A 'landmark piece of legislation'? The Modern Slavery Act

Many conversations about slavery and abolition feature the United Kingdom. This is because Britain was both the most successful slaver of the early modern Atlantic world and a central actor in the emergence and internationalisation of anti-slavery

(Quirk 2011: 23–112). This contentious record is frequently remembered selectively, provoking charges that the British have celebrated abolition while forgetting
enslavement (Hall 2007; Oldfield 2007). This selective orientation was recently on
display in 2016, when the newly appointed prime minister, Theresa May (2016),
declared her intention to build on Britain's 'historic stand to ban slavery two
centuries ago' and to 'once again lead the way in defeating modern slavery and
preserving . . . freedoms and values'. In addition to £33 million of funding, May
was keen to highlight the pioneering work of the then recently passed Modern
Slavery Act of 2015, which not only established 'tough new penalties' for modern
slavery offenders, but also introduced 'enhanced protection and support for victims
and a world-leading transparency requirement on businesses' (May 2016). The
Act has been favourably received in many circles and was recently celebrated as a
'landmark piece of legislation . . . the UK can build on internationally as it seeks
to reassert its place in international affairs following Brexit' (Grono 2017).

Both the origins and operations of the Modern Slavery Act have been closely
scrutinised, so this chapter will not delve into the finer procedural details here (see
Kotiswaran 2016). The primary goal is instead to reflect upon some of the main
ways in which this Act has been evaluated in terms of success or progress. On this
front, a representative point of departure comes from Andrew Wallis, the founder
and CEO of Unseen, an anti-slavery organisation based in Bristol. According to
Wallis (2015), it was important to 'pause and celebrate the United Kingdom's
Modern Slavery Act'. The main features of his overall evaluation are worth quoting
at length:

> So two years ago there was **nothing, zero, zip, no chance**. Fast forward two years
> and we have a Modern Slavery Act, a Commissioner, specific provision for children,
> a review of how we can effectively identify victims and a Transparency in Supply
> Chains clause in the act requiring large businesses to report what they are doing to
> ensure slavery cannot exist in its business practices and supply chains. Is the legisla-
> tion perfect? No of course not, but get real no legislation will ever be perfect! But
> two years ago we had **zero** and then we had the opportunity to aim for a **100%** and
> today we've ended up with **95%**. (Bold text in original.)

Wallis attributed this rapid transformation to the impact of the evidence produced
in a report entitled 'It Happens Here' by the Centre for Social Justice under the
auspices of a Slavery Working Group that he chaired (Centre for Social Justice
2013). This evidence is said to have been recognised by May as 'overwhelming',
to the point where 'doing nothing was clearly not an option' (Wallis 2015). While
accepting that '5%' remained outstanding, Wallis also declared that critics should
not allow this to overshadow the '95%' achieved to date and that we should remain
confident that 'we will get there eventually'.

Wallis' narrative contains a number of elements that are likely to be broadly
familiar. In keeping with now well-established conventions and expectations
regarding patterns of political activism, his narrative revolves around civil society

groups and researchers making a principled effort to change the world by initiating a campaign, which the state is subsequently obliged to respond to. Importantly, the response that follows is then conceptualised in terms of a feedback mechanism, wherein progress is measured against the key demands featured in the campaign. When political activism is defined in these terms, the evaluation of success or progress becomes a question of the relative distance between civil society activities and subsequent institutional responses. In addition, there is a further expectation that these responses will fall short to either a lesser or greater degree thanks to political and practical vagaries.

It is entirely possible to disagree with Wallis (see ITUC 2017) regarding the 'percentage' of progress achieved, yet nonetheless accept – either implicitly or explicitly – that the question of success or failure should be approached in these linear and reactive terms. As the above quotation makes clear, Wallis may well have wanted more 'progress' in an ideal world, but practical constraints meant that he remains 'thankful' for partial or imperfect success. There is no doubt that this formula is attractive, since it implies that no single solution will ever be definitive. However, as we shall see below, the assumption that 'we will get there eventually' is flawed.

What is most important for my purposes here is not whether or not Wallis is right regarding his own contribution, but that the Modern Slavery Act has been widely understood to be the product of a call which emerged from within civil society, and that the primary contribution of the British government was to respond to this call. This call and response model is not entirely without merit, but in this case and in other similar scenarios it ends up dramatically overstating the power and agency of civil society (and other non-state actors, such as academic researchers), while minimising the power and agency of the state. Whereas civil society activists and organisations are portrayed as *dynamic actors and initiators*, the state ends up being reduced to the position of a respondent that is *acted upon*. The contribution of civil society therefore ends up being overstated, and the role of the state in determining which issues are taken up and on what specific terms – both at a given moment and in the future – ends up being obscured or diminished. Civil society actors call for all kinds of reforms on a regular basis. Most of these calls have little to no effect on state policy. Civil society actors make all kinds of proposals regarding the overall design of policy. Most of these proposals are not taken up. Both the existence and the final form of the UK Modern Slavery Act are largely the products of calculations and agendas which have their origins *within* the British state, rather than being imperfect reflections of civil society campaigning.

We therefore need to understand the Modern Slavery Act in terms of the broader strategic purposes, policy priorities and ideological agendas of the British state. As both home secretary and prime minister, Theresa May has made a leading contribution to a government that is committed to deregulating the labour market, defending corporate and financial interests, cutting social services and workplace protections, and restricting, regulating and punishing international migrants (Strauss 2012: 180–97; Robinson 2015: 129–43). The dimensions and effects of the Modern Slavery Act must be understood in relation to this larger political agenda and ideological orientation. This wider context is especially significant in relation to migration, because the Modern Slavery Act was sandwiched between two closely related pieces of legislation: the Immigration Acts of 2014 and 2016.

Hostility towards migrant outsiders is now firmly established as a central driver of state policy in many countries. This trend has strong roots within the United Kingdom, where anti-immigrant sentiments were arguably the catalyst behind the 2016 vote to leave the European Union. These sentiments build upon a mutually reinforcing dynamic between politicians and the electorate, with the former seeking to mobilise the latter via anti-immigration appeals and the latter elevating politicians who are believed to share their anti-immigrant views. In this now highly charged environment, the imperative to 'get tough' on immigrants casts a long shadow over modern slavery, making it very difficult to distinguish between 'dangerous categories and categories in danger, between those destined for repression and those who inspire compassion' (Fassin 2015: 2; see also: Plambech 2014; O'Connell Davidson 2015a).

This distinction between a 'dangerous category' (migrants) and a 'category in danger' (prospective slavery, trafficking or forced labour victims) is worth developing. As we have already seen, activists such as Wallis often evaluate success in terms of the degree to which the British state reacted sufficiently to a call from civil society to protect and support modern slaves. However, the overall calculus shifts once broader policies and practices targeting migrants are added to the equation. From this vantage point, the key question is not only whether or not the British state has sufficiently reacted to campaigns to protect victims from 'danger', but also what role the state has played in creating the danger in question in the first place.

Take, by way of example, this assessment from Paul Blomfield (2015), a Labour member of the UK Parliament, who argued that the second Immigration Act:

> not only risk[s] forcing undocumented workers into exploitative employment relationships—supposedly outlawed by the Modern Slavery Act—but potentially give[s] abusive employers even more weapons with which to threaten employees.
>
> (Blomfield 2015)

Some of the key issues here concern the potential effects of weakening institutional protections for migrants and asylum seekers in conjunction with a further expansion of immigration inspections, controls and penalties. Importantly, these effects are not confined to victims of slavery, but extend to a much larger population of precarious migrants. One of the best-known examples of this far-reaching problem concerns overseas domestic workers, whose legal right to change employers under the terms of their visa was revoked in April 2012, thereby further constraining their capacity to protect and defend their rights. Theresa May and her colleagues repeatedly refused to restore this right, despite a campaign both within and outside Parliament, during the passage of the Modern Slavery Act in 2015 (Roberts 2015; Gausi 2015).

This overall line of argument also has additional applications when it comes to thinking about the future. As the Wallis example shows, it is sometimes asserted – or even assumed – that additional positive refinements will emerge in response to each new campaign, with each individual campaign representing a stepping-stone in a longer-term journey. If a particular state has appeared to be receptive, or at least susceptible, to a call for reform from civil society in the past, then doesn't this in turn create at least qualified grounds to be hopeful for further action in the future? Although this overall logic may well be applicable on some occasions, it nonetheless runs the risk of overestimating the political prospects of further or deeper reform. When civil society is given pride of place within the narrative, the internal reasons why states end up adopting some policies and approaches and not others can get lost.

It is one thing to pass legislation that narrowly targets 'exceptional' abuses for criminal sanction and quite another thing to pass further legislation that attempts to address the underlying sources of vulnerability, violence and marginalisation associated with punitive immigration regimes (or, alternatively, labour market deregulation and corporate complicity). Step one is relatively easy politically. Any further step that seeks to go substantially beyond the first is likely to be much more politically contentious. While the Modern Slavery Act and other similar pieces of anti-slavery or anti-trafficking legislation typically enjoy 'bipartisan' political support – and therefore typically secure parliamentary endorsement via large legislative majorities that cross party lines – this broad political support is almost entirely contingent upon the legislation in question not intruding too directly or significantly upon major political and economic interests and associated patterns of privilege.

There are a number of distinct arguments at work that are worth teasing out further here. First, the political popularity of anti-slavery/trafficking initiatives can frequently be traced to the fact that they have been narrowly targeted against 'exceptional' incidents, and therefore do not directly threaten major political and economic interests (Bunting & Quirk 2017). In some cases, such as the now ubiquitous model of discretionary Corporate Social Responsibility (CSR), the appeal of this politics of exception can also be traced to its strategic value in diluting or deflecting calls for more ambitious forms of regulation or reform (LeBaron & Quirk 2016; LeBaron & Lister 2015). Indeed, an initial step of voluntary CSR policy may ultimately end up working to undercut or displace other prospective future steps in terms of more robust regulation.

Second, we have the related argument that broader interests and ideologies – such as anti-immigrant sentiments, deregulation and corporate profits – are likely to create a hard ceiling when it comes to further steps that go beyond a narrow focus on 'exceptional' incidents or discretionary actions (O'Connell 2007). It is clear, for example, that collective bargaining and workplace organising via unions could potentially offer a degree of protection against severe labour exploitation, yet encouraging unionisation is unlikely to be an issue which commands bipartisan support. This ceiling is not necessarily absolute, but the degree of difficulty involved is likely to be much higher than was the case for the initial step. Bipartisan political support for (and/or corporate endorsement of) a specific course of action is frequently a sign that the political and economic stakes (i.e. who gets what, when and how) associated with a given policy or course of action are relatively low from a macro-economic standpoint. Policies which can command support from across the political spectrum do not easily or obviously pave the way for more ambitious policy proposals down the line. They may sometimes paradoxically end up doing the opposite.

Finally, and most importantly, we have the argument that the central challenge here is not simply that state responses have been imperfect or incomplete, but that we must also grapple with the degree to which states have directly contributed to the creation of a series of related problems in order to advance other political and economic interests and ideological agendas. While none of these arguments suggests that positive changes cannot take place via political activism and mobilisation, they nonetheless point to different criteria for both current and future success, wherein the state (and other institutions) must be understood to play a much more dynamic – and complicit – role than simply responding to principled calls for reform from civil society activists.

Viewed in terms of a conventional model of civil society activism and state reaction, the Modern Slavery Act appears a key example of success, or at least progress, which can in turn be expected to pave the way for other more positive steps in the future. The fundamental problem with this evaluative standard, however, is that it presents a model of 'success' which is likely to be both short term and superficial, since the central role of the state in both creating and sustaining larger patterns of vulnerability and exploitation remains at the margins of the overall equation. This omission is important, because it suggests that any evaluative framework and associated political strategy that fails to adequately engage with foundational issues of state agency and complicity is unlikely to offer a sufficient platform for political activism. As we shall see below, these considerations also extend to patterns of international advocacy, where a further division between 'good' and 'bad' states comes into focus.

The TIP Reports: new criminal sanctions and global good samaritans?

Numerous efforts to change the world have international dimensions, and thereby end up triggering political conversations amongst states, international organisations, corporations and representatives of global civil society. These conversations have attracted tremendous interest amongst researchers, with human rights and the environment emerging as focal points. In the case of human rights, which is the more relevant of the two themes here, we now have an extensive literature documenting how civil society coalitions and normative entrepreneurs have developed transnational advocacy networks through instruments such as information, alliances, shaming and leverage (Keck & Sikkink 1998; Della Porta & Diani 2015).

Much of this research into international activism has been informed by a broadly liberal sensibility, with a key goal being to demonstrate that numerous positive changes – i.e. 'moral victories' championed by 'global Good Samaritans' – have taken place, and that global political behaviour therefore cannot be reduced to material power and utilitarian calculations (Burgerman 2001; Brysk 2009). This liberal sensibility has also found expression in a recurring emphasis on 'successful' cases, wherein researchers seek to explain why and how specific political changes, such as the end of legal apartheid, banning landmines or the fall of communism, can be traced to patterns of global civil society activism, alliance formation and organisation (Klotz 1995; Price 1998; Thomas 2001). While such case studies played an especially important role in making the initial case for activism as a driver of positive change, it is also broadly agreed that '[h]umanitarian internationalism is more than episodic altruism – it is a pattern of persistent principled politics' (Brysk 2009: 3). Applied to anti-slavery and anti-trafficking, this liberal sensibility tends to promote a view of slavery as a principled issue that operates either outside or above 'day to day' politics.

This literature on international activism also points towards a model in which there are 'good' and 'bad' states when it comes to human rights, although these specific terms may not always be used explicitly. Global problems routinely generate multilateral conversations, where states come together to negotiate and evaluate all kinds of international instruments, and to help shape the activities of relevant international organisations. These multilateral conversations generate political platforms and agreements regarding standards, so they are invariably targeted by political campaigners who attempt to recruit sympathetic states to their cause via persuasion and pressure (Busby 2010; Haffner-Burton 2013). States that end up being successfully recruited – which are invariably a small minority – are then in turn classified as 'stewards', or 'Samaritans', with the main idea being that they come to (re)define their national interests in ways that incorporate specific human rights causes and campaigns. According to Emilie Haffner-Burton (2013: 150), stewardship involves states using 'muscle and money to advocate for the protection of human rights', with the two main mechanisms for effecting change being 'punishments and rewards'. These are not regarded as a substitute for civil society activism, but are viewed as augmenting and extending campaigns from the same.

Such viewpoints contribute to a picture of international activism wherein 'bad' or 'poor' performing states emerge as a key target. The most influential attempt to come to terms with this theme is the 'spiral model' of human rights change, which identifies a series of five potential stages – repression, denial, tactical concessions, prescriptive status and rule-consistent behaviour – which can be used to analyse how states respond to calls for change (Risse *et al.* 1999, 2013). This model chiefly classifies state behaviour in terms of defensive and reactive responses, at least in the early stages, which are primarily designed to repress, dilute or delay calls for change. These defensive reactions from intransigent states are said in turn to generate a 'boomerang effect', wherein '[n]ational opposition groups, NGOs, and social movements link up with transnational networks and INGOs who then convince international human rights organisations, donor institutions, and/or great powers to pressure norm-violating states' (Risse & Sikkink 2013: 18). Change is never certain, but to the extent that it does take place it is said to chiefly arise from cumulative efforts to overcome defensive responses from 'bad' states. If all goes well, this can pave the way for improved compliance (Smith-Cannoy 2012; Brysk 2013; Simmons 2009).

How and in what ways do these types of arguments, models and assumptions relate to the international politics of anti-trafficking and anti-slavery? To help answer this question, it is first necessary to make several brief observations regarding the global prevalence of these issues and the relative performance of states in addressing them. While most estimates of the global prevalence of slavery, trafficking and forced labour are speculative at best, they have nonetheless helped to promote an overall diagnosis that suggests that these problems are heavily concentrated in the Global South, or the developing world, along with specifically targeting countries such as India, Uzbekistan, Thailand and Haiti (Walk Free Foundation 2016; ILO 2012; US Department of State 2016). On the related question of performance, the pendulum generally swings the other way, with high-profile assessments by the US government and the Walk Free Foundation, amongst others, primarily but by no means exclusively endorsing the 'superior' performance of states in the Global North, or developed world. While there are some notable exceptions to this pattern, an impression has nonetheless been created that high performing/low prevalence states are concentrated in the Global North, while low performing/high prevalence states are in the Global South.

This global context is important, because it informs the ways in which many high-profile forms of anti-slavery and anti-trafficking activism have been formulated and evaluated. In keeping with broader patterns, international activism in this field is widely regarded as enlisting 'good' or 'high' performing states, which are chiefly located in the Global North, as allies in support of calls for change that are primarily directed towards 'bad' or 'poor' performing states, chiefly located in the Global South. Once the political issues at stake are diagnosed in these terms, one of the main evaluative standards for success and failure becomes the degree to which 'bad' states end up responding to calls for change. And since reform remains uncertain, both punishments and rewards also enter into the overall evaluation.

The most high-profile elephant in the room is the United States, which has had a far-reaching impact upon global behaviour for nearly two decades now through its self-appointed role as an anti-trafficking 'global sheriff' (Chuang 2006). The main vehicle for US anti-trafficking policy has been the annual Trafficking in Persons (TIP) Report, which has been published by the State Department since 2001, and which ranks governments based on their efforts to combat human trafficking. For the purposes of this chapter, the most consequential aspect of these reports is their role in seeking to monitor and evaluate global state performance. According to the 2016 report, the criteria used for these evaluations include state action in the enactment of new legislation, criminalisation and effective prosecution, victim identification, protection and reintegration, levels of funding and NGO partnerships, interventions to prevent predatory labour practices, and efforts to reduce the demand for commercial sex. Using a minimum standards model, the TIP Reports rank states using tiers based on whether they meet minimum standards (tier one), do not meet these standards but are making efforts (tier two), are making efforts yet have further problems (tier two watch list), or are not making significant efforts to adhere to the standards (tier three) (US State Department 2016: 36–7, 46–7, 55–61). As we will see below, the question of rankings has become politically contentious, with charges that foreign policy considerations have shaped rankings.

The structure and impact of the TIP system have been carefully scrutinised, with one of the most contentious issues being whether receiving a poor or declining ranking can have an impact upon state behaviour (Zaloznaya & Hagan 2012; Gallagher 2012). This question partly arises out of a well-known provision within the TIP system for the US to withdraw or withhold humanitarian foreign assistance in cases where states are ranked in tier three. However, this potential punishment has frequently proved to be a dead letter in practice, so the focus has instead shifted to the non-material reputational effects associated with changing rankings. One recent attempt to grapple with this question comes from Judith Kelley and Beth Simmons, who argue that the history of TIP rankings suggests that 'states are sensitive to monitoring, respond faster to harsher "grades," and react when their grade first drops below a socially significant threshold' (2015: 68). Their main metric in support of this conclusion is the degree to which domestic criminalisation of human trafficking can be connected to patterns of shaming and monitoring via TIP Reports. For Kelley and Simmons, the criminalisation of human trafficking should be regarded as a key marker of political success or progress. In support of this position, they argue that many states have been reluctant to embrace criminalisation, and that states are also likely to be resistant to shaming efforts thanks to the undemocratic and corrupt nature of their regimes. Social shaming via a poor or falling ranking is therefore argued to *'induce more compliant behavior'* (italics in original), despite political headwinds (Kelley & Simmons 2015: 61). Significantly, states are once again regarded as having been *acted upon*, with their behaviour being reduced to a largely defensive reaction to pressure and shaming.

Within the context of this chapter, the key question here is not whether or not Kelley and Simmons are correct in their analysis, but instead whether or not their underlying model for evaluating political success and progress can be regarded as useful or sufficient. To help answer this question, it is necessary to further expand upon some of the main arguments from the previous section, which are as follows:

1   The cause of combating slavery/trafficking frequently enjoys unusually high levels of 'bipartisan' political support in cases where it does not directly threaten major economic and political interests.
2   Criminal measures that are narrowly targeted against isolated and 'exceptional' cases will enjoy a much higher level of support and ideological acceptability than alternative or additional measures that attempt to challenge systems of exploitation and vulnerability.
3   Any analysis of state behaviour must take into account the key role of state complicity in enabling and sustaining conditions of exploitation and vulnerability in the first place.

These arguments direct our gaze towards issues that have been neglected or excluded from linear and reactive models of success. Firstly, they serve to highlight some of the problems inherent in treating the criminalisation of human trafficking as a decisive marker of progress or success. In 2016, the United Nations Office on Drugs and Crime (UNODC) reported that 158 states (88 per cent of a dataset covering 179 states) had introduced laws criminalising 'most forms of trafficking in persons', marking a remarkable jump from only 33 in 2003. However, this extraordinary growth of legislation is also reported to have resulted in 'very few convictions' (UNODC 2016: 12, 47–53). This new legislation may well have been driven by US policy and other lobbying efforts, but the fact that so many states have taken action within such a short space of time must also be attributed to an underlying strategic calculus suggesting that there are many political scenarios in which major political and economic interests are not threatened by the criminalisation of human trafficking.

This strategic calculus is also tied to the fact that recent laws against slavery or trafficking tend to be narrowly targeted against 'exceptional' cases, which are in turn said to be chiefly concentrated in 'developing' states located in the Global South and at the 'irregular' margins of the global economy. This politics of exception can have the indirect effect of excluding other 'normal' practices or 'lesser' problems that are said to fall short of an 'exceptional' or 'worst of the worst' normative threshold. There are currently hundreds of millions of 'free' labourers across the globe who routinely endure terrible wages, precarious conditions, unsafe and unhealthy workspaces, sexual harassment and assault, and bullying and abuse. They may well be formally 'free' to leave, in the sense that they can quit their jobs and seek other options, but their precarious status is nonetheless likely to make it very risky for them to quit, and their alternative options may be no better. Despite their predicament, recent campaigns against slavery and trafficking tend to exclude precarious 'free' labourers from their orbit of concern (Bunting & Quirk 2017).

This demarcation has considerable strategic and ideological appeal for many political and economic elites, especially in the Global North. This is because it portrays slavery and trafficking as forms of deviant criminal conduct that either disrupt or distort the operations of otherwise legitimate 'free' labour markets and 'voluntary' wage labour systems that remain foundational to global patterns of production, consumption and privilege. Any attempt to evaluate success or failure in this field must therefore grapple with the ideological and strategic appeal of slavery and human trafficking as a political platform, and with the extent to which investment and interest in this platform can end up deflecting or displacing activism on more challenging systemic issues. Whenever the globe is divided into 'good' and 'bad' states, there is invariably an element of (self-)validation and (self-)legitimation involved, wherein the privileged position occupied by states in the Global North is transformed into a positive attribute thanks to their 'good works' within the Global South.

The fundamental problem here, however, is that many problems in the world today persist *because of, rather than in spite of*, interventions and actions from the Global North (Broome & Quirk 2015: 829–33). Too many researchers and activists working on slavery, trafficking and forced labour structure their work around forms of methodological nationalism, where the sources of 'bad' performance are traced to internal failings of states and peoples within the Global South. Methodological nationalism tends to conflate performance and responsibility. Both 'good' and 'bad' states are assumed to be responsible for their relative performance, yet there are usually many factors and forces which are responsible for any given outcome, including numerous external interests, actions and institutions.

One of the main implications of this overall line of argument is that it does not necessarily or automatically follow that 'something is better than nothing'. Whenever we seek to evaluate the effects of political activism, we must at least entertain the prospect of some forms of activism ending up being compromised or counterproductive, rather than simply being ineffective, limited or grounded in tactical concessions, which are more familiar points of departure. As we have seen, the main issue here is the degree to which anti-trafficking and anti-slavery campaigns can end up being politically compromised by what they *do not say*, and with the types of underlying connections and associations that they *do not address* sufficiently.

The analysis of success and progress is further complicated by the argument that too many responses to human trafficking and slavery have ended up doing more harm than good, and therefore end up being counterproductive. Researchers have come to describe this disconnect between aims and outcomes in terms of 'collateral damage', which broadly refers to cases where state – and sometimes also private – interventions end up damaging marginalised and vulnerable populations that they are formally designed to help (Dottridge 2007). Common examples include police abusing those they are supposed to be assisting, immigration systems mistreating migrants with impunity, and people who have been 'rescued' from trafficking being subject to forms of incarceration, exploitation and abuse (Sharma 2005; Howard 2017; Bernstein 2012; Mahdavi 2011; Vance 2011; Musto 2016; Shih 2016). In addition to the collateral damage of specific policies, there is an additional critique concerned with how many anti-trafficking/-slavery campaigns have used a range of dubious 'statistics', self-serving narratives, and superficial and misleading images as part of their political advocacy, fundraising and awareness-raising efforts. Thanks to these sorts of distortions, it is argued that '[m]uch of what people think they know about trafficking and slavery is inaccurate, incomplete, or unfounded' (O'Connell Davidson & Quirk 2016: 11). This can in turn result in expectations of 'innocent' victimhood and deviant conduct that can complicate the identification and support of precarious and exploited individuals (Vance 2012; Soderlund 2011).

It is also worth emphasising, moreover, that there have been a number of occasions when anti-slavery and anti-trafficking rhetoric has been harnessed to justify and defend all kinds of uncomfortable agendas. Take, for example, the justification recently given by President Donald Trump in his executive order declaring his commitment to 'building a wall' in order to 'prevent illegal immigration, drug and human trafficking, and acts of terrorism' (White House 2017). Comparable language has also featured prominently in speeches by European politicians as part of the refugee crisis in the Mediterranean (O'Connell Davidson 2015b). If we look further back in history, we also encounter similar complications, such as the degree to which European colonial rule in Africa was justified in humanitarian terms, with the abolition of slavery playing a key ideological role in justifying unprovoked wars of conquest on the grounds that colonial rule would bring slavery to an end. However, this self-proclaimed 'civilising mission' was accompanied by massive violence, exploitation and dispossession, including the systematic use of forced labour under colonial rule. One especially notorious example of this trend concerns the devastating atrocities of the Congo Free State, a colony whose creation King Leopold of Belgium primarily justified to other European powers in anti-slavery terms (Quirk 2012).

As these sorts of examples help to illustrate, the politics of anti-trafficking and anti-slavery are not easily reduced to a compelling campaign for action from civil society and its 'Good Samaritan' allies which 'bad' states are obliged to reluctantly or defensively respond to. The politics of anti-slavery/trafficking are instead more akin to the politics of humanitarian intervention, or the war on terror (Mahdavi 2013), where we have a multi-faceted and deeply political project that remains heavily contested in terms of its dimensions and applications, and which numerous actors have attempted to strategically and selectively harness towards their own distinctive agendas and interests with varying degrees of success. While humanitarian intervention has helped to alleviate disaster on occasion, it has also generated precedents and arguments that were deployed to justify the disastrous invasion of Iraq. While global terrorism is undoubtedly a major challenge, the 'war' declared by the United States would also be co-opted by states who had a strategic interest in labelling ethnic separatists and political enemies as terrorists, and was also used to justify and legitimate further securitisation, xenophobia, repression and surveillance. In both of these cases it is now generally accepted that collateral damages, selective applications, and political co-optation must be included as part of any overall evaluation of political effects or success (Freedman 2005; Bricmont 2007). The same type of political sensitivity is required when thinking about success or progress in relation to political activism targeting slavery, trafficking and forced labour.

Conclusion

Many forms of political activism and mobilisation are increasingly constrained and enabled by technocratic schemes, neoliberal logics and Faustian alliances with corporate and institutional interests (Dauvergne & LeBaron 2014; Krause 2014; Chuang 2014, 2015). High-profile campaigns targeting slavery, trafficking and forced labour have often been closely aligned with this trend. Part of this alignment arises from the fact that anti-trafficking has been constructed as a bipartisan and 'non-ideological cause', which people of good will throughout the globe should be able to support regardless of their other differences. This image of anti-trafficking as an exceptional cause that stands apart from 'normal' politics has played a major role in helping to generate attention and investment, but this attention has too often come at the price of a superficial and short-term diagnosis of the fundamental issues at stake.

This state of affairs presents all kinds of challenges for both researchers and activists. It is no longer – and probably never was – useful to think in terms of a rough division of labour between researchers who gather and interpret information and front-line activists who advance the cause, drawing upon some of the information researchers have collected. If we accept, as I argued above, that one of the main goals of research should be to advance efforts to 'fight better', then researchers must in turn regard patterns of political activism and mobilisation as one of their core objects of concern, rather than a separate issue which is best left to others. Within this perspective, there are several specific issues that are also worth highlighting further. Making patterns of political activism a core object of concern cannot simply be an exercise in critique, but must also incorporate forms of strategic thinking and analysis that are designed to help improve, refine and advance efforts to change the world. In the specific case of anti-slavery and anti-trafficking, this frequently means focusing upon the type of things that high-profile campaigns do not say, and with the types of underlying connections and associations that they frequently struggle to acknowledge or address.

As we have seen, many high-profile anti-slavery and anti-trafficking campaigns fail to grapple with the underlying sources of forced labour, marginalisation and vulnerability, and thereby end up in pathways that target 'deviant exceptions' and 'bad' states. One of the core tasks of research should therefore be to develop and refine alternative starting points, strategies, alliances and arguments that contribute to a more significant and direct challenge to dominant political and economic interests. High-profile anti-slavery/trafficking campaigns enjoy high levels of support in many circles because they do not rock the boat politically or economically. How much can a campaign accomplish if much of its appeal stems from not making too many waves? Many widely celebrated markers of success, progress and 'bipatisan' support appear in a different light once underlying strategic calculations, ideological agendas and notable silences are factored into the overall equation.

References

Bernstein, E. (2012), 'Carceral Politics as Gender Justice? The "Traffic in Women" and Neoliberal Circuits of Crime, Sex, and Rights', *Theory and Society*, 41, 3: 233–59. DOI 10.1007/s11186-012-9165-9

Blomfield, P. (2015), 'The Immigration Bill 2015: Creating the Conditions for Exploitation?', *openDemocracy: Beyond Trafficking and Slavery* (11 December 2015), accessed 17 April 2017, https://www.opendemocracy.net/beyondslavery/paul-blomfield/immigration-bill-2015-creating-conditions-for-exploitation

Bricmont, J. (2007), *Humanitarian Imperialism: Using Human Rights to Sell War* (London, Monthly Review).

Broome, A. & Quirk, J. (2015), 'Governing the World at a Distance: The Practice of Global Benchmarking', *Review of International Studies*, 41, 5: 819–41. DOI 10.1017/S0260210515000340

Brysk, A. (2009), *Global Good Samaritans: Human Rights as Foreign Policy* (Oxford, Oxford University Press).

Brysk, A. (2013), *Speaking Will to Power: Constructing Political Will* (Oxford, Oxford University Press).

Bunting, A. & Quirk, J. (2017), 'Contemporary Slavery as More than Rhetorical Strategy? The Politics and Ideology of a New Political Cause', in A. Bunting & J. Quirk (eds), *Contemporary Slavery: Popular Rhetoric and Political Practice* (Vancouver, University of British Columbia Press).

Burgerman, S. (2001), *Moral Victories: How Activists Provoke Multilateral Action* (Ithaca, NY, Cornell University Press).

Busby, J. (2010), *Moral Movements and Foreign Policy* (Cambridge, Cambridge University Press).

Carpenter, C. (2014), *"Lost" Causes: Agenda Vetting in Global Issue Networks and the Shaping of Human Security* (Ithaca, NY, Cornell University Press).

Centre for Social Justice (2013), 'It Happens Here: Equipping the United Kingdom to Fight Modern Slavery, a Policy Report by the Slavery Working Group' (London).

Chuang, J. (2006), 'The United States as Global Sheriff: Using Unilateral Sanctions to Combat Human Trafficking', *Michigan Journal of International Law*, 27, 2: 437–94.

Chuang, J. (2014), 'Exploitation Creep and the Unmaking of Human Trafficking Law', *American Journal of International Law*, 108, 4: 609–49. DOI 10.5305/amerjintelaw.108.4.0609

Chuang, J. (2015), 'Giving as Governance? Philanthrocapitalism and Modern-Day Slavery Abolitionism', *UCLA Law Review*, 62, 6: 1516–56.

Dauvergne, P. & LeBaron, G. (2014), *Protest, Inc: The Corporatization of Activism* (Cambridge, Polity Press).

Della Porta, D. & Diani, M. (eds) (2015), *The Oxford Handbook of Social Movements* (Oxford, Oxford University Press).

Dottridge, M. (ed.) (2007), *Collateral Damage: The Impact of Anti-trafficking Measures on Human Rights around the World* (Bangkok, Global Alliance Against Traffic in Women).

Fassin, D. (2015), 'Introduction: Governing Precarity', in D. Fassin *et al.* (eds), *At the Heart of the State: The Moral World of Institutions* (London, Pluto Press).

Freedman, L. (2005), 'The Age of Liberal Wars', *Review of International Studies*, 31, 1: 93–107. DOI 10.1017/S0260210505006807

Gallagher, A. (2012), 'Human Rights and Human Trafficking: A Reflection on the influ-Ence and Evolution of the U.S. Trafficking in Persons Reports', in A. Choi-Fitzpatrick & A. Brysk (eds), *From Human Trafficking to Human Rights: Reframing Contemporary Slavery* (Philadelphia, University of Pennsylvania Press).

Gausi, T. (2015), 'Has the Modern Slavery Act left the UK's Most Exploited Workers Even More Vulnerable?', *Equal Times* (13 November 2015), accessed 24 April 2017, https://www.equaltimes.org/has-the-modern-slavery-act-left?lang=en#.WQG3YVJ7GgQ

Grono, N. (2017), 'Putting Slavery out of Business', *Thomson Reuters Foundation News* (12 January 2017), accessed 24 April 2017, http://news.trust.org/item/20170112113510-f94jk/

Haffner-Burton, E. (2013), *Making Human Rights a Reality* (Princeton, NJ, Princeton University Press).

Hall, C. (2007), 'Remembering 1807: Histories of the Slave Trade, Slavery and Abolition', *History Workshop Journal*, 64: 1–5. DOI 10.1093/hwj/dbm064

Howard, N. (2017), *Child Trafficking, Youth Labour Mobility and the Politics of Protection* (London, Palgrave).

ILO (2012), *Global Estimate of Forced Labour: Results and Methodology* (Geneva, ILO).

International Trade Union Confederation (2017), *Closing the Loopholes: How Legislators Can Build on the UK Modern Slavery Act* (Brussels, ITUC).

Jacobsen, K. & Landau, L. (2003), 'The Dual Imperative in Refugee Research: Some Methodological and Ethical Considerations in Social Science Research on Forced Migration', *Disasters*, 27, 3: 185–206. DOI 10.1111/1467-7717.00228

Keck, M. & Sikkink, K. (1998), *Activists beyond Borders: Advocacy Networks in International Politics* (Ithaca, NY, Cornell University Press).

Kelley, J. & Simmons, B. (2015), 'Politics by Number: Indicators as Social Pressure in International Relations', *American Journal of Political Science*, 59, 1: 55–70. DOI 10.1111/ajps.12119

Klotz, A. (1995), *Norms in International Relations: The Struggle against the Apartheid* (Ithaca, NY, Cornell University Press).

Kotiswaran, P. (2016), 'The Path to the UK's Modern Slavery Act 2015: An Oral History Project', *openDemocracy: Beyond Trafficking and Slavery* (26 September 2016), accessed 10 April 2017, https://www.opendemocracy.net/beyond-slavery-themes/msa-oral-history-project

Krause, M. (2014), *The Good Project: Humanitarian Relief NGOs and the Fragmentation of Reason* (Chicago, IL, University of Chicago Press).

LeBaron, G. & Lister, J. (2015), 'Benchmarking Global Supply Chains: The Power of the "Ethical Audit" Regime', *Review of International Studies*, 41, 5: 905–24. DOI 10.1017/S0260210515000388

LeBaron, G. & Quirk, J. (2016), 'Introducing the Terms of Debate: Regulation and Responsibility in Global Supply Chains', *openDemocracy: Beyond Trafficking and Slavery* (13 September 2016), https://www.opendemocracy.net/beyondslavery/gscpd/genevieve-lebaron-and-joel-quirk/genevieve-lebaron-and-joel-quirk-intro

Mahdavi, P. (2011), *Gridlock: Labor, Migration, and Human Trafficking in Dubai* (Palo Alto, CA, Stanford University Press).

Mahdavi, P. (2013), *From Trafficking to Terror: Constructing a Global Social Problem* (New York, Routledge).

May, T. (2016), 'My Government Will Lead the Way in Defeating Modern Slavery', *The Telegraph* (30 July 2016), accessed 10 April 2017, http://www.telegraph.co.uk/news/2016/07/30/we-will-lead-the-way-in-defeating-modern-slavery/

Mignolo, W. (2012), *Local Histories/Global Designs: Coloniality, Subaltern Knowledge, and Border Thinking* (Princeton, NJ, Princeton University Press).

Musto, J. (2016), *Control and Protect: Collaboration, Carceral Protection, and Domestic Sex Trafficking in the United States* (Berkley, University of California Press).

O'Connell, P. (2007), 'On Reconciling Irreconcilables: Neo-liberal Globalisation and Human Rights', *Human Rights Law Review*, 7, 3: 483–509. DOI 10.1093/hrlr/ngm015

O'Connell Davidson, J. (2015a), *Modern Slavery: The Margins of Freedom* (London, Palgrave).

O'Connell Davidson, J. (2015b), 'Mediterranean Migrants Are Not Slaves – Do Not Pervert History to Justify Military Action', *The Guardian* (17 May 2015), accessed 2 May 2017, https://www.theguardian.com/commentisfree/2015/may/17/mediterranean-migrants-slaves-history-military-action-eu-leaders-libya

O'Connell Davidson, J. & Quirk, J. (2016), 'Introduction: Moving beyond Popular Representations of Trafficking and Slavery', in J. O'Connell Davidson & J. Quirk (eds), *Popular and Political Representations: BTS Short Course Volume One* (London: openDemocracy).

Oldfield, J. (2007), *'Chords of Freedom': Commemoration, Ritual and British Transatlantic Slavery* (Manchester, Manchester University Press).

Plambech, S. (2014), 'Between "Victims" and "Criminals": Rescue, Deportation, and Everyday Violence among Nigerian Migrants', *Social Politics*, 21, 3: 382–402. DOI 10.1093/sp/jxu021

Price, R. (1998), 'Reversing the Gun Sights: Transnational Civil Society Targets Land Mines', *International Organization*, 52, 3: 613–44. DOI 10.1162/002081898550671

Quirk, J. (2011), *The Anti-Slavery Project: From the Slave Trade to Human Trafficking* (Philadelphia, Pennsylvania University Press).

Quirk, J. (2012), 'Uncomfortable Silences: Contemporary Slavery and the "Lessons" of History', in A. Brysk & A. Choi-Fitzpatrick (eds), *From Human Trafficking to Human Rights: Reframing Contemporary Slavery* (Philadelphia, University of Pennsylvania Press).

Risse, T., Ropp, T. & Sikkink, K. (eds) (1999), *The Power of Human Rights: International Norms and Domestic Change* (Cambridge, Cambridge University Press).

Risse, T., Ropp, T. & Sikkink, K. (eds) (2013), *The Persistent Power of Human Rights: From Commitment to Compliance* (Cambridge: Cambridge University Press).

Risse, T. & Sikkink, K. (2013), 'The Socialization of International Human Rights Norms into Domestic Practices: Introduction', in T. Risse, T. Ropp & K. Sikkink (eds), *The Persistent Power of Human Rights: From Commitment to Compliance* (Cambridge, Cambridge University Press).

Roberts, K. (2015), 'Modern Slavery Bill: Migrant Domestic Workers Fall through the Gaps', *openDemocracy: Beyond Trafficking and Slavery* (24 March 2015), accessed 24 April 2017, https://www.opendemocracy.net/beyondslavery/kate-roberts/modern-slavery-bill-migrant-domestic-workers-fall-through-gaps

Robinson, C. (2015), 'Claiming Space for Labour Rights within the United Kingdom Modern Slavery Crusade', *Anti-Trafficking Review*, 5: 129–43. DOI 10.14197/atr.20121558

Sharma, N. (2005), 'Anti-trafficking Rhetoric and the Making of a Global Apartheid', *NWSA Journal*, 17, 3: 88–111. DOI 10.1353/nwsa.2005.0076

Sharpe, C. (2016), *In the Wake: On Blackness and Being* (Durham, NC, Duke University Press).

Shaw, K. (2003), 'Whose Knowledge for What Politics?', *Review of International Studies*, 29: 199–21. DOI 10.1017/S0260210503005941

Shih, E. (2016), 'Not in My "Backyard Abolitionism"', *Sociological Perspectives*, 59, 1: 66–90. DOI 10.1177/0731121416628551

Simmons, B. (2009), *Mobilizing for Human Rights: International Law in Domestic Politics* (Cambridge, Cambridge University Press).

Smith-Cannoy, H. (2012), *Insincere Commitments: Human Rights Treaties, Abusive States, and Citizen Activism* (Washington, DC, Georgetown University Press).

Soderlund, G. (2011), 'The Rhetoric of Revelation: Sex Trafficking and the Journalistic Expose', *Humanity*, 2, 2: 193–211.

Strauss, K. (2012), 'Unfree Again: Social Reproduction, Flexible Labour Markets and the Resurgence of Gang Labour in the UK', *Antipode*, 45: 180–197. DOI 10.1111/j.1467-8330.2012.00997.x

Tarrow, S. (2011), *Power in Movement: Social Movements and Contentious Politics* (Cambridge, Cambridge University Press).

Thomas, D. (2001), *The Helsinki Effect: International Norms, Human Rights, and the Demise of Communism* (Princeton, NJ, Princeton University Press).

United Nations Office on Drugs and Crime (2016), *Global Report on Trafficking in Persons* (Vienna, UNODC).

US Department of State (2016), *Trafficking in Persons Report: June 2016*, accessed 11 April 2017, https://www.state.gov/j/tip/rls/tiprpt/2016/

Vance, C. (2011), 'States of Contradiction: Twelve Ways to Do Nothing about Trafficking While Pretending To', *Social Research*, 78, 3: 933–48.

Vance, C. (2012), 'Innocence and Experience: Melodramatic Narratives of Sex Trafficking and Their Consequences for Law and Policy', *History of the Present*, 2, 2: 200–18. DOI 10.5406/historypresent.2.2.0200

Walk Free Foundation (2016), *Global Slavery Index*, accessed 11 April 2017, https://www.globalslaveryindex.org/

Wallis, A. (2015), 'Modern Slavery Act – Be Thankful', *Unseen* (6 August 2015), accessed 11 April 2017, http://www.unseenuk.org/blog/modern-slavery-act-be-thankful

White House (2017), 'Executive Order 13767: Border Security and Immigration Enforcement Improvements', 25 January 2017, accessed 11 April 2017, https://www.whitehouse.gov/presidential-actions/executive-order-border-security-immigration-enforcement-improvements/

Wong, W. (2012), *Internal Affairs: How the Structure of NGOs Transforms Human Rights* (Ithaca, NY, Cornell University Press).

Zaloznaya, M. & Hagan, J. (2012), 'Fighting Human Trafficking or Instituting Authoritarian Control', in K. Davis, A. Fisher, B. Kingsbury & S. Engle Merry (eds), *Governance by Indicators: Global Power through Classification and Rankings* (Oxford, Oxford University Press).

5

What is Forced Labour?
A Practical Guide for Humanities
and Social Science Research

JEAN ALLAIN

Introduction

WHEN SEEKING TO STUDY a phenomenon, it is fundamental for researchers not only to capture its essence, but also to form a consensus around what this essence is constituted of. A baseline understanding of any concept is fundamental for ensuring methodological rigour. Beyond possible disagreements as to the particularities of forced labour or its conceptualisations across studies, it is imperative that researchers working in this area operate within, at the very least, a baseline understanding of the concept – for neglecting to do so may invite diminishing returns. In particular, the absence of an objective baseline understanding may produce studies that err on the side of subjectivity, which could consequently invite critique with regard to credibility, empirical rigour, the accuracy of representation, and the ability to identify cases of forced labour.

What is forced labour? Similarly to Marx, one could argue that wage slavery requires us all to engage in forced labour. However, this understanding negates the possibility of a standard against which society could measure whether labour is acceptable or coerced. History tells us that the designations of free and unfree labour are subjective. During much of the nineteenth century, indentured servitude was understood as free labour, as employees ostensibly consented freely to contracts that committed them to working for a set time period. By today's standards, such instances would fall under the category of forced labour, as the state guaranteed the terms of these contracts – regardless of how employees were treated – by physically returning, with the help of the police or the sheriff, those who sought to escape exploitative, abusive or brutish conditions, and by allowing employers to administer corporal punishment for breach of contract (Steinfeld 1991).

Proceedings of the British Academy, **220**, 79–93. © The British Academy 2018.

The move away from this type of contractual labour emerged in reaction to societal changes driven by labour movements and trade unions, resulting in labour standards to regulate industry, the end of indentured labour, and the limiting of employers' freedom to, among other things, contract above a maximum set of working hours and a minimum amount of pay, or compel forced labour. It is ultimately the state that, through law, establishes the societal standard for what constitutes forced labour and whose role it is to arbitrate between employers and workers when it is not met. The standard of forced labour emerged at the height of European colonialism and was first agreed to at the international level through its inclusion in the International Labour Organization's (ILO) 1930 Forced Labour Convention. Recently, further considerations regarding forced labour were concluded in the 2014 Protocol to the 1930 Forced Labour Convention.

The definition of forced labour from the 1930 Convention should not only serve as a baseline meaning of what constitutes forced labour, but also provide a starting point for research in the area of forced labour in any given academic discipline. In order to understand why this nearly century-old definition remains relevant, we must first consider the parameters of what constitutes forced labour.

What follows is meant to assist researchers in the humanities and social sciences studying forced labour by providing them with a method for establishing a shared, baseline understanding of what does – and what does not – constitute forced labour. In addition to offering a tool for individual researchers, it also provides a means for consistency across disciplines while ensuring cross-disciplinary accuracy; cross-over in the ability to use data across studies, both at the meta and anecdotal levels; and, ultimately, an anchor for the overall credibility of those studying forced labour.

What is forced labour?

The core definition of forced labour was first established by an international legal agreement in 1930. During these negotiations, it was understood that 'it was right that this Article should be of a very sweeping character and that we should include everything we could in the terms of the definition' (ILO 1930a: 269). However, as will become evident in the subsequent section – 'What is not forced labour?' – this definition also comes with a number of exceptions.

The understanding of forced labour, however, has not remained static over the years: authoritative bodies such as the ILO's Committee of Experts have updated the concept through their observations, as have regional human rights courts and the domestic courts of various countries. This process has therefore given more substance to the common understanding of forced labour beyond the bare bones of the definition established in 1930. While the ILO definition speaks of 'forced or compulsory labour', there is no legal distinction between 'forced' and 'compulsory' labour, which has resulted in the simple reference to 'forced labour'. The ILO definition of 'forced and compulsory labour' is found in the ILO Forced Labour Convention, 1930 (No. 29) in Article 2(1) and reads:

> All work or service which is exacted under menace of any penalty for its non-performance and for which the worker concerned does not offer himself voluntarily.

It is possible to establish a baseline understanding of what constitutes forced labour by breaking down this definition into its component parts:

1   'All work or service'
    The first of these components – 'all work or service' – may appear to be the most obvious of all: forced labour takes place through working relations, where any type of labour or service is being provided (ILO 1968). Yet, this acknowledgement places a fundamental limitation upon forced labour, as it requires the presence of an element of 'work or service'. Even at its very worst, forced labour remains a transgression of work, i.e. a contravention of acceptable practices within the context of an individual providing work or a service for another person. To go past the boundaries of such a situation removes us from the exclusive realm of forced labour, and brings us, as will be considered later, into the orbit of situations akin to slavery.

2   'Exacted under a menace of a penalty'
    The exacting of labour under the menace of a penalty is the means by which a person is compelled to perform forced labour (ILO 2005: 6). During the negotiation process of the 1930 Convention, it was recognised that this component entailed 'any penalty or punishment . . . whatever', including the 'loss of any rights or privileges' (ILO 1930b: 11). The ILO Committee of Experts, which evaluates bi-annually how states that have accepted the 1930 Convention as law carry out their legal obligations, has further elaborated upon the latter provision. To that end, the Committee of Experts has noted that a 'penalty' will include instances 'where persons who refuse to perform voluntary labour may lose certain rights, advantages or privileges' such as 'promotion, transfer, access to new employment, the acquisition of certain consumer goods, housing or participation in university programmes' (ILO 2007: 20).
       Beyond these considerations by the ILO, regional human rights courts have also elaborated upon what constitutes a 'menace of a penalty'. The European Court of Human Rights has determined that a menace need not amount to a threat uttered; a victim may encounter 'an equivalent situation in terms of the perceived seriousness of the threat' (*Siliadin* 2005: 37). In the case being referenced, which relates to a child who was a foreign domestic worker, it was deemed that the victim's fear of arrest by the police, as a migrant whose

illegal immigration status was nurtured by her employer, constituted a menace of a penalty.

In an extreme case of forced labour heard by the Inter-American Court of Human Rights, dozens of herders were forced to drive a thousand head of cattle at the demand of paramilitaries, whose menace of a penalty was of the 'most extreme form'; that is, that of 'direct or implicit threat of physical violence or death addressed to the victim or his next of kin'. In making this determination, the Court held that the phrase 'a menace of a penalty' 'can consist in the real and actual presence of a threat, which can assume different forms and degrees, of which the most extreme are those that imply coercion, physical violence, isolation or confinement, or the threat to kill the victim or his next of kin' (*Ituango* 2006: 79).

3   'Voluntary offer of labour'
The final component of the ILO definition of forced labour relates to consent (ILO 2005: 6). The ILO has noted that the element of 'voluntary offer of labour' overlaps with that of 'menace of any penalty' inasmuch as freedom to work cannot exist under threat (ILO 2007: 20). In many ways this component of the definition no longer holds, as consent to forced labour cannot justify the compelling of such labour. That said, if consent is to be offered, it must be set out in law. Thus, the ILO has determined that 'account must be taken of the legislative and practical framework which guarantees or limits that freedom' (ILO 2007: 20). In other words, if the type of consent that is sought after is not established in law, it will fall foul of this provision and will be deemed labour that is not voluntarily offered. Where consent is not forthcoming – and the other two component parts of the definition are satisfied – forced labour is present.

Beyond constraints established by law, the ILO Committee of Experts recognised that 'indirect coercion interfering with a worker's freedom to "offer himself voluntarily" may result . . . from an employer's practice, e.g. where migrant workers are induced by deceit, false promises and retention of identity documents or forced to remain at the disposal of an employer; such practices represent a clear violation of the Convention' (ILO 2007: 20). At the front end of taking on work, the regional Inter-American Court of Human Rights has noted that the lack of voluntary nature of the work 'consists in the absence of consent or free choice when the situation of forced labour begins or continues. This can occur for different reasons, such as illegal deprivation of liberty, deception or psychological coercion' (*Ituango* 2006: 79, 80).

With regard to the termination of labour, the ILO has stated that a worker's freedom to offer herself or himself voluntarily mandates that 'the workers' right to free choice of employment remains inalienable' and, as such, the introduction of 'statutory provisions preventing termination of employment of indefinite duration (or very long duration) upon notice of reasonable length is to turn a contractual relationship based on the will of the parties into service by compulsion of law, and is thus incompatible with the Convention'. Likewise, the requirement 'to serve beyond the expiry of a contract of fixed duration' would be incompatible with the provision of work that is 'voluntarily offered' (ILO 2007: 20).

In summary, the final component of forced labour should be understood in the following terms: the ability for a person to voluntarily offer her or his labour will be negated by any means or methods of coercion by an employer to compel said labour.

After having deconstructed the three constitutive parts of the legal definition of forced labour, it should be clear that using this definition to form a baseline understanding for humanities or social science research requires that: 1) forced labour transpires in the context of the provision of work or service; 2) it be compelled as a result of a threat; and 3) the threat in question coerces the victim into labouring against her or his will. If any of these three elements of the definition is not present, then neither is forced labour.

What is not forced labour?

Understanding the established, core meaning of forced labour also requires the appreciation of what does *not*, in legal terms, constitute forced labour. In the first instance, it should be understood that the concept of forced labour in the 1930 Forced Labour Convention was forged at the height of European colonialism, as a means to control the abuse of colonial labour, rather than as a measure to abolish forced labour. The Covenant of the League of Nations required that its members 'endeavour to secure and maintain fair and humane conditions of labour for men, women, and children' – both at home and in their colonies (Covenant 1920). The Covenant also created the mandate system, whereby a number of the colonial possessions of the vanquished were handed to the victors as a 'sacred trust of civilisation' which included, for specific mandate holders, the requirement to prohibit 'all forms of forced or compulsory labour, except for essential public works and services' (ILO 1929). There is, in this, therefore a prime consideration for developing an understanding of forced labour, which holds to this day: forced labour is not absolutely prohibited, but is rather permitted for specific, public, purposes.

This was made most evident during the negotiations of the 1930 Forced Labour Convention where, despite the professed aim to suppress forced labour, it was recognised that the Convention was tending 'towards a kind of codification of forced labour' for colonial purposes (ILO 1930b: 46). The codification in question established 'transitional provisions' which allowed for forced labour to occur, but regulated, for instance, the age, gender and provision of food, for those compelled to labour. However, a new instrument negotiated by the ILO was created in 2014 that repeals these provisions from the 1930 Convention; the Protocol of 2014 to the Forced Labour Convention effectively removes these transitional provisions, which constituted more than two-thirds of the original 1930 Convention (ILO 2014). As a result, what remains of the 1930 Forced Labour Convention is the obligation to criminalise forced labour, the definition of forced labour, as well as the exceptions to forced labour.

Despite the pledge in 1930 by states 'to suppress the use of forced or compulsory labour in all its forms within the shortest possible period', and to ensure that forced labour is used, solely 'during the transitional period, for public purposes only and as an exceptional measure' (ILO 1930c: Article 1(2)), the 2014 Protocol to the Forced Labour Convention excludes five institutions of public work from being considered as instances of forced labour – despite these being recognised as such by the ILO. These five formal exceptions to the general rule are: military conscription, civic duty, penal labour, emergency assistance and community service (see Appendix for full provisions). Thus, the legal definition established by the 1930 Forced Labour Convention does not consider these five exceptions to be manifestations of forced labour. Researchers must therefore frame their understanding of these practices within the realm of what specific uses of forced labour are allowed by states. Regarding how these five exceptions are understood beyond what is outlined by the 1930 Convention, the ILO Committee of Experts has gone to great lengths to set out the parameters of what kind of forced labour is deemed acceptable (Allain 2013).

Beyond these five formal exceptions, it should also be noted that labour that is considered degrading, exploitative or harsh does *not*, in and of itself, constitute forced labour. In this vein, the compulsion to work brought on by economic necessity – as opposed to, as set out in the previous section, a menace of a penalty by one person towards another – does not constitute forced labour. While one may lament structural inequality and the dire labour conditions found in the recesses of supply chains of a globalised economy, these do not, necessarily, equate to conditions of forced labour, as they are not considered to be instances where one person compels another to work. Where this transpires, a human rights violation will only take place where either a state agent is involved in such compulsion or there is 'acquiescence in fact' by the state (*Fazenda* 2016: 292).

Beyond forced labour

Having considered the various practices that do not legally constitute forced labour, it is now necessary to draw attention to the situations that go beyond instances of work or service, i.e. situations of slavery. Where slavery is present, forced labour is often also being compelled, as enslavement is in the main motivated by economic gain.

The relationship between the two practices is reflected in the 1926 Slavery Convention, which calls on countries 'to take all necessary measures to prevent compulsory or forced labour from developing into conditions analogous to slavery' (Slavery Convention 1926: Preamble and Article 5). This is not to say that forced labour is no longer present, but rather that it is often subsumed by the more serious manifestations of slavery.

While the internationally recognised definition of slavery is rather refractory and inelegant, scholars and practitioners have worked to provide it with clarity by way of the 2012 *Bellagio-Harvard Guidelines on the Legal Parameters of Slavery*. Similarly to the 1930 definition of forced labour, the legal definition initially set out in the 1926 Slavery Convention remains the legal standard by which to measure, in this instance, what constitutes slavery. It reads (Article 1(1)): 'slavery is the status or condition of a person over whom any or all of the powers attaching to the right of ownership are exercised'.

In 2016, the Inter-American Court of Human Rights considered this definition to be based on two fundamental elements: 1) 'the status or condition of an individual . . . refers to both *de jure* and *de facto* situations', in other words, that a person need not be legally owned but can be held in a condition of slavery; and 2) 'the exercise of the attributes of property rights' (*Fazenda* 2016: 269–70). Here, the Inter-American Court elevated the 2012 *Bellagio-Harvard Guidelines* from an academic suggestion to a legal pronouncement, as it reproduced and endorsed the *Guidelines*' reading of the exercise of the powers attached to the right of ownership, which:

> should be understood as constituting control over a person in such a way as to significantly deprive that person of his or her individual liberty, with the intent of exploitation through the use, management, profit, transfer or disposal of that person. Usually this exercise will be supported by and obtained through means such as violent force, deception and/or coercion.

In regard to this 'property' element, the Court noted that it 'must be understood in the phenomenon of slavery as "possession", that is, the demonstration of control of one person over another. Therefore, when determining the level of control required to consider an act as slavery . . . it could be equated with the loss of agency or a fundamental diminution of autonomy' (*Fazenda* 2016: 271).

Beyond establishing that a person need not be legally owned in order to be enslaved, the Inter-American Court of Human Rights demonstrated that slavery is fundamentally about an overarching control that prevents a person from walking away. Once that control is established, a person in the condition of slavery can be bought or sold, used, managed, profited from, or even used to exhaustion (Bellagio-Harvard 2012). With this in mind, it should be recognised that an exercise of control below this threshold can still be captured by the elements of the definition of forced labour.

The distinction between forced labour and slavery is that the latter is all-consuming. Enslavement not only entails – in a worst-case scenario – forced labour or service, but also effectively ensures that a person has no say in the other facets of her or his life. This level of control is equivalent to ownership, i.e. the type of despotic control that vitiates a human being's agency or autonomy. Taking this into consideration, a situation of forced labour may also constitute slavery, if forced labour is accompanied by an overarching control beyond the workplace, extending to fundamental control over a person's life choices.

This is most evident in situations where a person, depending on the nature of their work, is also living in their workplace. In such cases, if forced labour is present, enslavement also becomes a possibility. This vulnerability is mostly mani-fested in the context of foreign domestic workers or seafarers, which often involves particular features – including gender, class, nationality and language – that may be leveraged by an employer to establish the conditions for overarching control of the type recognised as enslavement. The same can be applied to situations where an employer provides ancillary services reaching beyond the workplace, such as accommodation, food or transportation.

Where empirical research is confronted with instances of enslavement, this need not be a barrier to also recognising forced labour. The method for deter-mining the contours of forced labour holds: consider the situation in light of the baseline understanding of forced labour, with its three defining elements. Where there is doubt or emphasis placed on forced labour, one may wish to provide a justification for why consideration is being given to forced labour rather than slavery.

Building on the baseline

There are many benefits to utilising the definition of forced labour that was originally set out in the 1930 Forced Labour Convention to form a baseline under-standing of the concept. When using a baseline definition with the intention of maintaining standards of rigour required by academic enquiry, it is worth empha-sising that generalities about whether certain practices or institutions constitute forced labour should be avoided. In other words, methodological rigour can be achieved by considering specific cases where, as we have seen, a person compels another to work against her or his will. This approach will speak to a valid find-ing, rather than a general, sweeping claim that an institution or practice such as child begging is, by its very nature, a manifestation of forced labour. Thus, cau-tion is required when making claims in the aggregate without substantiating such assertions or, where need be, qualifying them.

Further caution should be exerted when basing research on standards beyond the agreed definition of forced labour. Take, for instance, the 2012 *ILO Indicators of Forced Labour*, prepared by the ILO's Special Action Programme for Combating Forced Labour, which are meant to assist those at the coalface in 'identifying persons who are possibly trapped in forced labour situations'. 'These indicators', the ILO notes, 'represent the most common signs or "clues" that point to possible existence of a forced labour case' (ILO 2012: 2). While there is great value in these indicators, they nevertheless lack the sense of specificity required for asserted claims in humanities or social science research. In other words, while these indicators capture possible cases of forced labour, they cast a very wide net and, in doing so, also risk capturing situations that should *not* be considered as forced labour. A quick examination of these indicators is beneficial for assisting in the triage phase, before determining whether or not certain cases fall under the category of forced labour.

The ILO set out eleven indicators as 'the main possible elements of a forced labour situation, and hence . . . the basis to assess whether or not an individual worker is a victim of this crime' (ILO 2012: 3). While this claim may in and of itself be too strong, the following indicators are helpful for identifying potential cases where forced labour is present:

- abuse of vulnerability;
- deception;
- restriction of movement;
- isolation;
- physical and sexual violence;
- intimidation and threats;
- retention of identity documents;
- withholding of wages;
- debt bondage;
- abusive working and living conditions;
- excessive overtime.

It is worth pointing the reader to the commentary accompanying each of these *ILO Indicators of Forced Labour*, as they provide a framework for understanding the means by which forced labour is induced, or the methods used by those who seek to compel forced labour. Yet, reference to the last of these indicators, excessive overtime, brings into focus the distinction between an *indicator* of forced labour and forced labour. The commentary to this indicator reads:

> Forced labourers may be obliged to work excessive hours or days beyond the limits prescribed by national law or collective agreement. They can be denied breaks and days off, having to take over the shifts and working hours of colleagues who are absent, or by being on call 24 hours a day, 7 days a week.

> The determination of whether or not overtime constitutes a forced labour offence can be quite complex. As a rule of thumb, if employees have to work more overtime than is allowed under national law, under some form of threat (e.g. the threat of dismissal) or in order to earn at least the minimum wage, this amounts to forced labour.

After reading the first section of this chapter, which breaks down the three cornerstones of the definition of forced labour, it should be quite clear that what is described in this ILO commentary is *not* in fact forced labour. While it is accurate to say that a 'forced labourer may be obliged to work excessive hours', the reverse does not hold true: excessive hours do not constitute forced labour – unless by 'obliged' one means compelled by means of threat to work against one's will. Likewise, in regard to the second paragraph quoted above, forced labour does not arise 'if employees have to work more overtime than is allowed under national law' or 'in order to earn at least the minimum wage'; rather, these assertions would only hold true as forced labour if they transpired 'under some form of threat (e.g. of dismissal)' and where labour was not voluntarily offered. While these indicators may point to instances of exploitative labour or violations of national laws and international labour standards, their presence does not necessarily generate instances of forced labour.

Conclusion: the rationale for the legal definition as a baseline understanding

This chapter will conclude by providing a rationale for why the 1930 international legal definition should be used as a baseline for understanding what constitutes forced labour, be it in the humanities, the social sciences or beyond. This rationale is founded on the process by which states pass laws that shape societal norms and set legal standards for common conduct. The liberal international order recognises that establishing control over a territory and population, and being recognised by other states as having an effective government (democratic or otherwise), are essential constituents of modern states. Only then is an entity granted the right to speak on behalf of its citizenry in the determination of the normative content of the international order as expressed through international, legal, standards. Ordinarily the determination of those standards takes place through direct negotiations by diplomats, i.e. representatives of states.

However, where forced labour is concerned, it is not only the representatives of states who have a seat at the negotiating table. The ILO has a unique tripartite system of governance, wherein it is not only representatives of states that have a say in the elaboration of international standards – be they treaties or recommendations – but also representatives of employers and workers. Once an agreement is reached on a particular issue, for instance the 1930 Forced Labour Convention or its 2014 Protocol, then it is up to each state to consider whether or not it wishes to be party to this agreement, and to thus take on its requirements and integrate them into its domestic legal system. In the case of the 1930 Convention, 178 of 194 countries agreed to do so, and are thus required to incorporate the ILO's understanding of forced labour within their domestic framework, making it 'punishable as a penal offence' and ensuring that those 'penalties imposed by law are really adequate and are strictly enforced' (Article 25). Thus, for more than 85 years, a consensus has been maintained with regards to what constitutes forced labour, at both international and national levels.

There may be many challenges to the legitimacy of the international political process, including the colonial nature of the 'international community' as constituted in the 1930s and with regards to the plurality of various states' political systems. Furthermore, the legal definition of forced labour, including its fundamental, built-in exceptions and its original focus on legitimising coerced colonial labour, is ripe for disagreement. Yet, despite their limitations, the standards set by the 1930 ILO Convention ultimately find legitimacy in the fact that 178 countries have, through their domestic legislative process, accepted them as a binding legal instrument for their societies. Against the background of this consensus, researchers can forge ahead with their own readings of forced labour, but they do so at the risk of losing the methodological benefits of speaking a common language. This is not to say that the standard of the 1930 ILO definition is somehow 'correct' or 'right', but rather that it offers a baseline definition to use, critique and engage with. This baseline understanding ultimately provides a standard from which to explore forced labour – a starting point, rather than an end point – when conducting sound and rigorous research in the humanities or social sciences.

With this in mind, the following is a summary of practical points meant to assist those researching in the humanities or social sciences in developing a baseline understanding of forced labour.

Ten Practical Points for Understanding Forced Labour

1 The ILO definition of forced or compulsory labour includes three elements: '*All work or service* which is *exacted under menace of any penalty* for its non-performance and for which the worker concerned *does not offer himself voluntarily.*'

2 Forced labour is not absolutely prohibited; rather it is circumscribed, with exceptions allowing for specific public purposes: military conscription, civic duty, penal labour, emergency assistance, and community service.

3 Forced labour transpires through a working relationship.

4 A 'menace of any penalty' is *any* threat, be it direct or implicit, physical or otherwise, aimed at an employee and which is meant to compel labour.

5 The ability of a person to 'offer himself or herself voluntarily' will be negated by *any* means or methods of coercion used by an employer to compel labour.

6 Where any of the three elements of the definition are *not* present, neither is forced labour.

7 Degrading, exploitative or harsh labour will *not*, in and of itself, constitute forced labour.

8 Forced labour does not manifest itself by compulsion brought on by economic necessity; rather, the menace of a penalty needs to be attributable to a person or persons.

9 Forced labour will constitute a human rights violation where a state agent is involved or where forced labour is transpiring and is brought to the attention of the state, that state fails to investigate with due diligence.

10 A situation of forced labour will also constitute slavery, if the forced labour is accompanied by an overarching control beyond the workplace, extending to fundamental control over a person's daily life and life choices.

Appendix: selected international provisions related to forced labour

1930 Forced Labour Convention

Article 1

1   Each Member of the International Labour Organization which ratifies this Convention undertakes to suppress the use of forced or compulsory labour in all its forms within the shortest possible period . . .

Article 2

1   For the purposes of this Convention the term 'forced or compulsory labour' shall mean all work or service which is exacted from any person under the menace of any penalty and for which the said person has not offered himself voluntarily.

2   Nevertheless, for the purposes of this Convention the term 'forced or compulsory labour' shall not include:

(a) Any work or service exacted in virtue of compulsory military service laws for work of a purely military character;

(b) Any work or service which forms part of the normal civic obligations of the citizens of a fully self-governing country;

(c) Any work or service exacted from any person as a consequence of a conviction in a court of law, provided that the said work or service is carried out under the supervision and control of a public authority and that the said person is not hired to or placed at the disposal of private individuals, companies or associations;

(d) Any work or service exacted in cases of emergency, that is to say, in the event of war or of a calamity or threatened calamity, such as fire, flood, famine, earthquake, violent epidemic or epizootic diseases, invasion by animal, insect or vegetable pests, and in general any circumstance that would endanger the existence or the well-being of the whole or part of the population;

(e) Minor communal services of a kind which, being performed by the members of the community in the direct interest of the said community, can therefore be considered as normal civic obligations incumbent upon the members of the community, provided that the members of the community or their direct representatives shall have the right to be consulted in regard to the need for such services.

Protocol of 2014 to the Forced Labour Convention, 1930

Article 1

1   In giving effect to its obligations under the Convention to suppress forced or
     compulsory labour, each Member shall take effective measures to prevent and
     eliminate its use, to provide to victims protection and access to appropriate
     and effective remedies, such as compensation, and to sanction the perpetrators
     of forced or compulsory labour.
2   Each Member shall develop a national policy and plan of action for the effec-
     tive and sustained suppression of forced or compulsory labour in consultation
     with employers' and workers' organizations, which shall involve systematic
     action by the competent authorities and, as appropriate, in coordination with
     employers' and workers' organizations, as well as with other groups concerned.
3   The definition of forced or compulsory labour contained in the Convention
     is reaffirmed, and therefore the measures referred to in this Protocol shall
     include specific action against trafficking in persons for the purposes of forced
     or compulsory labour.

References

Allain, J. (2013), *Slavery in International Law: Of Human Exploitation and Trafficking*
    (Leiden, Martinus Nijhoff), 224–34.
Bellagio-Harvard (2012), *The 2012 Bellagio-Harvard Guidelines on the Legal Parameters of
    Slavery*, accessed 19 June 2017, https://www.qub.ac.uk/schools/SchoolofLaw/Research/
    HumanRights/bellagio/
Covenant (1920), Covenant of the League of Nations, Article 23(a), accessed 23 July 2018,
    http://avalon.law.yale.edu/20th_century/leagcov.asp
Fazenda (2016), Organization of American States, Inter-American Court of Human Rights,
    Workers of Fazenda Brasil Verde v Brazil, Judgement (Preliminary Objections, Merits,
    Reparations and Costs), 20 October 2016, 292.
ILO (International Labour Organization) (1929), International Labour Office, International
    Labour Conference, 12th Session, Forced Labour: Report and Draft Questionnaire,
    1929, 8.
ILO (1930a), International Labour Conference, 14th Session, Volume I: First and Second
    Part, Proceedings, Fifteenth Sitting, 1930, 269–70.
ILO (1930b), International Labour Conference, 14th Session, Item I, Report of the
    Committee on Forced Labour to the Twelfth Session of the Conference, Forced Labour,
    1930, 11.
ILO (1930c), Forced Labour Convention, 1930 (No. 29), Article 1(1) and 1(2), accessed 23
    July 2018, http://www.ilo.org/dyn/normlex/en/f?p=NORMLEXPUB:12100:0::NO::P1
    2100_ILO_CODE:C029
ILO (1968), International Labour Conference, 46th Session, Item III, Report of the
    Committee of Experts on the Application of Conventions and Recommendations,
    General Survey on the Reports Concerning Forced Labour Convention, 1930 (No. 29),

and the Abolition of Forced Labour Convention, 1957 (No. 105), Report III (Part IV), 187, n. 29.

ILO (2005), International Labour Conference, 93rd Session, Report of the Director-General: Global Report under the Follow-up to the ILO Declaration on Fundamental Principles and Rights at Work, Report I (B), 2005, 6.

ILO (2007), International Labour Conference, Eradication of Forced Labour, General Survey Concerning Forced Labour Convention, 1930 (No. 29), and the Abolition of Forced Labour Convention, 1957 (No. 105), Item III, Report of the Committee of Experts on the Application of Conventions and Recommendations, 2007.

ILO (2012), International Labour Office, Special Action Programme for Combating Forced Labour, *ILO Indicators of Forced Labour*, accessed 23 July 2018, http://www.ilo.org/wcmsp5/groups/public/---ed_norm/---declaration/documents/publication/wcms_203832.pdf

ILO (2014), Protocol of 2014 to the Forced Labour Convention, 1930, accessed 23 July 2018, http://www.ilo.org/dyn/normlex/en/f?p=NORMLEXPUB:12100:0::NO::P12100_ILO_CODE:P029

Ituango (2006), Organization of American States, Inter-American Court of Human Rights, *Ituango Massacres v Colombia*, Series C, No. 148, 1 July 2006, 79.

Siliadin (2005) Council of Europe, European Court of Human Rights, *Siliadin v France*, Application no. 73316/01, 26 July 2005, 37.

Slavery Convention (1926), The Slavery Convention, League of Nations, 1926, accessed 23 July 2018, https://www.ohchr.org/en/professionalinterest/pages/slaveryconvention.aspx

Steinfeld, J. (1991), *The Invention of Free Labour: The Employment Relations in English and American Law and Culture, 1350–1870* (Chapel Hill, University of North Carolina Press).

6

Confronting Bias in NGO
Research on Modern Slavery

SAMUEL OKYERE

Introduction

ARTICLE 2.1 OF THE ILO Forced Labour Convention, 1930 (No. 29) (recently updated
by the Protocol of 2014 to the Forced Labour Convention, 1930) defines forced
labour as 'all work or service which is exacted from any person under the menace
of any penalty and for which the said person has not offered himself voluntarily'.
Over the last few years, forced labour has been at the top of international human
rights, labour and political agendas, with ongoing efforts to better understand and
formulate policy on this phenomenon.

A notable obstacle to these efforts is the paucity of reliable evidence and data
on the phenomenon. Forced labour is said to be 'hard to see, harder to count' (ILO
2012). Some of the places where conditions deemed to constitute forced labour
occur (such as fishing boats, mining and construction sites, plantations, factories
and other private premises) are often inaccessible to researchers (Tyldum 2010;
Zhang *et al.* 2014; Penney 2014). Thus, existing forced labour statistics are criti-
cised as being 'guesstimates' or figures that may be politically appealing but are
inherently unreliable or flawed. The quest for better evidence and data on forced
labour is further compounded by conceptual and definitional ambiguities, as various scholars have observed (Farrell *et al.* 2008; O'Connell Davidson 2006, 2010).
The conflation of terminology and interchangeable use of terms such as 'trafficking', 'modern slavery' and 'forced labour' in some studies blurs the boundaries
between distinct phenomena (Weitzer 2012; Allain 2012; Chuang 2014; Zhang
et al. 2014) and makes uncertain what is actually being studied or measured.

This chapter argues that efforts to produce more comprehensive, reliable
knowledge and evidence on forced labour are further hampered by the uncritical
application of conventional concepts, frameworks and discourses in forced labour
studies. It identifies three major problems. First, the uncritical use of dominant or
conventional concepts, definitions and narratives on forced labour may reproduce

Proceedings of the British Academy, **220**, 94–109. © The British Academy 2018.

the same discourses and delegitimise divergent narratives. Thus, and second, it can foreclose the attainment of more in-depth or comprehensive understanding of the causes, nature, experiences and scope of forced labour. Third, at the policy and practice levels, it can yield measures which blame, stigmatise or penalise individuals and communities for problems which are largely caused by external economic and political forces.

The chapter accepts that conventional accounts and definitions can serve useful purposes in identifying conditions of forced labour. It is therefore not advocating for rejection of such definitions in forced labour research. Instead, it argues that use of conventional frameworks should not preclude serious engagement with counter-definitions and narratives on forced labour, especially those from communities and actors whose livelihoods and lived experiences are impacted by these definitions. It also cautions against the assumption that data or findings from studies which are based on conventional analysis, definitions and interpretations of forced labour are necessarily more rational, objective or legitimate than those which are not.

Background

This chapter draws on evidence from discourse analysis of textual data drawn primarily from materials published on the website of the non-governmental organisation (NGO) Free the Slaves (FTS). FTS was founded in 2000 and it currently operates in India, Nepal, Congo, Haiti and Ghana (FTS 2016). The information analysed for the chapter was mainly, but not exclusively, taken from two publicly accessible research reports on FTS-commissioned projects on child labour, child slavery and child exploitation. The two sources are the 'Child Slavery, Child Labour and Exploitation of Children in Mining Communities' report and the 'Child Rights in Mining: Pilot Project Results and Lessons Learned' report. The research underpinning both reports was carried out through a collaboration between FTS, Participatory Development Associates (PDA) and Social Support Foundation (SSF), to support FTS campaigns and interventions on the involvement of children in the Ghanaian artisanal gold mining sector.

The analysed materials were selected based on their reliance on conventional discourses as a framework underpinning the research projects. The projects were carried out over an 18-month period between November 2011 and April 2013. They formed part of FTS' ongoing Ghana Child Rights in Mining Project, which is primarily concerned with addressing 'modern forms of slavery, including child sex trafficking and the related and overlapping problem of hazardous child labour' (FTS 2013: 1), in the Ghanaian gold mining sector. Their principal aim was to document 'the dynamics of exploitation and abuse of children in and around Obuasi, Ghana, where informal small-scale and artisanal gold mining occurs', in order to 'understand the narratives of exploited and enslaved children to guide programs that strengthen community-based protection and prevention' (FTS 2013: 1). The language used throughout the description of the project's aims and objectives and employed throughout the published text underscores the positionality of FTS as a contemporary slavery abolitionist organisation. This positionality impacted on the study and its findings in many ways, as will be further addressed later in the chapter.

Methodologically, the study employed participatory rural appraisal, semi-structured interviews, trend analysis, focus group discussions, community mapping, body mapping, ranking and scoring, among other qualitative methods. Data collection involved three notable populations. Child research participants were first interviewed on their experiences of artisanal gold mining work. Data was also collected from community leaders, parents, miners and other stakeholders' understandings of the causes and consequences of the forms of child exploitation the study recorded in their community. Additionally, residents were interviewed and surveyed on their understanding and awareness of initiatives by the government and civil society organisations to address child exploitation in their community. Findings from these three strands of enquiry were used to develop an illustrated storybook for sensitisation workshops in the local communities (FTS 2014: 12).

The sensitisation workshops were the focus of phase two of the project, which involved 25 learning groups comprising over 350 residents who were brought together to discuss the storybooks. Prior to giving out the illustrated materials, the researchers conducted baseline surveys involving 21 open-ended questions. Three members of each learning group were also interviewed prior to their use of the books and afterwards. The objective of the surveys and interviews was to gauge the extent to which engagement with the illustrated materials could be deemed to have changed participants' attitudes and abilities 'to take the right steps to protect children from abuse' (FTS 2014: 13). Findings from both stages of the project were subsequently disseminated across the research settings, to policymakers and across the Internet as downloads via the FTS webpage.

Critical reflections on the FTS, PDA and SSF research

What follows in this section is a textual and discourse analysis critique of the texts and language employed in the reports, webpages and other published materials rather than a criticism of FTS, PDA, SSF and their researchers. The interest is in the meanings embodied in the material and the knowledge it provides about children's involvement in gold mining in Ghana and about the participants and their communities. Given the chapter's emphasis on the need for critical reflexivity in forced labour research, and in all research for that matter, it is important to acknowledge my own subjectivity and positionality in carrying out textual and discourse analysis of this kind. Subjectivity and politically grounded positions inevitably shape all research and analysis. Our normative judgements, political and moral assumptions and other human cognitive processes invariably guide how we collect, read and interpret information (Gouldner 1962; Aronowitz 1988; Gould 1996; Miller 1999; Crosby & Bearman 2006). It is therefore more credible to accept this aspect of the research process rather than assume that one can operate from a position of absolute neutrality or objectivity (Ramazanoglu 1992: 211).

On the strength of the above, this chapter is not seeking to supplant one objectivity fallacy with another; it is not calling the merits or findings by the FTS, PDA and SSF study into question. Far from purporting to speak from a more knowledgeable or credible position, the chapter proceeds on the basis that critical analysis of this nature is integral to academic debate and providing researchers with feedback (Polit & Beck 2004; Burns & Grove 2001). Critical analyses of textual data on forced labour research can also further illuminate the diverse opinions or perspectives on the issue and, consequently, the different trajectories that could be adopted by future studies. Indeed, such critiques are not uncommon. The Global Slavery Index (GSI), the Trafficking in Persons (TIP) Report, the ILO Indicators of Forced Labour and others are routinely scrutinised (COHA 2016; Andreas 2010; Weitzer 2014; Gallagher 2014, 2015; Quirk & Broome 2015; Crump 2016; Nair 2016). The chapter is therefore located in this tradition and body of critical work.

The rest of the section focuses on the consequences that can arise from exploring issues such as exploitative child labour exclusively through the lenses of dominant international definitions and discourses. Three key themes which emerged from the discourse and textual data will be discussed. First, uncritical reliance on mainstream discourses and definitions reinforces their dominance and further delegitimises counter-narratives; second, it gives rise to methodological issues that adversely affect research quality; and, third, it increases the risk of empirical findings being distorted or divergent findings ignored.

Uncritical application of popular discourses and definitions may simply reinforce these definitions and discourses

The FTS, PDA and SSF projects relied primarily on international conventions such as the ILO Forced Labour Convention, 1930 (No. 29) (recently updated by the Protocol of 2014 to the Forced Labour Convention, 1930) and the Worst Forms of Child Labour Convention, 1999 (No. 182), as well as FTS' own definition of modern slavery. They also drew heavily from conventional international discourses on children's involvement in artisanal gold mining work, which suggest that child labourers are unequivocally exploited, abused and denied their rights in this sector.

The textual data analysis shows that these discourses profoundly shaped the project and its conclusions. The language employed throughout the report embraces the discourse of pathology, exploitation and crisis. Words and phrases such as 'exploited children', 'enslaved children', 'slavery', 'abused children' and 'forced children' pervade the projects' aims, research questions and objectives in the published materials. They are also persistently used in reference to the child research participants throughout the reports. The unequivocal use of such terms or descriptions for the child research participants (before the data was even collected to confirm that the children were 'exploited', 'enslaved', 'abused' and 'forced') can suggest that foregone conclusions had been made about their situation or status in advance of the study.

The pervasive use of words such as 'slaves', 'slavery' and 'enslaved' for describing the child research participants throughout the published materials also reflects FTS' own mission. The prolific use of these qualifiers underscores a congruency between the *raison d'être* of FTS – an abolitionist organisation – and the objectives of the study it commissioned. The positionality and political assumptions of the research sponsor cum lead organisation for the project were made evident through these terms. Further, no real distinctions were made between child exploitation, child slavery, forced labour, worst forms of child labour and other terminology, all used interchangeably throughout the text. As noted in the chapter's introductory paragraphs, lack of precision and conflation of terminology have serious implications for the findings of studies of this nature (Kapur 2002; Galma & Finckenauer 2005; Snajdr 2013; McGrath & Mieres 2014, Pieper *et al.* 2015).

Methodological dilemma: delegitimising of counter-narratives and epistemologies

A second theme which emerged from the discourse and textual analysis was a tendency to privilege dominant international definitions and discourses over local views and interpretations of children's involvement in artisanal gold mining work. This finding raises methodological questions. As noted earlier, the study's use of mixed-methods research design offered opportunities for methodological rigour, data triangulation and enhanced understanding of the issues it set out to study (Tashakkori & Teddlie 2003; Onwuegbuzie & Leech 2004; Chow *et al.* 2010). The participatory methodological strategy which was employed for the qualitative component is also regarded as a means of democratising knowledge and the process of knowledge production (Habermas 1971). Participatory approaches can facilitate equal partnerships in research and co-production of knowledge between researchers and participants (Curtis 1995; Chambers 2008; Cook 2012). They can also empower or amplify the voices of marginalised communities (Oakley *et al.* 1991; Chambers 1994; Agrawal 1995).

On the strengths of the above, the study was well placed methodologically to produce vivid, nuanced and holistic accounts of the issues in question. However, the unquestioned use of mainstream and FTS' own definitions and accounts, coupled with terminological conflations throughout the texts, held back this potential.

The manner of the community's involvement in the study permitted neither the balancing or equalising of power relationships in the research process nor due consideration of their voices and narratives. From the textual and discourse analysis, it emerged that, far from democratising the knowledge production process by opening up hegemonic positions to scrutiny, the community's analysis, interpretations and contributions were rather routinely discredited and delegitimised. The participatory approach thus merely served as a process to entrench and legitimise ideologies and the conventional ideas, discourses and understandings which had been adopted for the project at the outset. It also served to support FTS' own positions adopted prior to the study instead of prying these open to participants' and the community's scrutiny in much the same way as the research sought to interrogate those of participants and their communities.

Questions about power, voice and credibility in research were therefore among the important observations which emerged from the textual and discourse analysis. The manner in which participants' and the community's voices were routinely questioned – while those of the researchers were taken as facts – carries an implicit assumption that the latter are necessarily more knowledgeable or better informed on the issue of children's involvement in artisanal gold mining work than the community and participants whose daily lives were characterised by this activity, and whose lived experiences the study was actually trying to understand. A significant and long-standing body of work in the fields of international development studies and practice has similarly rightly raised concerns that participatory research has become yet another means of legitimising researchers' and NGOs' preconceptions or ideas rather than attaining the advertised emancipatory or collaborative goals (White 2010; Chambers 1997; Richards 1993, 1995; Leurs 1998; Green 2000; Kothari 2001; Leal 2007). The stated aim of giving participants, especially those from marginalised groups, a voice as true partners in research and developmental projects through participatory methods is sometimes merely a façade for pushing through top-down ideas and agendas, as Cooke and Kothari (2001) also note.

An area of the analysis where these observations were most evident was the report's section on the understanding of childhood within the research communities versus that promoted by the dominant international discourse employed by the study. The project adopted the definition offered by Article 1 of the United Nations Convention on the Rights of the Child (UNCRC), which stipulates that 'a "*child*" is a person below the age of 18, unless the laws of a particular country set the legal age for adulthood younger'. Results from baseline surveys carried out during the second project showed that respondents overwhelmingly rejected this conventional international understanding. The report does not stipulate the specific number of survey respondents. However, it does indicate that only 18 per cent of the survey respondents agreed with the view that the age of 18 represents the boundary between childhood and adulthood (FTS 2014: 14). Upon sensitising the community with the illustrated booklets and re-administering the survey, only 39 per cent agreed with this conventional definition (FTS 2014: 14).

It was therefore evident that the community did not agree with this understanding of childhood or the use of chronological age alone as a basis for determining a person's maturity. This discord between the dominant international definition of childhood and understandings of the concept across diverse cultures, spaces and times has been widely discussed in sociological and anthropological texts (James & Prout 1997; Punch 2003; Gadda 2008). The differences could have been acknowledged as an example of the ways in which alternative understandings of childhood and maturity might inform the entry of children and youth into conditions of labour deemed hazardous, exploitative or forced, given that the community did not regard that category of teenagers who were involved in artisanal mining work as children in the same way as those aged 10 and below. However, the published materials held it up as a sign of parental and community naivety or ignorance. Parents were described as 'lacking knowledge about their roles as parents, and the rights and welfare of their children' (FTS 2014: 5), simply because their views on the definition or nature of childhood and appropriate work for children contrasted with those that had been adopted for the research. In contrast, in a manner which follows what Van Dijk (1993) describes as positive self-representation and negative other-representation, FTS is held up in the texts as being more objective, better informed and in a position to address the parents' and community's perceived 'ignorance' about their children's rights. Thus, as stated in dissemination material on the NGO's website: 'Free the Slaves is building awareness about child rights in source communities that send children to work at mines. Many parents lack detailed knowledge about their roles and responsibilities in promoting child welfare, and there is a general lack of awareness about government resources to address child abuse.'

Genuine participatory research is guided by an understanding that informants are knowing subjects whose ideas, analysis and interpretations must be meaningfully considered and represented in the findings. It also embodies respect for participants and their communities, as well as commitment to inclusion of participants' voices and insights in the knowledge researchers create and share about participants' lives. Where evident power imbalances exist between the two, this approach to research can serve as a means of equalising or minimising power differentials between research participants and researchers; the two are co-equals or collaborators in producing knowledge. From the textual and discourse analysis, it is evident that the manner and extent to which participants' views are elicited, and whether their ideas are inculcated into the knowledge produced, still exclusively rests with the researcher. The community's opinions about childhood, hazardous work, exploitative labour, forced labour and other phenomena were delegitimised in the knowledge produced and disseminated by the project. A hierarchy of credibility (Becker 1967) was evident in the texts, demonstrated by a tendency to affirm and accentuate assumptions held by the researchers while discrediting local ideas as naive or ignorant, especially where they deviated from the positions which guided the study.

Distorting or ignoring of empirical findings

A third theme from the discourse and textual analyses is that notable empirical findings could be skewed or ignored if they do not fit with the assumptions guiding the study. Earlier, the chapter mentioned that one of the most prominent observations about the discourse and textual data was the gratuitous use of words and phrases such as 'child slavery', 'child sex slavery' and 'exploitative labour', among others. These characterisations reflect the positionality of FTS as an abolitionist organisation which has long argued that Ghanaian children working in quarries and informal mining, including diamond and gold mines, are forced, exploited and 'enslaved' and that girls are subject to sexual exploitation and prostitution (FTS 2014: 8). Indeed, this long-held assumption partly underpins the NGO's presence in Ghana. The research studies were also commissioned in part with the aim of finding evidence to support FTS' claims of child enslavement in these economic sectors of the country.

It is instructive to note that the two studies did not find a single case or instance of 'child sexual slavery', 'child prostitution', 'child sexual exploitation' or 'forced labour', despite the repeated assertions of the existence of these phenomena by FTS. This lack of supporting evidence is noted in the report: 'while grassroots working in these mining areas believe many children end up working in the mines because they have been coerced by parents or relatives through explicit or implicit mental or physical threat, and thus would be classified as being in child labour slavery, such cases were not documented through this formative research' (FTS 2014: 8). Given the fact that a principal reason for the 18-month project was to document such cases, it is puzzling that this important discovery about the lack of supporting evidence is largely underplayed in the texts and dissemination material. In contrast, despite the lack of evidence, the prominent and persistent use of the terms 'child sexual slavery', 'child labour slavery', 'child prostitution', 'child sexual exploitation' and others is maintained throughout the texts and publicity materials about the study. A less critical reader, or one who does not spot the couple of lines acknowledging the lack of evidence for these pathological and stigmatising descriptions, might assume that FTS' long-held claims of widespread 'child slavery' and 'forced labour' in the Ghanaian artisanal gold mining sector have been substantiated when this is far from the case. In fact, the report's insistence on these terms despite the lack of evidence seems to be premised on the assumption that the 'worst forms of child labor often occur simultaneously with child labor slavery' (FTS 2014: 8). The research findings are therefore underplayed for the benefit of FTS' long-standing assumptions.

Such distortions in the presentation of empirical findings speak to concerns about the use of hyperbole, guesstimates, melodramatics and unfounded assumptions in the place of dispassionate analysis and data on forced labour, human trafficking and other related issues (Andrijasevic & Mai 2016). It is particularly troubling because although such data produced by NGOs for their own awareness raising, training and fundraising campaigns may be poor quality, these studies and claims now inform rankings on the GSI, the TIP Report and other metrics which have serious economic, political and reputational implications for what are often relatively poor countries. Just as guesstimates and fictitious figures on forced labour are repeated until they begin to appear as truths (Yea 2017: 1), so too, it seems, the text from the FTS, PDA and SSF materials reinforces unfounded assumptions of widespread child slavery in the Ghanaian gold mining sector. Children's work in artisanal gold mining can be unsafe and needs urgent solutions. However, the manner in which the issue is presented in the dissemination materials is still problematic, given the lack of evidence to support the original assumptions of 'child slavery' and forced child labour in this sector. The persistence of these claims in FTS' ongoing campaigns in relation to the Ghanaian artisanal gold mining communities creates a false image that stigmatises, and could contribute to economic sanctions and other penalties against, a country that is already struggling to meet the welfare needs of its citizens such as those who participated in the study.

Forced labour research and (NGO) bias and politics

The observations discussed in the previous section highlight a blind spot in the text concerning the ways in which researcher subjectivity and political and moral assumptions shape or constrain efforts to produce more inclusive and comprehensive knowledge of forced labour. Partisanship is not inherently ineffective (Becker 1967). Indeed, from a feminist theoretical perspective, supporting an underdog or a marginalised group, or seeking to challenge manifest inequality and injustice through research, is desirable (Brewer 2000; Skeggs 2007: 432). It has long been accepted that our individual identities, emotions, values and cognitive processes always have an impact on the research we carry out (Gouldner 1962; May 1993; Finlay 2002; Ferrell & Hamm 1998: 257; Lumsden 2013). However, as part of what has been termed the reflective turn or 'reflective partisanship' (Gouldner 1973: 53), contemporary social researchers must be open about which side they have taken, if so. They must also reflect on how their own (and others') values, beliefs and identities influence the design, conduct and dissemination of research (Coffey 1999: 5; Heartz 1997; Nightingale & Cromby 1999; Brewer 2000).

From the dissemination materials, it is evident that the community's values and ideologies are subjected to critical scrutiny at every point in the research. However, the text is markedly silent on how the researchers' own ideologies, politics and standpoints shaped the study and their interrogation of the former's ideas. The text suggests a foregone conclusion that views held by parents and the community are necessarily less valid relative to those held by the researchers. Linked to this is an implicit assumption of moral superiority. Subjective moral judgements are cast on the parenting skills, knowledge and abilities of those who participated in the study. Whole communities are tainted with the brush of ignorance because their views happened to challenge or contradict those held by the researchers. However, the ideology, positionality and agenda of the latter were not similarly held up for scrutiny in the text and considered in terms of their rationality, naivety or otherwise in the context and circumstances within which the views of parents and the community were formed.

In Yea's (2017) view, this issue is especially prominent in NGO/non-academic studies. Many do not appear to have much time for or see much value in critically examining how researcher identity and position inform findings, despite the importance of such considerations in all social research (Yea 2017: 1). Evidently, use of the most innovative or sophisticated methodology may still fail to yield inclusive or comprehensive knowledge when researchers are unwilling to challenge their own preconceptions, agendas, terminologies and concepts. The FTS, PDA and SSF project was premised on a belief in the existence of forced labour and 'child slavery' in the Ghanaian artisanal gold mining sector. The project's stated objective at the very outset was to 'understand the narratives of exploited and enslaved children' (FTS 2014: 2), a foregone conclusion on the existence of 'enslaved children' that was maintained even when no evidence was found. Taking a critical reflexive approach to the study by questioning the assumptions, identities and positionality of the organisations involved may have helped to correct the distortions.

The distortion of empirical findings also occurred because, to put it bluntly, organisations such as FTS have clear vested interests in the conceptualisation or construction of the problems they set out to study and in the findings of such studies (Weitzer 2014: 7). They assert the existence of 'child slavery' or forced labour in order to attract attention and support from the media, national governments and other stakeholders for fundraising and other purposes. FTS is at the forefront of modern abolitionist organisations in Ghana, and one of the areas where it is mainly focused is the artisanal gold mining sector. Contradictions to its long-held beliefs and persistent claims on the existence of widespread 'forced labour' and 'child slavery' in this sector would not necessarily be helpful to the NGO's case. To publicise the fact that an 18-month project commissioned to document instances of 'forced labour' and 'child slavery' did not find a single case could have implications for its ability to raise funds for this work and ultimately affect its credibility. Such vested interest also explains the blurring of boundaries and conflation of terminology in this field, as others have discussed (Musto 2009; O'Connell Davidson 2006, 2010; Pieper *et al.* 2015). The report not only speaks of 'child labour' or 'worst forms of child labour' but also introduces terms such as 'child labour slavery' and 'sexual slavery' as if these are different or distinct phenomena which have been found by the study.

Conclusion

This chapter has extended critiques of definitional and conceptual frameworks as potential obstacles for attaining more inclusive, comprehensive data and knowledge on forced labour. Critical appraisal of discourse and textual data was employed in support of the chapter's arguments. I have presented three principal problems that might occur in the application of broad, international definitions, concepts and discourses without due regard for how such work is conceived, rationalised or understood by those involved and by the communities in which it occurs. The underlying problem, the chapter has argued, is that this inadvertently privileges mainstream discourses, international legislation and interpretations over local voices. Researchers, NGOs and other actors who subscribe unequivocally to the mainstream international definitions and discourses may also presume that they are better informed and unbiased, or that their opinions are more rational and legitimate than those held by the people whose lived experiences they seek to study.

Chambers (1997) has presented a similar critique. Voices from below – and particularly participants whose accounts deviate from the orthodoxy – are unlikely to be given due consideration even if their opinions were elicited and reflected in research and policymaking. To receive the due attention and support, their accounts and portrayals must fit with those recognised by the dominant discourse. For NGOs, which have to solicit for funds, a story about 'forced child labour' or 'child mining slaves' in a poor African country seems much easier to promote compared to a narrative about children who have not been coerced or compelled by a third party but have exercised constrained agency and choice to seek work in difficult, dangerous and hazardous conditions such as artisanal gold mining. Likewise, greater sympathy might be gained from governments and donors by individualising the cause of this problem or attributing it to parental or communal ignorance and callousness rather than the outcome of structural problems, such as governmental failure and socio-economic injustices created by neoliberal reforms imposed on countries like Ghana. Ultimately, what gets counted as valid and authoritative knowledge for policymaking on forced labour are invariably ideas, values and opinions which fit with those preferred by national governments and international organisations. Studies which produce contrasting or non-conventional categorisations are unlikely to be taken on board.

The chapter accepts that international definitions, categorisations and discourses can serve useful purposes. It is therefore not advocating for a complete rejection of such definitions in research. However, the chapter cautions against the assumption that such discourses are essential, neutral or universal. They reflect particular ideological, political and socio-cultural interests and must therefore be critically considered in the same way as divergent narratives and discourses encountered in the field. Additionally, forced labour research, like any other social research activity, is located in – and loaded with – diverse socio-political and moral meanings. All these meanings must be carefully considered for a more holistic understanding of the issue and responses to it.

References

Agrawal, A. (1995), 'Dismantling the Divide between Indigenous and Scientific Knowledge', *Development and Change*, 26: 413–39.

Aird, S. C. (1999), 'Ghana's Slaves to the Gods', *Human Rights Brief*, 7, 1: 6–8, accessed 2 May 2017, http://www.wcl.american.edu/hrbrief/07/1ghana.cfm

Akyeampong, E. (2001), 'History, Memory, Slave-Trade and Slavery in Anlo (Ghana)', *Slavery and Abolition*, 22, 3: 1–24. DOI 10.1080/714005205

Allain, J. (2012), 'Combating Trafficking in Human Beings for Labour Exploitation', *International Journal of Refugee Law*, 24, 1: 161–4. DOI 10.1093/ijrl/ees002

Andreas, P. (2010), 'The Politics of Measuring Illicit Flows and Policy Effectiveness', in P. Andreas & K. Greenhill (eds), *Sex, Drugs, and Body Counts: The Politics of Numbers in Global Crime and Conflict* (Ithaca, NY, Cornell University Press), 23–45.

Andrijasevic, R. & Mai, N. (2016), 'Editorial: Trafficking (in) Representations: Understanding the Recurring Appeal of Victimhood and Slavery in Neoliberal Times', *Anti-Trafficking Review*, 7: 1–10.

Aronowitz, S. (1988), *Science as Power: Discourse and Ideology in Modern Society* (Minneapolis, University of Minnesota Press).

Becker, H. (1967) 'Whose Side Are We On?', *Social Problems*, 14: 239–47.

Berlan, A. (2009), 'Child Labour and Cocoa: Whose Voices Prevail?', *International Journal of Sociology and Social Policy*, 29, 3/4: 141–51. DOI 10.1108/01443330910947516

Blanchette, T. G. & da Silva, A. P. (2012), 'On Bullshit and the Trafficking of Women: Moral Entrepreneurs and the Invention of Trafficking of Persons in Brazil', *Dialectical Anthropology*, 36, 1/2: 107–25. DOI 10.1007/s10624-012-9268-8

Blunt, L. (2000), 'The Bitter Taste of Child Slavery', *BBC News* (28 Sept. 2000), accessed 16 June 2017, http://news.bbc.co.uk/1/hi/world/africa/946952.stm

Boaten, B. A. (2001), 'The Trokosi System in Ghana: Discrimination against Women', in A. Rwomire (ed.), *African Women and Children: Critical Response* (Santa Barbara, CA, Praeger), 91–103.

Brewer, J. D. (2000), *Ethnography* (Buckingham, Open University Press).

Burns, N. & Grove, S. K. (2001), *The Practice of Nursing Research: Conduct, Critique and Utilisation*, 4th edn (Philadelphia, PA, W.B Saunders Company).

Chambers, R. (1994), 'Participatory Rural Appraisal (PRA): Challenges, Potentials and Paradigm', *World Development*, 22, 10: 1437–54.

Chambers, R. (1997), *Whose Reality Counts? Putting the First Last* (London, Intermediate Technology Publications).

Chambers, R. (2008), 'PRA, PLA and Pluralism: Practice and Theory', in P. Reason & H. Bradbury (eds), *The Sage Handbook of Action Research: Participative Inquiry and Practice*, 2nd edn (London, Sage), 297–318.

Chow, M. Y., Quine, S. & Li, M. (2010), 'The Benefits of Using a Mixed Methods Approach—Quantitative with Qualitative—to Identify Client Satisfaction and Unmet Needs in an HIV Healthcare Centre', *AIDS Care*, 22, 4: 491–8. DOI 10.1080/09540120903214371

Chuang, J. (2006), 'The United States as Global Sheriff: Using Unilateral Sanctions to Combat Human Trafficking', *Michigan Journal of International Law*, 25, 2: 437–94.

Chuang, J. (2014), 'Exploitation Creep and the Unmaking of Human Trafficking Law', *American Journal of International Law*, 108, 4: 609–49. DOI 10.5305/amerjintelaw.108.4.0609

Coffey, A. (1999), *The Ethnographic Self* (London, Sage).

COHA (2016), 'The Trafficking in Persons Report: Who Is the United States to Judge?', accessed 21 November 2016, http://www.coha.org/the-trafficking-in-persons-report-who-is the United-states-to-judge/

Cook, T. (2012), 'Where Participatory Approaches Meet Pragmatism in Funded (Health) Research: The Challenge of Finding Meaningful Spaces', *Forum Qualitative Sozialforschung/Forum: Qualitative Social Research*, 13, 1, article 18. DOI http://dx.doi.org/10.17169/fqs-13.1.1783

Cooke, B. & Kothari, U. (eds), *Participation: The New Tyranny?* (London, Zed Books).

Crosby, F. J. & Bearman, S. (2006), 'The Uses of a Good Theory', *Journal of Social Issues*, 19: 413–37.

Crump, J. (2016), 'The Global Slavery Index: Helpful or Harmful?', *Human Trafficking Centre Blog*, accessed 16 June 2016, http://humantraffickingcenter.org/global-slavery-index-helpful-harmful/

Curtis, D. (1995), 'Power to the People: Rethinking Community Development', in N. Nelson & S. Wright (eds), *Power and Participatory Development* (London, Intermediate Technology Publications), 115–24.

Farrell, A., McDevitt, J. & Fahy, S. (2008), *Understanding and Improving Law Enforcement Responses to Human Trafficking* (Boston, MA, Institute on Race and Justice).

Ferrell, J. & Hamm, M. S. (eds) (1998), *Ethnography at the Edge: Crime, Deviance, and Field Research* (Boston, MA, Northeastern University).

Finlay, L. (2002), 'Negotiating the Swamp: The Opportunity and Challenge of Reflexivity in Research Practice', *Qualitative Research*, 2, 2: 209–30.

Free the Slaves (2013), 'Child Slavery, Child Labour and Exploitation of Children in Mining Communities', accessed 1 November 2016, http://www.freetheslaves.net/wp-content/uploads/2013/08/Summary-of-Findings-Child-Rights-in-Mining-Ghana-January-2013.pdf

Free the Slaves (2014), 'Child Rights in Mining Pilot Project Results and Lessons Learned', accessed 1 November 2016, https://www.freetheslaves.net/wp-content/uploads/2015/03/ChildRightsinMiningPilotProjectOverview.pdf

Free the Slaves (2016), 'Our Formula for Freedom', accessed 1 November 2016, https://www.freetheslaves.net/wp-content/uploads/2016/03/FTS-One-Pager-Revised2016.pdf

Gadda, A. (2008), 'Rights, Foucault and Power: A Critical Analysis of the United Nations Convention on the Rights of the Child', *Edinburgh Working Papers in Sociology*, No. 31. Social and Political Studies, University of Edinburgh.

Gallagher, A. (2014), 'The Global Slavery Index: Seduction and Obfuscation', *The Guardian* (4 December 2014), accessed 15 May 2017, https://www.theguardian.com/

global-development/poverty-matters/2014/nov/28/global-slavery-index-walk-free-human-trafficking-anne-gallagher

Gallagher, A. T. (2015), 'Exploitation in Migration: Unacceptable but Inevitable', *Journal of International Affairs*, 68, 2: 55–74.

Galma, J. & Finckenauer, J. (2005), 'Representations and Misrepresentations of Human Trafficking', *Trends in Organized Crime*, 8: 24–40. DOI 10.1007/s12117-005-1035-7

Gillard, M. L. (2010), *Trokosi: Slave of the Gods* (USA, Xulon Press).

Gould, S. (1996), *The Mismeasure of Man* (New York, W. W. Norton).

Gouldner, A. (1962), 'Anti-Minotaur: The Myth of a Value-Free Sociology', *Social Problems*, 9: 199–213. DOI 10.2307/799230

Gouldner, A. (1973), *For Sociology* (London, Allen Lane).

Green, M. (2000), 'Participatory Development and the Appropriation of Agency in Southern Tanzania', *Critique of Anthropology*, 20, 1: 67–89. DOI 10.1177/0308275X0002000105

Green, P. (1993), 'Taking Sides: Partisan Research on the 1984–1985 Miners Strike', in D. Hobbs and T. May (eds), *Interpreting the Field* (Oxford, Oxford University Press).

Habermas, J. (1971), *Knowledge and Human Interests*, trans. J. Shapiro (Boston, MA, Beacon Press).

Hawksley, H. (2002), 'Meeting the "Chocolate Slaves"', *BBC News* (13 June 2002), accessed 31 May 2017, http://news.bbc.co.uk/1/hi/world/africa/2042474.stm

Heartz, R. (1997), *Reflexivity and Voice* (Thousand Oaks, CA, Sage).

Hilson, G. (2010), 'Child Labour in African Artisanal Mining Communities: Experiences from Northern Ghana', *Development and Change*, 41, 3: 445–73. DOI 10.1111/j.1467-7660.2010.01646.x

ILO (2012), *Hard to See, Harder to Count: Survey Guidelines to Estimate Forced Labour of Adults and Children* (Geneva, ILO).

James, A. & Prout, A. (1997*), Constructing and Reconstructing Childhood: Contemporary Issues in the Sociological Study of Childhood* (London, Falmer Press).

Kapur, R. (2002), 'The Tragedy of Victimization Rhetoric: Resurrecting the "Native" Subject in International Post-colonial Feminist Legal Politics', *Harvard Human Rights Journal*, 15: 1–38.

Kempadoo, K. (2016), 'Revitalizing Imperialism: Contemporary Campaigns against Sex Trafficking and Modern Slavery', *Cadernos Pagu*, 47. DOI 10.1590/180944492016 00470008

Kothari, U. (2001), 'Participatory Development: Power, Knowledge and Social Control', in B. Cooke & U. Kothari (eds), *Participation: The New Tyranny?* (London, Zed Books).

Lamb, C. (2001), 'The Child Slaves of the Ivory Coast: Bought and Sold for as Little as £40', *The Telegraph* (27 April 2001).

Leal, P. A. (2007), 'Participation: The Ascendancy of a Buzzword in the Neo-liberal Era', *Development in Practice* 17, 4/5: 539–48. DOI 10.1080/09614520701469518

Leurs, R. (1998), 'Current Challenges Facing Participatory Rural Appraisal', in J. Blackburn & J. Holland (eds), *Who Changes? Institutionalizing Participation in Development* (London, Intermediate Technology Publications).

Lumsden, K. (2013), '"You Are What You Research": Researcher Partisanship and the Sociology of the Underdog', *Qualitative Research*, 13, 1: 3–18.

McGrath, S. & Mieres, F. (2014), 'Mapping the Politics of National Rankings in the Movement against "Modern Slavery"', *openDemocracy: Beyond Trafficking and Slavery* (14 December 2014).

May, T. (1993), 'Feelings Matter: Inverting the Hidden Equation', in D. Hobbs and T. May (eds), *Interpreting the Field* (Oxford, Oxford University Press).

Mfum-Mensah, O. (2003), 'Fostering Educational Participation in Pastoral Communities through Non-formal Education: The Ghanaian Perspective', *International Journal of Educational Development*, 23: 661–77. DOI 10.1016/S0738-0593(03)00102-0

Miller, D. (1999), *Principles of Social Justice* (Cambridge, MA, Harvard University Press), 42–60.

Mohan, G. (2001), 'Beyond Participation: Strategies for Deeper Empowerment', in U. Kothari & B. Cooke (eds), *Participation: The New Tyranny?* (London, Zed Books), 153–67.

Musto, J. L. (2009), 'What's in a Name? Conflations and Contradictions in Contemporary U.S. Discourses of Human Trafficking', *Women's Studies International Forum* 32, 4: 281–7. DOI 10.1016/j.wsif.2009.05.016

Nair, C. (2016), 'The Developed World Is Missing the Point about Modern Slavery', *Time Magazine* (20 June 2016).

Nightingale, D. & Cromby, J. (eds) (1999), *Social Constructionist Psychology* (Buckingham, Open University Press).

Oakley, P. *et al.* (1991), *Projects with People: The Practice of Participation in Rural Development* (Geneva, ILO).

O'Connell Davidson, J. (2006), 'Will the Real Sex Slave Please Stand Up?', *Feminist Review*, 83, 1: 4–22. DOI 10.1057/palgrave.fr.9400278

O'Connell Davidson, J. (2010), 'New Slavery, Old Binaries: Human Trafficking and the Borders of "Freedom"', *Global Networks*, 10, 2: 244–61. DOI 10.1111/j.1471-0374.2010.00284.x

Onwuegbuzie, A. J. & Leech, N. L. (2004), 'Enhancing the Interpretation of Significant Findings: The Role of Mixed Methods Research', *Qualitative Report*, 9, 4: 770–92.

Penney, T. L. (2014), 'Dark Figure of Crime (Problems of Estimation)', in J. S. Albanese (ed.), *The Encyclopedia of Criminology and Criminal Justice* (Chichester, Wiley Blackwell).

Pieper, N., Segrave, M. & Moore, R. N. (2015), 'Editorial: What's in a Name? Distinguishing Forced Labour, Trafficking and Slavery', *Anti-Trafficking Review*, 5: 1–9.

Polit, D. F. & Beck, C. T. (2004), *Nursing Research: Appraising Evidence for Nursing Practice*, 7th edn (Philadelphia, PA, Wolters Klower).

Punch, S. (2003), 'Childhoods in the Majority World: Miniature Adults or Tribal Children?', *Sociology*, 37, 2: 277–95. DOI 10.1177/0038038503037002004

Quirk, J. & Broome, A. (2015), 'The Politics of Numbers: The Global Slavery Index and the Marketplace of Activism', *openDemocracy: Beyond Trafficking and Slavery* (10 March 2015).

Ramazanoglu, C. (1992), 'On Feminist Methodology: Male Reason versus Female Empowerment', *Sociology*, 26, 2: 207–12. DOI 10.1177/0038038592026002003

Richards, P. (1993), 'Cultivation: Knowledge or Performance?', in M. Hobart (ed.), *An Anthropological Critique of Development: The Growth of Ignorance* (London, Routledge), 60–78.

Richards, P. (1995), 'Participatory Rural Appraisal: A Quick and Dirty Critique', *PLA Notes*, 24: 13–16.

Skeggs, B. (2007[2001]) 'Feminist Ethnography', in P. Atkinson, A. Coffey, S. Delamont, J. Lofland & L. Lofland (eds), *Handbook of Ethnography* (London, Sage), 426–42.

Small Bilyeu, A. (1999), 'Trokosi—the Practice of Sexual Slavery in Ghana: Religious and Cultural Freedom vs Human Rights', *Indiana International & Comparative Law Review*, 9, 2: 457–504.

Snajdr, E. (2013), 'Beneath the Master Narrative: Human Trafficking, Myths of Sexual Slavery, and Ethnographic Realities', *Dialectical Anthropology*, 37: 229–56. DOI 10.1007/s10624-013-9292-3

Steinfatt, T. (2011), 'Sex Trafficking in Cambodia: Fabricated Numbers versus Empirical Evidence', *Crime, Law, and Social Change*, 56: 443–62. DOI 10.1007/s10611-011-9328-z

Tashakkori, A. & Teddlie, C. (eds) (2003), *Handbook of Mixed Methods in Social and Behavioral Research* (Thousand Oaks, CA, Sage).

Tyldum, G. (2010), 'Limitations in Research on Human Trafficking', *International Migration*, 48, 5: 1–13.

Valente, S. (2003), 'Research Dissemination and Utilization: Improving Care at the Bedside', *Journal of Nursing Care Quality*, 18, 2: 114–21.

Van Dijk, T. A. (1993), 'Principles of Critical Discourse Analysis', *Discourse & Society*, 4, 2: 249–83.

Weitzer, R. (2012), 'Sex Trafficking and the Sex Industry: The Need for Evidence Based Theory and Legislation', *Journal of Criminal Law and Criminology*, 101, 4: 1337–69.

Weitzer, R. (2014), 'New Directions in Research on Human Trafficking', *Annals of the American Academy of Political and Social Science*, 653, 1: 6–24. DOI 10.1177/0002716214521562

White, S. C. (2010), 'Depoliticising Development: The Uses and Abuses of Participation', *Development in Practice*, 6, 1: 6–15. DOI 10.1080/0961452961000157564

Yea, S. (2017), 'Editorial: The Politics of Evidence, Data and Research in Anti-trafficking Work', *Anti-Trafficking Review*, 8: 1–13.

Zhang, S., Spiller, M., Finch, B. & Qin, Y. (2014), 'Estimating Labor Trafficking among Unauthorized Migrant Workers in San Diego', *Annals of the American Academy of Political and Social Science*, 653, 1: 65–86. DOI 10.1177/0002716213519237

Part II

Frontiers of Forced Labour Research and Methods

7

Why (and How) We Need
to Talk to 'the Victims'

NEIL HOWARD

Introduction

IT IS NOW COMMONLY accepted that we possess generally poor quality data on the triad of 'extreme labour exploitation' that are 'human trafficking', 'forced labour' and 'modern slavery'. The United Nations (UN) has frequently decried the data deficit (e.g. ILO 2012), Western governments have called for more to be done, and academics – including those who feature in this volume – have lamented our lack of information. In recent years, high-profile efforts have been made to address these gaps. The UN Global Initiative to Fight Human Trafficking (UN. GIFT) has developed a widely cited global estimate of human trafficking prevalence, the International Labour Organization (ILO) has done similarly with regard to forced labour, and the Walk Free Foundation has launched the Global Slavery Index (GSI) to great fanfare. Yet each of these initiatives has been critiqued for their myriad methodological flaws, with the GSI lambasted for its fundamental lack of rigour (Weitzer 2014) and the UN.GIFT report derided even by those involved in producing it (Howard 2016). Furthermore, certain of these failings are replicated in academic work. Many 'big picture' scholars – including economists, political economists and political scientists – rely on (and thus reproduce) unverified, inaccurate and sensationalist reports of 'forced labour' and 'slavery' in their otherwise valiant attempts to hold the holders of social or economic power to account (Kielland & Sanogo 2002; Crane 2013).[1]

This chapter contends that a major explanation for why extreme exploitation is so frequently misrepresented lies in the very simple fact that far too few researchers actually talk to the people they wish to understand, analyse or represent when

[1] A classic example here is the so-called 'child trafficking' or 'slavery' which has widely been said to plague the cocoa plantations of Ghana and Côte d'Ivoire – a claim discredited by much anthropological research (e.g. Berlan 2013).

Proceedings of the British Academy, **220**, 113–129. © The British Academy 2018.

researching the shadow economy. Such is the contemporary fetishisation of quantitative data and so un-reflexive the acceptance of received institutional (or media)
reports that scholars and institutions alike often overlook the most basic of research
approaches: talking to those especially concerned by any particular phenomenon.
This chapter will make the case that qualitative research with so-called victims of
trafficking, forced labour and modern slavery can provide a major corrective to
these current empirical shortcomings. In giving voice to those that one wishes
to understand by using techniques such as interviewing, participant observation or
focus group discussions, it is possible for the researcher to build a picture of life
as a severely exploited or coerced labourer and of the factors leading workers to
work in such circumstances. In making this case, the chapter will draw in places
on my original qualitative research in West Africa with young migrant labourers
identified by authorities including UN agencies and non-governmental organisations (NGOs) as 'victims of child trafficking'. That research took place in multiple
stages, and over many years, between 2005 and 2013 as part of my professional
work in Benin, my Master's and ultimately my PhD. It involved interviews and
focus group discussions with over 150 Beninese youth currently or previously
involved in labour mobility equated with 'child trafficking', including many on
site and at work in artisanal quarries in Nigeria.

Collateral damage

There are at least four reasons why our current informational inadequacies are so
significant. These are empirical, political, ethical and epistemological. The first two
are reasonably self-evident: from an empirical standpoint, if we wish to understand
a phenomenon with any degree of confidence, we need precise measurements,
triangulation of observations and depth to our perspective. Similarly, from a practical or political standpoint, if we wish to design effective interventions that have
the desired outcome, we need sound understandings: the more we know about any
given phenomenon, the more control we are likely to have when taking action to
affect it.

Sound understandings are also an *ethical* imperative, given that often political
or project interventions to 'save' unfree or exploited workers cause what Dottridge
(2007) has rightly called 'collateral damage' to those workers themselves. Acting
on the basis of poor-quality data or unchecked assumptions, national and international policymakers, and even well-intentioned humanitarians, have historically
pioneered blunderous interventions that have actually made life worse for the very
people they were supposed to be assisting (see Bourdillon *et al.* 2011 for a series
of painful examples). The current author saw this at close quarters in Benin and
Nigeria, where the explosion of the child-trafficking discourse in the early 2000s
led donors, UN agencies, NGOs and some scholars to effectively tar all under-age

mobility as the equivalent of child trafficking, with draconian policy consequences including the promulgation of an anti-trafficking law that effectively illegalised unaccompanied child migration and rendered any adult 'accomplice' a *de facto* trafficker (Morganti 2011; Howard 2013). Many innocent people were arrested at the borders as a result, many willing young migrants were either obstructed in their migration or forcibly repatriated, and hundreds of thousands of dollars were absorbed into a quixotic civil society effort to get the Beninese to stay 'at home'.

This relates to the fourth, epistemological reason. In contrast to more traditional, positivistic understandings of the social world, the post-structuralist starting point holds that meaning is always and everywhere relational, a consequence of social and discursive practice. On this understanding, concepts do not possess any definitive 'essence'; rather, they are 'fixed' only ever partially and as a consequence of the ongoing exercise of power. This is significant because power is never evenly distributed: different actors within the social field have differential meaning-making capabilities. For instance, the poor, black, African adolescents with whom this researcher worked across the Benin–Nigeria border had far less influence over their definition as 'victims of trafficking' within international child-protection circles than did the rich, white, non-African aid workers most frequently using that label. This itself is important for a number of reasons. First, a democratic egalitarian epistemology *requires* us to take into account the definitional perspectives of those whose lived realities we wish to 'understand' or label – and indeed to build meaning dialogically with them. Second, failing to do so carries with it the risk of legitimising and sedimenting problematic, disempowering and at times dangerous discourses about people disenfranchised from the meaning-making process. The consequences of this have been most clearly documented when it comes to young people and their suffering at the hands of the international anti-child labour architecture. That architecture has been critiqued by anthropologists from around the world for its ethnocentric bias, relying as it does on a liberal, capitalist and particularly Western understanding of human social, cultural and biological maturation (James & Prout 1997; Wells 2009). It characterises under-18s as inherently vulnerable, lacking in the agency (and thus the rights) that pertain to adulthood, and therefore in need of 'protection' *qua* exclusion from the dangers of the labour market. When operationalised, this vision of childhood has caused poor children – whose positionality within global capitalism requires them to work for a living – major 'collateral damage', in particular by legitimating policy interventions that exclude them from paid work (Bourdillon *et al.* 2011). Worse still, it also *systemically* disempowers *all* children and communities whose livelihood practices do not conform to the dominant norm of a Western, workless childhood and who will thus eventually face 'intervention' at the hands of those whose task it is to 'save' them (Boyden 1997). The non-participatory epistemological approach to research thus carries with it major ethical dangers.

'Talk to us' – the importance of qualitative research

One simple and potentially powerful way to correct these failings is to talk directly to the individuals who are aggregated into the statistics that shape law, policy and projects – observing their lives and their interactions over time, and reflecting on one's observations with them. This can be challenging. Most researchers face both time and money limitations, and it takes skill and courage to gain access to certain sites of the informal economy. But those challenges can be overcome, even in the context of under-resourced projects like the average PhD. The rest of this chapter will reflect on how and why this can be done and, in doing so, will draw from the author's previous research into child trafficking and youth labour mobility in West Africa. Below is a brief description of that research in order to situate the reader.

Overview of the research project informing this chapter

In 2005, I volunteered for a small Beninese NGO engaged in anti-trafficking work in Cotonou. It became clear to me that mainstream anti-trafficking discourse said very different things about youth labour mobility to what was said by the young labour migrants I encountered in my work. Whereas dominant discourse painted young migrants as vulnerable and likely to experience abuse, young people told stories of growth or emancipation, or of voyages that were no more than a 'normal' expression of their economic needs. In order to understand the reasons behind these discrepancies, I adopted a case-study approach, identifying a paradigmatic example of a putative trafficking flow: the crossing of boys from the Za-Kpota region of the Beninese South to the artisanal gravel quarries of Abeokuta, Nigeria. Much had been written about this flow and even World Bank economists had been dispatched to run large-scale surveys in order to ascertain relevant causal trends (Ouensavi & Kielland 2000). Yet surprisingly no one had ever spoken directly to the migrant boys themselves, or visited their places of work. For my PhD research between 2009 and 2012, I therefore selected four source villages using a local research assistant who was subcontracted from an NGO working in the area, and together we snowball-sampled former teenage migrant labourers who had returned from the quarries, others considering leaving, parents and local social authorities. We subsequently complemented this sending-zone research with research in the receiving zone, in the quarries that were the destination for these adolescent migrants. Here again, we used snowball sampling to identify important figures from the local socio-economic hierarchy, and we talked with over 40 working boys on site and at work, over a total period of around 12 months between 2009 and 2012. Interviewees were accessed through the mediation of a locally active NGO which had good relations with the quarry power hierarchy. Naturally, interviews were conducted with consent and at a safe site of the boy's choosing.

Our findings flatly contradicted the dominant discourse, which held that these teenagers had been forced or tricked into their work and mobility. Our data said otherwise, revealing their labour mobility to be situated within complex socio-economic webs that were at times both exploitative and supportive. For example, although the men employing these boys all made more money from their work than the boys did, they also provided the boys with food, lodging and protection. Moreover, by giving them work they offered them an important, established path to the social manhood they were seeking. In turn, our findings pointed to policy and project interventions that were very different from those of the reigning orthodoxy, which sought to shut borders or stifle movement. What talking to young migrant workers revealed was that simply providing alternative employment options in Benin or labour protection in Nigeria would have been a more welcome approach. Although that story has been told more fully elsewhere (Howard 2016), below I will reflect on certain methods used to construct it and that other researchers can use to conduct similar research into the shadow economy.

Interviews

Without doubt, the primary research tool for in-depth qualitative research is the interview. The reasons for this are threefold. First is the aforementioned epistemo-logical standpoint that research must be '[about] the "generation" of knowledge, rather than its capture or extraction' (Veale in Campbell & Trotter 2007: 33). Many qualitative researchers consider it a moral-ethical imperative to gather the personal testimonies of those whose life-worlds they wish to understand. And my research with young migrant labourers suggests that they do too. On more than one occa-sion, the uniqueness of the fact that I was asking them how they made sense of their experiences led them to hug, clap and cheer me. In one instance in Abeokuta, a group of normally very sceptical young workers actually even downed tools to break into a Fon song of thanks. This reflects the sheer emotional importance of giving people the opportunity to speak on their own behalf, instead of perpetuating power imbalances by having others speak for them.

Second, interviews can often provide more accurate data than other methodo-logical tools such as surveys, since they allow one to access the unique, personal perspective of the individuals under analysis. A useful example of this can be provided by contrasting a qualitative approach such as the one advocated in this chapter and the survey approach employed by Ouensavi and Kielland (2000) in their classic World Bank study on the same flow of teenage migrant workers that I researched from Benin to Nigeria. Ouensavi and Kielland had sought to understand why young people leave home in such large numbers in this region and to do so they systematically sampled mothers – and only mothers – asking them why their child had left. The logic behind their approach was twofold: first, that statistical sampling yields more accurate data than qualitative research and, second, that 'a mother always knows best' why her child has decided to migrate (Ouensavi & Kielland 2000). Their findings were standard – poverty being given as the prime reason for a child's departure.

Yet their findings have major limitations. First is a chronic lack of depth. My research also showed poverty to be a key motivation for young migrant workers, with nearly all claiming that earning money was their key goal when they left. The difference, however, is that talking to them allowed me to contextualise this search in myriad social and cultural processes that gave meaning to it. For instance, some boys left so that they could earn enough money to return to school. Others went to earn money for marriage or to contribute to their family households. None of this complexity was captured by Ouensavi and Kielland, whose conclusions pointed simplistically towards desperation or starvation as the meaning of the word 'poverty'. A second limitation of their approach relates to the constitution of their sample. They chose mothers because 'a mother always knows best'. But qualitative research on youth mobility from across West Africa shows that mothers in the region are often the *last* people to know why their children have migrated, with adolescents frequently absconding without asking parental permission (e.g. Hashim & Thorsen 2011). As such, although their statistical approach may have yielded a far greater sample size, the assumptions embedded in the composition of their sample ensured that the findings were entirely unreliable. Had they interviewed young migrant workers themselves, by contrast, their findings would have been very different indeed.

The third major reason for employing interviews as a core research method is that, in researching dynamic realities of the kinds involved in much of the shadow economy (such as networks of illegal labour mobility), breadth is as important as depth, and it is the interview which most clearly allows one to develop understandings across a broad sweep of time and space when unlimited resources are not available. Although only long-term ethnographic study can allow for the generation of 'deep', 'thick' data of the kind advocated most famously by Clifford Geertz (1994), in the absence of such extended time periods, a large number of well-chosen interviews can provide a very rich dataset indeed.

The interview is not without its problems, however, and should not be understood as a panacea. As Heissler highlights (2009: 144), the quality of data gathered through interviews can often be undermined by a participant's failing memory or indeed by the picture of themselves that the present leads them to wish to convey. Respondent 'reactivity' and narrative 'accuracy' are thus genuine issues in interview research, which must be accounted for when triangulating one's research design. In my case, triangulation was achieved through speaking to a large number of differently positioned people (over 300) in each of our research sites and cross-checking their many claims against each other. For example, in checking the validity of a former child migrant's claim, we were able to cross-check that with his peers, family members or former employer. Likewise, in assessing the accuracy of a parental evaluation, we could include the perspective of neighbours, local authority figures or young migrants themselves. Numbers are important, therefore, even in qualitative methodologies.

In terms of the conduct of interviews themselves, there are many different approaches that one can take, ranging from the closed questioning of traditional surveys to the entirely open-ended meander of a more ethnographic conversation. Each has its merits. In my fieldwork, I endeavoured to employ what Levy and Hollan describe as a 'person-centred approach', which involves more open-ended questions that invite participants to elaborate the interview in ways they see fit, rather than being fully directed (and thus constrained) by the researcher (1998). This is incredibly useful because it allows participants to exercise much more agency in shaping the research encounter, which can in turn provide more (and more contextual) data than can be obtained through the closed questioning of surveys (Boyden & Ennew 1997: 8). An example of how useful this can be from my study came when I interviewed a group of men formally recognised as 'traffickers' for their role in the migrant labour network linking Za-Kpota to Abeokuta. Having spent much of our meeting asking them questions about working conditions in the quarries, I eventually asked them what they thought I should be asking – and they promptly told me all I needed to know about the labour recruitment process.

While it is useful, therefore, for interviews to be person-centred and to a large extent interviewee-guided, it is often sensible for them to be at least *semi-structured*, with the interviewer working loosely around a number of central themes. This is important when the researcher has a number of core topics to address with each interviewee and at each site. Similarly, it can be useful with influential and often busy interviewees, for whom purely open-ended questioning might become frustrating, since it can appear too directionless when one has limited time available.

Group interviews or focus groups

A second core qualitative methodology for researching the shadow economy, and especially for achieving a compromise between breadth and depth, is the group interview or focus group discussion, which I utilised on a number of occasions in and around my case study villages in Benin, and across the border in Nigeria. This method of interviewing can be particularly helpful when seeking to obtain village or community-level data, or when investigating collective perceptions or commonly held norms structuring important social practices. The following extract from my field notes demonstrates how this technique can work in practice. I was conducting a group interview with a collection of non-schooled adolescents in Tenga village, trying to understand how young people like them perceive the concept of migration and relate to the idea of 'elsewhere', which is of critical importance when seeking to understand phenomena labelled as 'trafficking'. Having initially struggled to make myself understood with questions such as 'How do you feel about the idea of leaving home for work?', I turned to word association and asked everyone to shout out the first thing that came to mind when I mentioned the names of common migrant destinations.

What do you think of when I say the word 'Cotonou'?

–   One boy said that he thinks there are lots of opportunities down there. They have electricity, they have radios. He himself wants to go there and get a job, but since he didn't go to school and learn French he knows it will be hard.
–   Another said that when he hears the word 'Cotonou', he thinks of a place that everyone dreams of going to. He would like to go there, to discover it and enjoy the amenities, but he would also like Tenga to develop into a Cotonou itself.
–   A third boy also said he'd like to work there.

What about Europe, translated as 'yovotomè' – 'home of the white man'?

–   The boy who spoke good French and had clearly been better schooled than most said, "When we say *yovotomè*, I think there is money there."
–   Another said that there is loads of business there, loads of work, and that that is what we need in Benin.

(Interview with Group 11, Tenga Village, 14 May 2010)

This excerpt offers a useful indication of how effective collective interviews can be at generating deep data of the kind often missed either in survey research or in research that relies too heavily on second-hand data. But collective interviews also have other advantages. One is accuracy; at least with village-level data, responses can be and are cross-referenced and validated by those present. For example, if one wishes to have a sense of the availability of land for purchase, or of the period of greatest rainfall or highest out-migration, a collection of local voices will likely provide a more accurate response. Additionally, interviewing in numbers can provide greater comfort for younger, adolescent or otherwise socially 'subordinate' participants. Many commentators have noted that, given the social power imbalance between adults and children or between men and women, some participants will be more at ease when surrounded by their peers, which is also very likely to be the case when researching among those who are fearful given their work status. This was something I often found with young migrants at their place of work – when interviewed in groups, boys more easily opened up about their experiences, their challenges, their joys and their motivations.

None of this should be read, however, as implying that group interviews or focus groups are without their pitfalls. Like any other method, they have their limitations. For one, without careful moderation such encounters can often find themselves dominated by one or two particularly vocal individuals who drown out other participants. For another, the chances of participant reactivity are arguably much higher in such settings than they are in one-on-one encounters – it is not difficult to imagine, for example, a scared worker offering opinions that are more safe than honest when in the presence of those who may report her to her employer, which again points to the importance of quality triangulation.

Interview issues

Although individual and collective interviews do therefore have much promise when researching the shadow economy, it should be noted that conducting them effectively on matters of illegality also comes with various challenges. One relates to data recording. Some claim that data recorders are essential in interviews in order to generate reliable transcripts and texts that can then be verified by secondary sources. Others, by contrast, reject recorders out of hand as likely to alienate or endanger participants. Both arguments have their merits. Nevertheless, although mindful of the greater accuracy offered by voice recordings, I opted against recording interviews in Benin and Nigeria, largely because I wanted to avoid estranging or endangering participants. I understood that those who were or had been previously engaged in illicit activity might be wary of the trappings of officialdom, and I was fearful that the existence of voice recordings could compromise their security.

Another essential challenge for conducting this kind of interview-based qualitative research is language, and the need to work through an interpreter if one is not fluent in the respondent's native tongue. Levy and Hollan note that 'it is deeply distorting not to work in the respondent's core language' (1998: 338), and there is no doubt that my own inability to grasp all the socio-cultural nuances embedded in the Fon words that my interviewees were using in Benin and Nigeria distanced me from the fullness of what they were saying. This will have been compounded by the presence of my research assistant, who literally embodied the structural gap between them and me, as well as between what they said and me (Fontana & Frey 2003: 77). Moreover, as Morrissey observes, 'instead of being passive conveyors of knowledge, [translators/interpreters] actually constitute active participants in the research process and make important judgements about what information is conveyed. As a result, what is commonly thought of as passive translation might actually constitute an active transformation of the messages that are being conveyed' (2010: 148–9). This ultimately means that everything I was told at village level was refracted through the subjectivity of my research assistant, with the consequence that his positionality inflects and affects all of the data I gathered during this project. Such an obstacle simply cannot be overcome when one wishes to deploy the interview to research the shadow economy, and it must be accounted for in both design and analysis phases.

Yet it should not be assumed that the presence of an interpreter or research assistant is always and everywhere a drawback for qualitative research. In most cases, research of the kind I have described would simply not be possible without such support. Similarly, a well-trained assistant can add greatly to the research process, providing nuanced interpretations, grounded insights and, of course, access. In my own case, my assistant was both a close friend and a well-established social worker within the Beninese anti-trafficking field. As such, he was well trained in working as an interpreter and in anthropological methods and consequently proved to be an enormous source of personal and professional support throughout our fieldwork. For example, as a result of his positionality, our relationship and the freedom I offered him during the research, he would frequently pick up on noteworthy information shared by interviewees and would take the initiative in exploring propitious research angles. This often led us to obtain information that I otherwise would not have accessed. For example, when examining migrant boys' motivations for their mobility, it was only his situated knowledge that allowed us to tease out the frustrations teenage boys often felt at their subordinate position within the home and the liberation thus constituted by their migration. This is a detail that is also inevitably missed by quantitative research. My research assistant also had myriad useful interpretations, anecdotes and reflections to share about both our research encounters and the wider field we were examining. Moreover, as a community 'insider', he proved invaluable in facilitating my entry to – and acceptance by – the communities with which I engaged, serving therefore as far more than a mere linguistic bridge between my interlocutors and me. Indeed, when researching the shadow economy, such a human 'bridge' is often essential.

Participant observation or 'hanging out'

Interviews may well be the cornerstone of much qualitative research, then, but the structured and artificial nature of the interview set-up means that, even when it is person-centred and open-ended, it can only take you so far. To go further, the researcher needs what Bernard describes as the 'sine qua non of anthropological fieldwork' (1998: 16): participant observation. According to Atkinson and Hammersley, all 'social research is a form of participant observation because we cannot study the world without being a part of it'. In this view, 'participant observation is not a particular research technique but a mode of being-in-the-world characteristic of researchers' (1994: 249), or what Mosse would call 'participant deconstruction' (2005: 13). It involves spending time with research participants, joining in with their activities, asking questions whilst taking part, wearing both of the hats of insider and critical observer at one and the same time, and developing as much of a 'feel' for what it is to *be* an insider as one can. In my view, this is critical to in-depth qualitative research and it represents a crucial complement to interviewing. It was fundamental to my work in Benin and Nigeria.

What does it entail? In my case, during the first round of my research and before I chose my case-study villages or my cross-border destination site, it involved

living for six months immersed among Fon families in Cotonou, working in a
shelter for young people identified as 'trafficked' from areas including Za-Kpota,
engaging in the daily rituals of community life, working, talking, playing with
Beninese children and young people, and 'hanging out' in the ethnographic sense
of the term. This allowed me to familiarise myself with many of the rhythms,
norms and behaviours of the case-study communities I wished to understand
before even arriving. That familiarity, in turn, facilitated my speedy acceptance –
to my ethnographic delight, 'He's already a Beninese', 'He's definitely not a real
white man' and 'He's just like us' were some of the refrains I heard when displaying
my *initié* status through cultural performances that a non-*initié* simply would not
have been able to offer.

In my case-study villages themselves and across the border in Nigeria, the fact
that I chose to divide myself between four villages and a destination zone meant
that I was unable to live truly 'inside' any of these communities as a participant
observer in the way that I would like to have done, or in the way that a researcher
conducting fully ethnographic research would do. This remains a regret, since
I know that it affected the depth of the data I was able to gather, and meant that I
missed certain nuances or micro processes that are important to understand when
building a 'thick' description of any social world. Nevertheless, the fact that I lived
for six months in a settlement located at an equal distance from each of my research
villages, and thus spent many long days and nights in and between each, meant that
I was still able to observe and participate in a great deal of social life. Certain of my
most revealing conversations came whilst shelling peanuts or drinking beer at the
local *buvette*, while others happened on random walks through the villages. This
depth is simply impossible for the kinds of large-scale 'in–out' research beloved
of survey-reliant economists, or for those political scientists who rely on second-
hand accounts of life inside the shadow economy produced by the likes of the
UN. As the dialogue with Trevor demonstrates (see below), long-term presence
as a participant in a community can open doors to the kinds of critical and hugely
informative social encounters that can truly deepen analysis. In this case, the depth
related both to the performativity of those engaged in shadow-economy activities
when encountering figures of power, and to the sheer lack of comprehension on the
part of those powerful figures attempting to influence the shadow economy. Neither
of these nuances could ever be grasped at surface level and without time and trust.

Indeed, trust is an absolutely critical factor in the practice of participant observation, since without it one is often unable to access informants, research sites
or research moments that are truly revealing. This is especially the case when
researching illegal or illicit activity, and when the 'stakes' of letting a researcher
in can be very high for participants. One of the major advantages of the long-term
fieldwork that is at the heart of participant observation is thus precisely that it gives
the researcher the time necessary to build this trust and thus gain that access. In
my case, had I not been able to build trust, I would have faced a near impossible

battle to get beyond the mere 'surface' of what people chose to share with me and enjoy insights of the kind expressed below. In fact, I was once told by one of my research participants that when he first saw me, all he thought was money. 'You were', he explained, 'no more than a dollar bill', and it was only the fact that I got to know him and his community over time that enabled me to make the cross-over into trusted acquaintance.

Personal positionality

Two final considerations are important in this discussion, as they are in any qualitative research project – and especially with potentially 'vulnerable' partici-pants such as many of those populating the shadow economy – and they are the researcher's personal positionality and the ethics of the research process. In her seminal piece on the importance of understanding one's positionality in research, Beverley Mullings defines the term as denoting the 'unique mix of race, class, gender, nationality, sexuality and other identifiers', each of which can shift fluidly with time and place, and each of which can interact and intersect with the vari-ous vectors of other people's identities in a way that necessarily impacts on one's research understandings (1999: 337).

In my case as a white, male, adult, graduate student from a Minority World, Anglophone society, I inhabited identities during research which were different from the black, Francophone, African, frequently unschooled young people whose labour migration I was studying. This unquestionably impacted on the nature of the bonds I was able to form and thus on the understandings they enabled me to cultivate, though not only in a negative fashion. For Mullings, it is not simply that 'insiders' or 'outsiders' get better information, because in different contexts being 'the same' or 'different' can help or hinder the research process in equal measure. While identity is multiple and fluid, what is most important is to seek common ground which can 'engender trust and co-operation' (1999: 340) or, in Berreman's famous terms, to learn 'impression management' (1972) and to activate different aspects of one's identity at different points in order to better relate to different others.

In managing my own impressions during research, different aspects of myself (or selves) came to the fore at different times. In my case-study villages and in Abeokuta, for instance, explaining clearly that I was a researcher vehemently opposed to the dominant anti-movement emphasis of anti-trafficking policy, and that I advocated for changes in that policy, was integral to my gaining the trust and acceptance of interviewees and to being able to transcend the socio-economic baggage of being a white man in an African country. The following example clearly illustrates this, as it involves my emphasising these aspects of myself in order to persuade one of my key informants to help me assemble and interview a group of men involved in the migrant labour network linking Za-Kpota to Abeokuta and thus formally and legally identified as 'traffickers':

Neil: Trevor, my friend, who else do you think should I talk to [vis-à-vis 'trafficking' and the structure of the migrant labour network]?

Trevor: Hmm, it's going to be difficult to talk to anyone really, because people will definitely lie to you. No matter what you say, they'll think you're going to arrest them, or that you're going to report them to NGOs or the police . . .

Neil: Oh come on, man, you know that's not me!!!

Trevor: Yes, but I really don't think there's anything you can do. Even me, I was only honest with you originally because I've left this activity behind.

Neil: But you know I'm not with the police . . .

Trevor: Sure, but the problem is that people here don't respect your word when you give it. It's not like where you're from where you can trust someone. Here people lie, they don't trust each other. Even the President lies. He came here promising to pave our roads and he never did a thing!

Neil: I know, but I think I really need to at least talk to *some* of the guys involved in Abeokuta, taking kids across and avoiding the authorities, you know?

Trevor: Yes, I do see that . . .

Neil: So how about this, then – you know what I'm researching, that I'm against the way you and your boys have been defined as 'traffickers' and also that I'm against the attempts to stop people moving. Can you try and round up some of your people, tell them and emphasise this, emphasise that I'm just here to learn what they think and show the world a different picture, and then see what they say?

Trevor: [After a pause] Alright, I can try that, I'll vouch for you and we'll see what we can do. [We then agreed to meet next Wednesday at 10, with about four or five of his friends, for a beer at the Maison du Peuple.]

(Interview with Trevor, Za-Kpota, 7 April 2010)

Crucial here was my activating the part of my identity that coincided with Trevor's: as someone frustrated by dominant policy and keen to challenge it. This fact was critical, no doubt along with my maleness and the repartee this also generated between us.[2]

---

[2] In my case, a further particularly interesting aspect of my research positionality was the frequently liminal space I inhabited and which I believe allowed many people to feel comfortable with me in ways that would not have been possible, had I been definitively one or another thing. For example, in Benin, being a Francophone enabled me to converse freely with people in a way that an Anglophone could not, but, in being British, I was able to avoid the negative colonial and post-colonial associations of French politics in the region. Furthermore, the fact that I had lived and worked in Benin previously and thus already attained a certain level of intimacy with Beninese cultures meant that, in contrast to many researchers, I was an *initié* to a number of the situations I was experiencing. This undoubtedly worked in my favour, just as my being both an academic and a pseudo-member of the anti-trafficking community led many anti-trafficking actors to see me both as 'one of them' and as an informed observer whose opinions were worthy of respect. While not all researchers will necessarily enjoy such liminality in their research in shadow-economy activities, all have choice over which aspects of their selves to articulate in order to establish the bonds necessary to achieve mutual understanding.

Ethical considerations

Finally, it is important to emphasise that qualitative research with potentially vulnerable populations such as those engaged in the shadow economy involves a number of serious ethical considerations. Chief among these is always the obtainment of informed consent. As Boyden and Ennew argue, this 'is especially important in research involving children because they are much less able than adults to exercise, or indeed recognise, their right to refuse to participate' (1997: 41), though as much can be said for any subordinate individuals. Throughout my own fieldwork, I was careful to obtain and continually renegotiate consent and thus took great care to ensure that everybody I worked with was both aware of this right *and* fully informed as to what the research entailed when exercising it. One useful means for achieving this is to ask people if they can explain what they think you are trying to understand after having introduced your work. Another is to ensure that they are offered the opportunity to reaffirm or withdraw consent at different points throughout the research interaction. Given what is at stake in researching the shadow economy, I typically do this verbally instead of obtaining written consent, since written consent can either alienate participants for whom literacy is low or cause discomfort among those unfamiliar (or too familiar) with institutional authority.

Another critical ethical concern in this kind of research is guaranteeing the security and safety of all participants. Doing this necessarily depends on the context and the particular dangers faced by each participant. In my case and in villages or at teenage boys' place of work, I took care to conduct research encounters in as safe and comfortable a setting as possible, which was commonly a shaded location of their choosing, to which we repaired after authority figures had been suitably convinced of what we were doing. Now, away from fieldwork sites, I have continued to protect the identity of my respondents and any sensitive data they gave me, by coding and securing my notes and by anonymising anything that could potentially point to the identity of individual participants or places. This is essential if you possess material that could be incriminating.

A further ethical issue in this kind of research is reciprocity. In line with critical theorists from Horkheimer to Habermas, sociologists including Bourdieu and Wacquant, and anthropologists from across the board, it is my belief that research should be both 'action-oriented' and beneficial or empowering for participants. In the words of Seymour-Smith, researchers must try to 'perform some useful or valued service in return for the collaboration require[d]' (in Robben & Sluka 2007: 9). This can take a number of forms. In my case, at its most basic it involved treating all participants as equals entitled to my respect. With the young and with my case-study communities, this began by asking for their views on their life-worlds, a practice all too uncommon among those who generally create 'knowledge' around the trafficked or vulnerable to trafficking, and one that was consequently received with genuine gratitude. Similarly, in such encounters, I endeavoured to validate my interlocutors by mirroring their behaviour. An example of this would include my drinking from the same cup as interviewees and also pouring a drop of water on the ground in honour of our shared ancestors. Beyond such symbolism, though I never offered payment to anyone involved in my research, I expressed my gratitude materially by buying coffee or lunch, by giving things such as footballs to groups of young people, or by buying and sharing either a round of drinks or a bottle of *sodabi*, which is Benin's famed palm wine. I felt this to be a much more equal gesture, and the joy with which it was generally greeted suggests that it was perceived as such as well.

My attempts to ensure reciprocity have also continued long after the end of the fieldwork. Research participants often asked me to 'tell the truth' or to 'get this information out there', reflecting at once the need to be heard and the desire to change hegemonic practices, which are maintained precisely because such voices are not frequently heard. I have therefore written newspaper articles, published open-source academic papers, established with the editor of this volume the Beyond Trafficking and Slavery website (https://opendemocracy.net/beyondslavery), worked on a documentary film, and engaged in persistent corridor advocacy to see institutional discourses, policies and practices shift in the direction that both I and the majority of those who participated in my study believe that they must.

Relatedly, my last crucial ethical concern is with the politics of representation. Hastrup and Elass (1999) show how, even when advocating for a group (or for a more 'accurate' representation of that group), one has to be careful to avoid the homogenising tendencies of almost all representation. With a group as broad and, frankly, externally defined as 'trafficked children' (and their communities) this is especially true. In order to avoid misrepresentation, therefore, I took pains to discuss and reassess my interpretations with my research participants as I was making them and am still in contact with many of them, with whom I continue to discuss and elaborate my position.

Conclusion

Qualitative research is not, and cannot be, a panacea for all that is wrong with research on the shadow economy. Interviews and participant observation data can be difficult to scale up and often fail to convince the powerful, for whom numbers are the stock tools of trade. Yet such research is essential for understanding the nuances of both the lived experience of exploitation and the conditions that lead to it. It is essential for overturning the assumptions of the blundering policy elite and the well-meaning scholars who at times unwittingly exacerbate the blundering. Most importantly of all, such research is necessary for developing the situated and effective interventions likely to avoid collateral damage. A sensible beginning for anyone interested in understanding or addressing 'forced labour', 'trafficking' or 'slavery' would be to do everything possible to talk to and observe the workers themselves. What is more, doing so might just change the researcher's received understandings.

References

Atkinson, P. & Hammersley, M. (1994), 'Ethnography and Participant Observation', in N. K. Denzin & Y. S. Lincoln (eds), *Handbook of Qualitative Research* (Thousand Oaks, CA, Sage Publications), 248–61.

Berlan, A. (2013), 'Social Sustainability in Agriculture: An Anthropological Perspective on Child Labour in Cocoa Production in Ghana', *Journal of Development Studies*, 49, 4: 1088–100.

Bernard, H. R. (ed.) (1998), *Handbook of Methods in Cultural Anthropology* (London, Sage/ AltaMira Press).

Berreman, G. D. (1972), 'Prologue. Behind Many Masks: Ethnography and Impression Management', in G. D. Berreman (ed.), *Hindus of the Himalayas: Ethnography and Change* (Berkeley, University of California Press), xvii–lvii.

Bourdillon, M., Levison, D., Myers, W. & White, B. (2011), *Rights and Wrongs of Children's Work* (New Brunswick, NJ, Rutgers University Press).

Boyden, J. (1997), 'Childhood and the Policy Makers: A Comparative Perspective on the Globalisation of Childhood', in A. James & A. Prout (eds), *Constructing and Reconstructing Childhood: Contemporary Issues in the Sociological Study of Childhood* (London, Falmer Press), 190–216.

Boyden, J. & Ennew, J. (1997), *Children in Focus: A Manual for Participatory Research with Children* (Stockholm, Radda Barnen).

Campbell, C. & Trotter, J. (2007), '"Invisible" Young People: The Paradox of Participation in Research', *Vulnerable Children and Youth Studies*, 2, 1: 32–9.

Crane, A. (2013), 'Modern Slavery as a Management Practice: Exploring the Conditions and Capabilities for Human Exploitation', *Academy of Management Review*, 38, 1: 45–69.

Dottridge, M. (ed.) (2007), *Collateral Damage: The Impact of Anti-trafficking Measures on Human Rights around the World* (Bangkok, GAATW).

Fontana, A. & Frey, J. H. (2003), 'The Interview: From Structured Questions to Negotiated Text', in N. K. Denzin & Y. S. Lincoln (eds), *Collecting and Interpreting Qualitative Materials* (Thousand Oaks, CA, Sage Publications), 645–73.

Geertz, C. (1994), 'Thick Description: Toward an Interpretive Theory of Culture', in M. Martin & L. Mcintyre (eds), *Readings in the Philosophy of Social Science* (Cambridge, MIT Press), 213–33.

Hashim, I. & Thorsen, D. (2011), *Child Migration in Africa* (London, Zed Books).

Hastrup, K. & Elass, P. (1999), 'Anthropological Advocacy: A Contradiction in Terms', *Current Anthropology*, 31, 3: 301–11.

Heissler, K. (2009), 'On Being 'Good' in Bangladesh: Child Labour Migration and Choice in Madhupur Upazila', unpublished DPhil thesis, University of Oxford, UK.

Howard, N. (2013), 'Promoting "Healthy Childhoods" and Keeping Children "At Home": Beninese Anti-trafficking Policy in Times of Neoliberalism', *International Migration*, 51, 4: 87–102.

Howard, N. (2016), *Child Trafficking, Youth Labour Mobility and the Politics of Protection* (London, Palgrave Macmillan).

ILO (2012), *Hard to See, Harder to Count: Survey Guidelines to Estimate Forced Labour of Adults and Children* (Geneva, ILO).

James, A. & Prout, A. (eds), *Constructing and Reconstructing Childhood: Contemporary Issues in the Sociological Study of Childhood* (London, Falmer Press).

Kielland, A. & Sanogo, I. (2002), *Burkina Faso: Child Labour Migration from Rural Areas: The Magnitude and the Determinants* (Ouagadougou, World Bank).

Levy, R. & Hollan, W. H. (1998), 'Person-Centered Interviewing', in H. R. Bernard (ed.), *Handbook of Methods in Cultural Anthropology* (London, Sage/AltaMira Press), 333–65.

Morganti, S. (2011), 'La Mobilit à dei Minori in Benin: Migrazione o Tratta?', in A. Bellagamba (ed.), *Migrazioni: Dal lato dell'Africa* (Padova, Edizioni Altravista), 127–56.

Morrissey, J. (2010), 'Mobility in Context: Exploring the Impact of Environmental Stress on Mobility Decisions in Northern Ethiopia', unpublished DPhil thesis, University of Oxford, UK.

Mosse, D. (2005), *Cultivating Development: An Ethnography of Aid and Practice* (London, Pluto Press).

Mullings, B. (1999), 'Insider or Outsider, Both or Neither: Some Dilemmas in Interviewing in a Cross-Cultural Setting', *Geoforum*, 30: 337–50.

Ouensavi, R. & Kielland, A. (2000), *Le Phénomène des Enfants Travailleurs Migrants du Bénin: Ampleur et Déterminants* (Cotonou, World Bank/CEO).

Robben, A. C. G. M. & Sluka, J. (2007), *Ethnographic Fieldwork: An Anthropological Reader* (Oxford, Blackwell Publishing).

Weitzer, R. (2014), 'Miscounting Human Trafficking and Slavery', *openDemocracy: Beyond Trafficking and Slavery* (8 October 2014), accessed 8 October 2016, https://www.opendemocracy.net/beyondslavery/ronald-weitzer/miscounting-human-trafficking-and-slavery

Wells, K. (2009), *Childhood in a Global Perspective* (Cambridge, Polity Press).

8

Researching Unfree Student Labour in Apple's Supply Chain

JENNY CHAN[1]

Introduction

STUDENT INTERNSHIPS ARE TYPICALLY required for meeting educational qualifications in the fields of medicine, hospitality and tourism, creative industries, and media and communication studies, among many others. In China, such internships are mandatory in the realm of vocational education. With the availability of a potential labour pool of nearly 20 million vocational school students nationwide, some employers such as Foxconn Technology Group – the world's largest manufacturer of high-tech electronics products on contract with Apple and other global brands – have coerced student interns to work day and night on the assembly line. Working and living in the factory-cum-dormitory complexes, the young students must comply with the Foxconn internship programme on pain of not graduating. At a time of rising costs and an aging population, companies are incentivised to tap into the cheap productive labour of interning students to maximise their profits. Student interns are unfree labourers, who face multi-layered pressures from schools, companies and local governments in transnational manufacturing. This chapter further assesses how this emerging student worker regime impacts labour standards and the future development of a globalised economy.

[1] I thank Ngai Pun, Mark Selden, Ferruccio Gambino, Devi Sacchetto, Rutvica Andrijasevic, Jan Drahokoupil, Cindy Yin-Wah Chu, Amanda Bell, Jeff Hermanson, Greg Fay, Chris Smith, Rachel Murphy, Nandini Gooptu, Philip Huang, Richard Gunde, Richard Appelbaum, Nelson Lichtenstein, SACOM (Students and Scholars against Corporate Misbehavior), and anonymous reviewers for the *Proceedings of the British Academy* series for their intellectual support. Genevieve LeBaron gave helpful feedback throughout the writing process. Penelope Kyritsis and Fintan Power provided assistance with copy-editing. This publication arises from research funded by the John Fell Oxford University Press Research Fund, the United Board for Christian Higher Education in Asia, the Department of Applied Social Sciences of the Hong Kong Polytechnic University, and the Early Career Scheme (2018–20) of the Hong Kong Research Grants Council.

Proceedings of the British Academy, **220**, 130–147. © The British Academy 2018.

Previous research on the commodification of education has shown that, under China's market reforms since the 1970s, vocational schools have diversified their funding sources by expanding student enrolment and engaging in business partnerships (Kuczera & Field 2010; Li & Sheldon 2014; Loyalka *et al.* 2015). The quality of teaching and learning varies widely. In under-resourced and poorly governed schools, many students play with handsets and online games, read comic books and even sleep through ill-prepared lectures, with disillusioned students dropping out altogether. Vocational schools are thus stigmatised as 'holding tanks' for 'bad students' who have failed in the mainstream education system (Woronov 2016; Ling 2015).

When looking at the school-to-work transition, I focus on the institutional practices of student internship programmes and the lived experiences of interns. Under Chinese law interning students are *not* classified as employees: the legal status of interns remains that of students (Ministries of Education and Finance 2007; Ministry of Education *et al.* 2016). For Guy Standing (2011: 16), 'internships are potentially a vehicle for channelling youths into the precariat', which begs the questions: is a precarious intern economy comprised of teenage vocational students expanding in China? Are businesses within global supply chains becoming dependent on China's intern economy?

Fieldwork in China

While investigating the loss of more than a dozen employees' lives in a spate of workplace suicides at Foxconn throughout 2010, I came to learn about workers' struggles, including the struggles of interning students. Between 2011 and 2012, I interviewed 38 student interns from working-class rural migrant families and 14 teachers from eight vocational schools participating in an internship programme at Foxconn, the largest student internship programme in the world. In addition to face-to-face interviews, I did undercover research inside Foxconn dormitories and worker communities. In food outlets, Internet cafes, basketball courts, discos, shopping malls, parks and the Foxconn Employees Care Center, I met with workers and student interns, as well as a smaller number of human resources managers, teachers and government educational officials. The interns were eager to talk about their studies, working lives and anxieties about their future. I supplemented semi-structured interviews with workers' monthly wage statements, employment contracts, internship agreements, employees' handbooks, company publications (including newspapers, magazines, recruitment posters, notices, annual reports and press releases) and government data (including educational directives and labour laws and regulations). It became clear to me that provincial governments provide special funds for schools that meet Foxconn's labour quotas, thus firming up close ties linking local governments, schools and corporations.

As I expanded my field research from Sichuan and Guangdong to the eastern coastal provinces of Jiangsu and Zhejiang in August and November 2016, I learned that labour agencies – also known as dispatch firms – have undertaken new forms of labour subcontracting, including the dispatch of student interns to factories and service workplaces (see also: Crane & LeBaron in this volume). The quasi-employment arrangements of interns, who occupy an ambiguous space between being a student and a worker, result in the super-exploitation of Chinese youth whose internship opportunities are being squandered, and who with ever greater frequency serve as cheap and disposable labour – all while learning no marketable skills.

Student internship and labour informalisation

China's educational and labour systems in student internship governance have been changing rapidly. Until the early 1990s, graduates from vocational schools were assigned to urban state-owned enterprises and hence enjoyed a high level of job security. With the increase of economic reforms, privatisation and enterprise restructuring, this government-planned job assignment system was phased out (Hoffman 2001). A fresh graduate is now assumed to have full responsibility for his or her own career in a competitive labour market. Different terms of work and employment, differentiated by one's educational credentials and social status, thrive in 'flexible' workplaces (Kuruvilla *et al.* 2011).

The mass recruitment of students as 'interns', 'trainees' and 'apprentices' has increasingly drawn attention from academics and labour non-governmental organisations. Lu Zhang (2015) showed that the ranks of 'temporary workers' – such as agency labourers and student interns – had been growing in step with pressure on industry to cut costs and intensify labour. At the assembly factories Zhang surveyed, temps earned one half to two-thirds of formal employees' wages and received far fewer welfare benefits. In particular, auto production has been further streamlined by the use of lower-cost contingent or non-standard workers, on the one hand, and the application of advanced robotic technologies replacing human labour, on the other hand. Eli Friedman and Ching Kwan Lee (2010: 513) insightfully summarise that the multi-tiered employment system is problematic not just from the perspective of subcontracted workers who lack job security, but also from that of regular employees, who encounter greater difficulty in making 'collective demands on their employers', as they now must compete with student interns and dispatch labourers.

The current author, Ngai Pun and Mark Selden (2015a) drew on their multi-year investigation of the labour conditions at Foxconn to highlight the critical role played by Chinese local governments in manipulating internships through direct school policy interventions. After the tragedy of 12 young worker suicides at

Foxconn from January to May 2010, the company temporarily halted open recruitment of labour at its large facilities in South China. A human resources manager dismissively commented that the policy was to prevent the entry of those who would jump to their death for company compensation. However, Foxconn did not halt the employment of teenage student interns from all over the country. If a student is found emotionally unstable or seriously ill, the front-line manager can ask the responsible teacher to take the student back. In this way Foxconn attempts to avert the risk of suicide and monitor labour conditions with the assistance of teachers, who report to company managers and stay on site throughout the internship (Smith & Chan 2015). Moreover, government officials take the initiative to assist big investors to recruit student interns on demand. Interns, unlike their co-workers, are *not* free to leave work at any time upon reasonable notice. The students must comply with the Foxconn internship programme in order to graduate. Working hand in glove with provincial, municipal, district, and township and village governments, Foxconn blatantly subverts China's internship regulations designed to protect students and assure that their career needs are served.

Student interns often face restrictions on their ability to exert rights, but on occasions when they have organised, they have exercised power and leverage within global supply chains. Student interns and their co-workers at the Honda (Nanhai) auto-parts plant, for example, went on strike between May and June 2010, paralysing the entire close-knit, just-in-time supply network of Honda from within China (Chan & Hui 2014; Pringle 2017). At the time, interns made up the majority of the 1,800-person labour force (Lyddon *et al.* 2015). In the labour process 'foremen offer little in the way of instruction despite the fact that the work at the factory is considered to be a part of the interns' education' (Butollo & ten Brink 2012: 426). In spite of the power asymmetry between managers and workers, including interns, the strikers – with support from concerned academics and labour activists – won a big wage increase for both workers and interns. Importantly, the interns and workers interacted as friends and colleagues, going to work every day by company shuttle buses and living in the same collective dormitories. Such an environment can prove conducive to strategising solidarity actions (Friedman 2014), but since interns are typically only short term, sustainable organising with other workers can be difficult (SACOM 2012; DanWatch 2015; China Labor Watch 2016, 2017).

What remains understudied is the complex power structure faced by unskilled student interns amid the growing competition for good jobs, and the deepening collusion between vocational schools, labour agencies and local governments in shaping the internship system. As my research data reveal, employers utilise student labour, which is coordinated by local officials as well as by private agencies through subcontracting, to maximise staffing flexibility and profitability. This constitutes a manifestation of the persistent labour unfreedom and inequalities in a volatile global market.

The disconnect between students' majors and internships

Chinese vocational schools offer employment-oriented courses for eligible applicants who have completed nine years of schooling. While the number of vocational high-school students (grades 10–12) doubled from 11.7 million in 2001 to 22.4 million in 2010, by 2014 it had dropped to 18 million nationwide (Ministry of Education 2015). The official goal for 2020 is to reverse this trend by recruiting 23.5 million students – i.e. 50 per cent of the nation's senior secondary student population (Ministry of Education 2010a: table 1) – into three-year vocational programmes.

Vocational schools follow the work–study model, emphasising the integration of education with production, as stated in China's 1996 Vocational Education Law. For students, the key question is the quality of teaching in the classroom and in internships among a wide range of vocational training programmes. A 6,000-student vocational school that trains equipment and machinery technicians proclaims its mission to be: 'Master one skill, create a career. Master one skill, make a blue sky.' Similarly, in a larger school specialising in auto repair and mobile mechanics, the recruitment brochure elaborates on the importance of studying real skills:

> Our country has a good policy so that families in difficulty pay no tuition!
> To look for a job without learning technical skills is a lifelong mistake!
> It is best to have a skill in this world, to save you if times get tough!
> Parents with foresight have their children learn skills![2]

The schools' marketing campaigns focus on offering prospective students the skills to provide a solid foundation for career building and lifelong security. According to the government, good internship programmes are participatory, contribute to students' growth and development, and relate to their field of study. By contrast, my first-hand research reveals that the interns' work positions at Foxconn are *not* related to their field of study, nor are they designed to develop lifelong skills for student interns.

In Foxconn's integrated Digital Product Business Group (iDPBG), exclusively serving Apple, 28,044 'student interns' from over 200 schools were working alongside employees in Shenzhen city in 2010. This was a sixfold increase from 4,539 interns in 2007 (Foxconn Technology Group 2010a: 23). Nationwide, Foxconn used the labour of 150,000 student interns – 15 per cent of its entire million-strong Chinese workforce – during the summer of 2010 (Foxconn Technology Group 2010b: 2), dwarfing Disney's College Program, often cited as one of the world's largest internship programmes with more than 50,000 cumulative interns over 30 years (Perlin 2012: 6).

---

[2] The vocational school brochure, in the original Chinese, is on file with the author.

In the eight vocational schools, between 2011 and 2012, 38 interviewed interns were studying arts, construction, petrochemistry, automotive repair, herbal medicine, horticulture, secretarial services, computer science, business management, accounting, textiles, electronics and mechanics, among others. Only eight of them, barely one-fifth, were in their third and final year, i.e. when internships are supposed to take place. Their average age was 16.5, just above China's statutory minimum working age of 16. In terms of the length of internship, the 14 teachers I interviewed who were dispatched to Foxconn revealed that the company internships were often extended to meet production needs, ranging from three months to a full year, with scant regard for the students' training needs. A 16-year-old Foxconn intern said:

> Come on, what do you think we've learned standing for more than ten hours a day manning machines on the line? What's an internship? There's no relation to what we study in school. Every day is just a repetition of one or two simple motions, like a robot.
>
> (29 November 2011, Shenzhen city, Guangdong province)

Interns at Foxconn are required to work 10–12 hour shifts, six or seven days a week during peak production months. The 2007 Administrative Measures for Internships, however, state that 'interns shall not work more than eight hours a day', and the 2010 Education Circular specifies 'interns shall not work overtime beyond the eight-hour workday' (Ministries of Education and Finance 2007; Ministry of Education 2010b). Not only must interns' shifts be limited to eight hours, but all their training is required to take place during the day to ensure students' safety and physical and mental health, in accordance with the Law on the Protection of Minors. This law – which was revised in 2012 and promulgated in 2013 – aims to protect young people under the age of 18 and ensure their balanced development and healthy growth (Standing Committee of the National People's Congress 2012). Article 20 stipulates that schools, including vocational schools, shall 'cooperate with the parents or other guardians of minor students to guarantee the students' time for sleeping, recreational activities and physical exercise, and may not increase their burden of study'. In reality, Foxconn student interns aged from 16 to 18 were subjected to the same working conditions as regular workers, including alternating day and night shifts and extensive overtime, defying the letter and the spirit of the law.

In explaining the design and purpose of internships, a teacher showed me the following school letter addressed to parents:

> Participation in this internship will advance students' respect and appreciation of employment, their honesty and integrity as the main part of a vocational moral education, will help students understand enterprise and become familiar with a business environment and culture, will lead students to develop employee awareness in both practice through study and learning by doing, will cultivate students' comprehensive career capabilities, and will integrate their overall qualities and inure them to

hardship and promote endurance so that in the future they will enter the job market with a solid foundation.

(5 December 2011, Chengdu city, Sichuan province)

With its highly moral tone, this letter claims that, through the school's assigned internship, students' 'employability' in the market will be enhanced; yet it does not specify the curriculum, nor provide any information about the content of the technical training.

A 17-year-old student interviewee recalled his internship experience: 'I enrolled in an automotive repair course in September 2009 and, according to the curriculum, the specialised course lasts for three years, with two years at school and a final year of internship.' But less than a year into the programme, in June 2010, he and his fellow classmates were sent to Foxconn's production site to intern for seven months. Rather than working on automobiles, he worked on iPhones. 'It's exhausting. It's a waste of time', he concluded.

Not long after the students' return to school, the administration began arranging more internships. He recalled:

> The school had still not finished planning our specialised classes, but they began setting up internship assignments. We haven't yet completed even the core classes in our specialisation, nor have we grasped the basic skills of automotive repair. How are we going to handle an internship in an auto company?

The student was very upset. He explained:

> We followed the rules and paid for three years of tuition, but we haven't completed the professional training. The school violated the most basic agreement, contradicted the student recruitment brochure, arbitrarily changed the curriculum, treated its students' future like a plaything, and failed in its responsibility to us. We students have not attained sufficient knowledge in our education, and come time for employment, we'll have no competitive advantage.

(4 December 2011, Chengdu city, Sichuan province)

One school's mission statement says: 'Unification of school and business, unification of theory and practice, unification of teacher and technician, and unification of student and employee.' However, this is not a seamless unification, and the discrepancy between their promise and the reality faced by interns could scarcely be larger. The responses of several interns, such as playing video games all night and not going to work on time, as well as slowing down due to loss of motivation to work, have remained a consistent pattern. Foxconn's presentation of honorary titles such as the Outstanding Student Intern Awards – also known as the 'hardworking bee' prize – failed to instil stronger commitment and loyalty among interns who perceived the internship programme as squandering their education and found the work demeaning.

Forced internships

One Chinese literature teacher observed that the student intern system is not unlike the 'contract labour system' of the 1930s (Honig 1983). He drew a parallel with the desperate Occupation-era children and teenagers from poverty-stricken villages who were sold to labour contractors and dispatched to toil day and night under harsh conditions in Japanese-owned cotton mills in Shanghai. Laughing bitterly, he confides, 'I'm a modern day contractor', referring to his role as a coordinator of the internship programme. He said:

> My daughter is seventeen years old, my only daughter. She's now preparing for the national college entrance exam. No matter what the result is, I won't let her come to intern, or work, for this company.
>
> (16 December 2011, Chengdu city, Sichuan province)

More importantly, he states that, 'at Foxconn, there's no real learning through integration of classroom and workshop. The distortion of vocational education in today's China runs deep.'

None of the 38 interviewed interns expressed any interest in working for Foxconn after graduation. If they were interested in low-skilled, low-paid assembly line jobs, one of them told me, they 'would have started working straight away after finishing junior secondary school rather than seeking specialised training in multiple fields'. In January 2011, new workers and student interns at Foxconn's 'iPad city' in Chengdu, the provincial capital of Sichuan, were paid the same 950 yuan per month as everyone else, but, unlike regular workers, interns were not entitled to a 400 yuan per month skills subsidy, despite having passed a three-month probationary period. Foxconn justifies this tiered treatment by referring to the legal requirement to 'pay reasonably for the labour of interns', wherein what constitutes 'reasonable pay' went unspecified under the national regulations at that time.

Teachers are assigned by their schools to accompany student interns to their work sites. They play two roles: one is to ensure that student interns follow factory rules; the second is to help students deal with feelings of dejection at their work situation. During the entire internship, the teacher focuses on managing students' emotions, as maintaining high morale was key to assuring a high retention rate of student interns, which was a primary criterion for assessing teacher performance. A 26-year-old teacher spoke of some students who were reluctant to go to work during the first week after arriving at the Foxconn factory:

> I asked my students to manage their emotions. Calm down. Think carefully if you want to leave; won't your parents be disappointed? I visited my students in the dorm to see if they felt okay on Tuesday night. They answered 'not too bad'. I met them again on Friday night. They said 'fine'. They've gradually gotten used to the work rhythm. Finally, when I asked if they want to leave, they replied 'no'.
>
> (14 December 2011, Chengdu city, Sichuan province)

A number of teacher interviewees, I eventually learned, concealed the absence of educational value in the programme in part because they were being paid not only their regular monthly salary by their schools but also an additional salary from Foxconn for their supervisory service during the internship period. During the school year of 2011–12, each teacher received an extra 2,000 yuan per month from Foxconn for their role in strengthening labour control. The student interns were therefore pressured not only by the company but also by their teachers to accept internships that violated the educational criteria of their vocational programmes.

Often when interning students fell ill, neither their teachers nor the company supervisors seemed to be able to help them. A 16-year-old girl suffered from abnormal menstrual pains while she was assigned to the packaging workshop:

> I used to have relatively regular menstrual periods, but this time my period was delayed until the first week in October. I was frightened. I had such severe cramps that I was covered with sweat on the line, where it's air-conditioned. In November and December, my irregularity and pain persisted . . . My line leader is a young man with whom I don't feel comfortable talking about a 'girl matter'. Further, I didn't report my sickness to my teacher for the same kind of embarrassment.
>
> (14 December 2011, Chengdu city, Sichuan province)

In the broader social structure, teachers were pressured to coordinate internships tailored to Foxconn, an influential corporate player in the local political economy. A teacher explained:

> There's a need to respond to the Education Department's call to get the whole class of students organised. To take action uniformly. Because an internship is not a summer job that one gets on one's own. Between September 2011 and January 2012, a school semester, more than 7,000 students – approximately 10 per cent of the labour force – were working on the assembly line in Foxconn's Chengdu factories.
>
> (2 February 2012, Chengdu city, Sichuan province)

His school sent 162 students on 22 September 2011 to undertake three-month internships that were subsequently extended in accordance with iPad production needs. Another larger school recruited 309 students, who were accompanied by only three male and three female teachers for the entire internship. This is typical of the 1:50 teacher–student ratio maintained throughout the Foxconn Chengdu internship programme in 2011–12.

Contrary to my findings, the Fair Labor Association (FLA) (2013: 5) 'found *no interns* had been engaged at [Foxconn] Chengdu since September 2011' (my emphasis). Having received annual membership dues of US$250,000 from Apple, plus well into six-figure audit fees for conducting their investigation at the Foxconn facilities (Weir 2012), the FLA had ignored the exploitative features of China's internship programmes.

Ralph Litzinger (2013: 176) aptly notes that 'Apple is a master at blurring truth and fiction – through its advertising, its Genius Bars, its secrecy, and its brilliantly spun corporate responsibility reports.' In October 2016, Apple terminated its membership of the FLA,[3] after learning that it had aligned with 'the FLA code elements related to employment relationship; non-discrimination; harassment or abuse; forced labor; and health, safety, and environment' (Fair Labor Association 2016: 1). Ironically, instead of terminating the abusive student internship programmes, in 2016 Apple modified its Supplier Code of Conduct provisions to ensure that suppliers were 'compensating student workers comparable to regular workers' (Apple 2017: 30). The result was to tacitly legitimate Foxconn's continued abuse of the labour of young students in the absence of any genuine internship training and in violation of prohibitions on overtime work for interns. Whether Apple's suppliers will actually pay student interns up to the *same* wages as their co-workers remains a pressing issue to be investigated.

With the loss of the capacity to control the timing, location and training content of the internships, a student interviewee vented his pent-up anger by condemning the Foxconn programme for offering 'fake internships' and 'forced internships'.

The labour dispatch of student interns

One compelling feature of the intern programme for Foxconn and other corporations is that student interns offer cheap labour. Because student interns are not classified as employees – even though they perform identical work to other production workers – employers *do not* enrol them in government-administered social security, which covers medical insurance, work injury insurance, unemployment benefits, maternity insurance and old age pensions. By dispensing with all of these benefits, the company ultimately saves money.[4]

During my follow-up fieldwork in the summer and autumn of 2016, I observed that several vocational schools had engaged with for-profit labour agencies to supply students to workplaces in return for labour service fees. Under the dispatch work relationship, 'the contracting and managing entities are constructed to be severed from one another' (Huang 2017: 250). If the dispatched student-workers were injured at work, neither Foxconn, the managing entity nor the agency would feel the need to take any responsibility, given the ambiguity and complexity of the triangular labour relations.

In China, dispatch workers had long been excluded from legal protections prior to the implementation of the Labour Contract Law, which was promulgated in June

---

[3] In the aftermath of young Chinese worker suicides in 2010 and an aluminium-dust explosion at the Foxconn Chengdu iPad factory in May 2011, Apple – the biggest business partner of Foxconn – was compelled to join in 2012 the auditing programmes led by the Washington, DC-based Fair Labor Association to protect its corporate image (Chan 2013; Chan *et al.* 2015b; Pun *et al.* 2016).

[4] As of 2015, in Guangdong province, employers were required to contribute 29.2 per cent and employees 11 per cent of the employee's wages to social insurance on a monthly basis (Hong Kong Confederation of Trade Unions 2015).

2007 and came into force in January 2008 (Chan 2009; Xu 2014; Zhang 2015). Under this new law, hiring agencies and client firms share joint legal responsibilities, and dispatch workers are entitled to receive the same pay for doing the same work as directly employed workers. The law restricts labour dispatch for 'temporary, supplementary or substitute work', thereby placing certain limits on labour informalisation while providing organisational flexibility. However, huge discrepancies exist between workers' formal employment rights and the enforcement of these rights (Liu 2014; Cairns 2015).

Student interns are joining the ranks of the rapidly expanding labour dispatch force. In the city of Danyang, Jiangsu province, the private labour agency paid the student-employees an 'internship subsidy' of 10 yuan per hour (compared to the 15.5 yuan local minimum hourly wage standard), with the longest working month of 308 hours (under the Chinese labour law the normal working time should be 174 hours a month, plus no more than 36 hours' overtime in any month). The labour agency pocketed the difference between the interning students' 'standard hourly pay' (i.e. 10 yuan per hour) and the factory rate (which is negotiated on a case-by-case basis). For the factory boss, the use of dispatched or outsourced student workers helps to cut both administrative and labour costs.

The corporate use of student interns is now widely taken as a quick fix to the difficulties posed by rising labour costs and a tightening labour market. China's basic wage levels, particularly in large cities, have risen substantially to reach the mid-range of Asian countries, higher than those for manufacturing workers in Cambodia, Pakistan, Vietnam and other developing countries, but far below those in Hong Kong, Singapore, Japan and South Korea (ILO 2016: 2). While the numbers of Chinese internal migrant workers reached 282 million in 2016, the annual rate of growth of rural migrant labour had declined from 5.4 per cent in 2010 to 1.5 per cent in 2016 (National Bureau of Statistics of the People's Republic of China 2010, 2017).

Barry Naughton (2014: 14, 21) shows that the Chinese economy sustained average growth of 10.4 per cent per annum between 2003 and 2012, while real wages for rural migrant workers increased by 2.5 times in the course of the decade. With the exception of 2008–9, during the deepest world recession since World War II, increases in statutory minimum wages steadily boosted Chinese workers' incomes as the government sought to stimulate domestic consumption and lessen over-reliance on exports (Li 2016; Hung & Selden 2017). In many cities, statutory minimum wages rose almost every year. In 2014, the minimum wages in 19 municipalities, autonomous regions and provinces increased by an average of 14.1 per cent, and in 2015 the minimum wage in 27 regions increased by an average of 14 per cent (*Xinhua* 2016).

Under these circumstances the researched private labour agency has been responsive to growing human resources needs at 'competitive rates'. It takes care of the hiring and management of student interns, such as the signing of labour dispatch agreements and the payment of wages in a one-stop service, for its clients. In my interview, the human resources manager was excited to talk about his business expansion strategies. He also commented on the entrepreneurial, rather than educational, role of the teachers:

> Teachers are interested in getting a cut [from student internships], too. We either have to make a good deal, or reach out to students directly through our local agents, whom we call downstream suppliers, but not via the school teacher gatekeepers. In this way, we don't have to pay them commissions. You know what, meeting with teachers means spending on cigarettes, food and drinks, KTVs . . . all this will cost you quite a lot before you'll get any return.
>
> (28 August 2016, Danyang city, Jiangsu province)

Student internships are profoundly marketised. As an experiment, the dispatch agency has invested in a vocational school at the Lianyungang Economic and Technological Development Zone. The agency sends students directly to employing units in return for labour service payments from the enterprises.

Regulating China's intern economy

Legal practitioners Earl Brown and Kyle deCant (2014: 195) argue that when internship programmes are 'devoid of any relevant educational component and maintained solely for the benefit of the employer's bottom line . . . interns should be afforded the full protection of China's labor laws'. Exposés by the media have shown that Chinese interns – the youngest ones being only 14 years old – are essentially engaged in thinly disguised child labour (BBC 2012). In these 'sheep-like internships', interns are confused and helpless, like sheep without a shepherd. In response, the central government finally took some measures in 2016 to protect the basic rights of student interns, who were being increasingly exploited as low-cost workers in factories, express delivery companies, restaurants, hotels, metro stations and other workplaces (*China Daily* opinion 2016; Lin 2016; Horwitz & Huang 2015).

Specifically, vocational schools were instructed to manage student internships in accordance with the latest regulations jointly promulgated by the Ministry of Education, the Ministry of Finance, the Ministry of Human Resources and Social Security, the State Administration of Work Safety and the China Insurance Regulatory Commission, which superseded the 2007 Administrative Measures and came into force on 11 April 2016. Under the 'Regulations on the Management of Vocational School Student Internships' (Ministry of Education *et al.* 2016), the duration of workplace-based internships should normally be six months. On insurance benefits, vocational schools and enterprises are required to undertake 'joint responsibility' to provide interns with commercial general liability insurance. Moreover, the regulations require that student internships have substantial educational content and work-skills training provisions, along with comprehensive labour protections for student interns such as eight-hour working days, no overtime and no night shifts. Above all, no more than 10 per cent of the labour force at 'any given facility', or no more than 20 per cent of the workers in 'any given work position', should consist of student interns at any point in time.

However, the Chinese central government has left intact incentives for corporations to continue to prioritise intern labour as cheap labour. With the passage of the 2016 Regulations, the statutory minimum level for paying interns is clearly specified: 'Wages shall be *at least* 80 per cent of that of employees during the probationary period' (italics added). In other words, employers are permitted to give student interns only 80 per cent of the income offered to full employees on the job, whether or not students' productivity is less.

Fundamentally, the intricate interests shared by companies, vocational schools and local governments will not be done away with easily. Rob Lederer, the executive director of the Electronic Industry Citizenship Coalition (EICC), an industry association with more than 100 members around the world, acknowledged that 'one large potential source of reliable, quality labor may be student workers' (EICC & REAP 2015: 2). At the invitation of the EICC, Scott Rozelle, co-director of the Rural Education Action Program (REAP) at Stanford University, assisted in designing a monitoring and evaluation programme for China's vocational schooling system since 2013 (Apple 2013: 19). The major objective is to achieve 'responsible vocational education', beginning with a pilot project of 118 vocational high schools in the heavily populated Henan province in central China. In July 2016, the American academic research team, with support from leaders from the provincial Department of Education, created a list of 22 credentialled vocational schools to benchmark teaching standards, school resources and student learning experiences against a set of criteria (EICC & REAP 2016).

The local government encouraged companies to select students and graduates from quality schools for internships, thereby providing economic incentives for both teachers and students to improve their performance. Cooperating schools were also promised increased government funding for long-term educational development. This is framed by the Stanford University research team as a 'win–win–win action research' to strengthen collaboration between the government, schools and companies (Rozelle *et al.* 2013). In engaging with the world's largest electronics association, the researchers took aim at vocational schools, holding them accountable for bad learning experiences and poor internship arrangements. They have not, however, addressed the managerial abuses involving the violation of China's internship provisions at the workplace level that I have shown to be the product of collaboration between local governments and corporate giants.

Conclusion

Student interns have become an important source of precarious workers that is growing in step with the expansion of vocational education and the informalisation of employment in China. Greig de Peuter, Nicole Cohen and Enda Brophy (2015: 331) observe that internships are 'an entry point for interrogating contested conditions of life, labour, and learning at a historical moment when precarity is an encroaching structure of feeling'. Young and inexperienced students, along with many other kinds of low-skilled workers, face formidable challenges in the face of credential inflation, ineffective governance and the flexibilisation of production of services and goods (Lee 2016; Chan and Selden 2017). In the name of internship, they are thrust into menial work without training, or transfer, of useful skills.

Ross Perlin (2012: 23) comments that the 'very significance of the word *intern* lies in its ambiguity'. Facing financial and political pressures from local government, many schools – even the better ones – are unable to shield students from internships that violate the law. At the same time, some employers went as far as renaming 'internships' as 'social practice programmes' and 'service learning' to evade the new law and public monitoring.

On reflection, at a time of slowing economic growth, a shrinking pool of workers and an aging population, interning students and graduates could play a significant role in China's economic and technological development if they are protected against violations of China's labour law, and particularly if they were to receive appropriate training leading to better jobs and higher levels of technology. Stronger labour protections – especially for teenage student workers – will require much more sustained joint efforts from the state, companies and civil society.

References

All website URLs were accessed on 19 July 2018.

Apple (2013), 'Apple Supplier Responsibility: 2013 Progress Report', http://images.apple.com/supplier-responsibility/pdf/Apple_SR_2013_Progress_Report.pdf

Apple (2017), 'Apple Supplier Responsibility: 2017 Progress Report', http://images.apple.com/supplier-responsibility/pdf/Apple-Progress-Report-2017.pdf

BBC (2012), 'Foxconn Admits Employing Under-Age Interns', *BBC News* (16 October 2012), http://www.bbc.com/news/technology-19965641

Brown Jr., E. V. & deCant, K. A. (2014), 'Exploiting Chinese Interns as Unprotected Industrial Labor', *Asian-Pacific Law and Policy Journal*, 15, 2: 150–95.

Butollo, F. & ten Brink, T. (2012), 'Challenging the Atomization of Discontent: Patterns of Migrant-Worker Protest in China during the Series of Strikes in 2010', *Critical Asian Studies*, 44, 3: 419–40. DOI 10.1080/14672715.2012.711978

Cairns, D. S. S. (2015), 'New Formalities for Casual Labor: Addressing Unintended Consequences of China's Labor Contract Law', *Washington International Law Journal*, 24, 1: 219–52.

Chan, C. K.-C. & Hui, E. S.-I. (2014), 'The Development of Collective Bargaining in China: From "Collective Bargaining by Riot" to "Party State-Led Wage Bargaining"', *China Quarterly*, 217: 221–42. DOI 10.1017/S0305741013001409

Chan, J. (2009), 'Meaningful Progress or Illusory Reform? Analyzing China's Labor Contract Law', *New Labor Forum*, 18, 2: 43–51. DOI 10.4179/NLF.182.0000006

Chan, J. (2013), 'A Suicide Survivor: The Life of a Chinese Worker', *New Technology, Worker and Employment*, 28, 2: 84–99. DOI 10.1111/ntwe.12007

Chan, J., Pun, N. & Selden, M. (2015a), 'Interns or Workers? China's Student Labor Regime', *Asian Studies*, 1, 1: 69–98. DOI 10.6551/AS.0101.04

Chan, J., Pun, N. & Selden, M. (2015b), 'Apple's iPad City: Subcontracting Exploitation to China', in K. van der Pijl (ed.), *Handbook of the International Political Economy of Production* (Cheltenham, Edward Elgar), 76–97.

Chan, J. & Selden, M. (2017), 'The Labour Politics of China's Rural Migrant Workers', *Globalizations*, 14, 2, 259–71. DOI 10.1080/14747731.2016.1200263

China Daily opinion (2016), 'Student Labor Shows Dark Side of E-commerce', *China Daily* (22 November 2016), http://www.chinadaily.com.cn/opinion/2016-11/22/content_27448767.htm

China Labor Watch (2016), 'Labor Rights Violations in Walmart and Home Depot's Supplier Factory' (1 December 2016), http://www.chinalaborwatch.org/upfile/2016_11_29/Report.pdf

China Labor Watch (2017), 'China: Factory Fully Pays Some Student Workers' (13 January 2017), http://www.chinalaborwatch.org/newscast/620

DanWatch (2015), 'Servants of Servers: Rights Violations and Forced Labour in the Supply Chain of ICT (Information and Communications Technology) Equipment in European Universities' (5 October 2015), https://www.danwatch.dk/en/undersogelse/servants-of-servers/

de Peuter, G., Cohen, N. S. & Brophy, E. (eds) (2015), 'Introduction—Interrogating Internships: Unpaid Work, Creative Industries, and Higher Education', *tripleC: Communication, Capitalism and Critique*, 13, 2: 329–35.

EICC & REAP (Electronic Industry Citizenship Coalition & Stanford University's Rural Education Action Program) (2015), 'Creating and Evaluating a Credentialing System for Vocational Schools in China', Phase 2 final report, http://www.eiccoalition.org/media/docs/publications/EICC-REAPreport2015.pdf

EICC & REAP (Electronic Industry Citizenship Coalition & Stanford University's Rural Education Action Program) (2016), 'Electronics Industry Recognizes Vocational Schools in China for Excellence', http://www.eiccoalition.org/news-and-events/news/credentialed-schools-china/

Fair Labor Association (2013), 'Second Foxconn Verification Status Report', http://www.fairlabor.org/sites/default/files/documents/reports/second_foxconn_verification_status_report_0.pdf#overlay-context

Fair Labor Association (2016), 'Alignment with the FLA Workplace Code of Conduct as of October 2016', http://www.fairlabor.org/sites/default/files/documents/reports/alignment_with_the_fla_workplace_code_of_conduct_october_2016.pdf

Foxconn Technology Group (2010a), '"Win–win cooperation": iDPBG Convenes the Intern Appraisal and Awards Ceremony', *Foxconn Bridgeworkers*, 183 (31 December 2010), print edition (in Chinese).

Foxconn Technology Group (2010b), 'Foxconn Is Committed to a Safe and Positive Working Environment' (11 October 2010), http://regmedia.co.uk/2010/10/12/foxconn_media_statement.pdf

Friedman, E. (2014), *Insurgency Trap: Labor Politics in Postsocialist China* (Ithaca, NY, Cornell University Press).

Friedman, E. & Lee, C. K. (2010), 'Remaking the World of Chinese Labour: A 30-Year Retrospective', *British Journal of Industrial Relations*, 48, 3: 507–33. DOI 10.1111/j.1467-8543.2010.00814.x

Hoffman, L. (2001), 'Guiding College Graduates to Work: Social Constructions of Labor Markets in Dalian', in N. N. Chen, C. D. Clark, S. Z. Gottschang & L. Jeffery (eds), *China Urban: Ethnographies of Contemporary Culture* (Durham, NC, Duke University Press), 43–66.

Hong Kong Confederation of Trade Unions (2015), 'One Year Anniversary of the Yue Yuen Workers' Strike: Conditions and Voices of Workers', http://en.hkctu.org.hk/mainland-china/labour-news/one-year-anniversary-of-the-yue-yuen-workers-strike-conditions-and-voices-of-workers

Honig, E. (1983), 'The Contract Labor System and Women Workers: Pre-liberation Cotton Mills of Shanghai', *Modern China*, 9, 4: 421–54. DOI 10.1177/009770048300900402

Horwitz, J. & Huang, E. (2015), 'Uber's Business in China Is Built on Exploiting Armies of Underpaid, Overworked Interns', *Quartz* (16 December 2015), https://qz.com/573103/ubers-business-in-china-is-built-on-exploiting-armies-of-underpaid-overworked-interns

Huang, P. C. C. (2017), 'Dispatch Work in China: A Study from Case Records, Part I', *Modern China*, 43, 3: 247–87. DOI 10.1177/0097700417693590

Hung, H.-F. & Selden, M. (2017), 'China's Postsocialist Transformation and Global Resurgence: Political Economy and Geopolitics', in J. Fürst, S. Pons & M. Selden (eds), *The Cambridge History of Communism. Volume III: Endgames? Late Communism in Global Perspective, 1968 to the Present* (Cambridge, Cambridge University Press), 502–28.

ILO (2016), 'Wages, Productivity and Labour Share in China' (April), http://www.ilo.org/wcmsp5/groups/public/---asia/---ro-bangkok/documents/publication/wcms_475254.pdf

Kuczera, M. & Field, S. (2010), 'Learning for Jobs: OECD Reviews of Vocational Education and Training—Options for China', OECD (Organization for Economic Cooperation and Development), http://www.oecd.org/china/45486493.pdf

Kuruvilla, S., Lee, C. K. & Gallagher, M. E. (eds) (2011), *From Iron Rice Bowl to Informalization: Markets, Workers, and the State in a Changing China* (Ithaca, NY, Cornell University Press).

Lee, C. K. (2016), 'Precarization or Empowerment? Reflections on Recent Labor Unrest in China', *Journal of Asian Studies*, 75, 2: 317–33. DOI 10.1017/S0021911815002132

Li, M. (2016), *China and the 21st Century Crisis* (London, Pluto Press).

Li, Y. & Sheldon, P. (2014), 'Collaborations between Foreign-Invested Enterprises and China's VET Schools: Making the System Work amid Localised Skill Shortages', *Journal of Vocational Education & Training*, 66, 3: 311–29. DOI 10.1080/13636820.2014.908939

Lin, W. (2016), 'How Interns in China Spend Their Singles Day', *Asia Times* (11 November 2016), http://www.atimes.com/article/crazy-china-single-day-online-shopping/

Ling, M. (2015), '"Bad Students Go to Vocational Schools!": Education, Social Reproduction and Migrant Youth in Urban China', *China Journal*, 73: 108–31. DOI 10.1086/679271

Litzinger, R. A. (2013), 'The Labor Question in China: Apple and Beyond', *South Atlantic Quarterly*, 112, 1: 172–8. DOI 10.1215/00382876-1891314

Liu, G. (2014), 'Private Employment Agencies and Labour Dispatch in China', SECTOR Working Paper No. 293 (Geneva, ILO), http://www.ilo.org/wcmsp5/groups/public/-ed_dialogue/-sector/documents/publication/wcms_246921.pdf

Loyalka, P., Huang, X., Zhang, L., Wei, J., Yi, H., Song, Y., Shi, Y. & Chu, J. (2015), 'The Impact of Vocational Schooling on Human Capital Development in Developing Countries: Evidence from China', *World Bank Economic Review*, 30, 1: 143–70. DOI 10.1093/wber/lhv050

Lyddon, D., Cao, X., Meng, Q. & Lu, J. (2015), 'A Strike of "Unorganized" Workers in a Chinese Car Factory: The Nanhai Honda Events of 2010', *Industrial Relations Journal*, 46, 2: 134–52. DOI 10.1111/irj.12089

Ministries of Education and Finance of the People's Republic of China (2007), 'Administrative Measures for Internships at Secondary Vocational Schools' (in Chinese), http://www. moe.gov.cn/publicfiles/business/htmlfiles/moe/s3566/201001/xxgk_79114.html

Ministry of Education of the People's Republic of China (2010a), 'Outline of China's National Plan for Medium and Long-Term Education Reform and Development, 2010–2020' (in Chinese), http://www.gov.cn/jrzg/2010-07/29/content_1667143.htm

Ministry of Education of the People's Republic of China (2010b), 'Circular on Further Improving the Work of Secondary Vocational School Student Internships Regarding the Skilled Labor Shortage of Enterprises' (in Chinese), http://www.moe.edu.cn/publicfiles/ business/htmlfiles/moe/s3044/201005/87769.html

Ministry of Education of the People's Republic of China (2015), 'Composition of Students in Senior Secondary Schools', http://en.moe.gov.cn/Resources/Statistics/edu_ stat_2014/2014_en01/201509/t20150902_205030.html

Ministry of Education, Ministry of Finance, Ministry of Human Resources and Social Security, the State Administration of Work Safety, and the China Insurance Regulatory Commission (2016), 'Regulations on the Management of Vocational School Student Internships', (in Chinese), http://www.moe.edu.cn/srcsite/A07/moe_950/moe_721/ 201604/t20160426_240252.html

National Bureau of Statistics of the People's Republic of China (2010), 'Investigative Report on the Monitoring of Chinese Rural Migrant Workers in 2009' (10 March 2010) (in Chinese), http://www.stats.gov.cn/ztjc/ztfx/fxbg/201003/t20100319_16135.html

National Bureau of Statistics of the People's Republic of China (2017), 'Statistical Communiqué of the People's Republic of China on the 2016 National Economic and Social Development' (28 February 2017), http://www.stats.gov.cn/english/pressrelease/ 201702/t20170228_1467503.html

Naughton, B. (2014), 'China's Economy: Complacency, Crisis & the Challenge of Reform', *Daedalus: Journal of the American Academy of Arts & Sciences*, 143, 2: 14–25. DOI 10.1162/DAED_a_00269

Perlin, R. (2012), *Intern Nation: How to Earn Nothing and Learn Little in the Brave New Economy*, updated edn (London, Verso).

Pringle, T. (2017), 'A Class against Capital: Class and Collective Bargaining in Guangdong', *Globalizations*, 14, 2, 245–58. DOI 10.1080/14747731.2016.1205811

Pun, N., Shen, Y., Guo, Y., Lu, H., Chan, J. & Selden, M. (2016), 'Apple, Foxconn, and Chinese Workers' Struggles from a Global Labor Perspective', *Inter-Asia Cultural Studies*, 17, 2: 166–85. DOI 10.1080/14649373.2016.1170961

Rozelle, S., Loyalka, P. & Chu, J. (2013), 'China's Human Capital Challenge and What Can Be Done about It', presentation on 'Responsible Electronics 2013: Student Workers' (2 October 2013), http://www.slideshare.net/EICCoalition/responsible-electronics-2013-student-workers

SACOM (Students and Scholars against Corporate Misbehavior) (2012), 'Students and Scholars Demand Tim Cook Stop Using Student Workers and Ensure Decent Working

Conditions at Apple Suppliers!' (9 February 2012), http://sacom.hk/petition-an-open-letter-to-apple-ceo-tim-cook/

Smith, C. & Chan, J. (2015), 'Working for Two Bosses: Student Interns as Constrained Labour in China', *Human Relations*, 68, 2: 305–26. DOI 10.1177/0018726714557013

Standing Committee of the National People's Congress (2012), 'Decision on Revising the Law of the People's Republic of China on the Protection of Minors' (revised 26 October 2012, came into force 1 January 2013), http://www.chinalaw.gov.cn/article/fgkd/xfg/fl/201211/20121100377788.shtml

Standing, G. (2011), *The Precariat: The New Dangerous Class* (London, Bloomsbury Academic).

Weir, B. (2012), 'A Trip to the iFactory', *ABC News* (21 February 2012), http://news.yahoo.com/trip-ifactory-nightline-gets-unprecedented-glimpse-inside-apples-001926196--abc-news.html

Woronov, T. E. (2016), *Class Work: Vocational Schools and China's Urban Youth* (Stanford, CA, Stanford University Press).

Xinhua (2016), 'Only Nine Provincial Regions in China Raise Minimum Wage: Ministry', *China Daily* (14 December 2016), http://usa.chinadaily.com.cn/business/2016-12/14/content_27661945.htm

Xu, F. (2014), 'Temporary Work in China: Precarity in an Emerging Labor Market', in J. Fudge & K. Strauss (eds), *Temporary Work, Agencies, and Unfree Labor: Insecurity in the New World of Work* (New York, Routledge), 143–63.

Zhang, L. (2015), *Inside China's Automobile Factories: The Politics of Labor and Worker Resistance* (New York, Cambridge University Press).

9

Transparent Companies? Legal Research Strategies to Understand Forced Labour in Global Supply Chains

ANDREAS RÜHMKORF[1]

Introduction

MOST MULTINATIONAL ENTERPRISES HAVE policies to combat forced labour in their global supply chain. These policies are often included in their supplier code of conduct and/or the terms and conditions of purchase that they impose on their suppliers. Whilst corporate social responsibility (CSR) has traditionally fallen under the purview of private governance schemes, more recently governments have started to implement public legislation around these issues. For example, the United Kingdom passed the UK Modern Slavery Act 2015 to address the way companies account for forced labour in their global supply chains. This raises the question of how this type of legislation has impacted private commercial relationships, and in particular regarding the issue of forced labour. Given that the UK Modern Slavery Act and similar legislation are triggering companies to publish disclosure statements, update policies and generally increase their transparency with regard to measures they are or are not taking to combat forced labour in their global supply chains, this body of legislation also opens up a new source of information for researchers.

This chapter focuses on how legal research can secure and analyse data about how companies address forced labour in their global supply chains. Related to this question, the chapter seeks to demonstrate how such methods can complement research on the business models of forced labour in global supply chains in disciplines such as politics and management studies (Crane & LeBaron 2018).

Securing reliable data on the commercial relationships between buyers and suppliers poses several challenges, however, particularly as supply chain relations

[1] Dr Andreas Rühmkorf is a member of Sustainable Market Actors for Responsible Trade (SMART) (smart.uio.no). SMART has received funding from the European Union's Horizon 2020 research and innovation programme under grant agreement No. 693642, and we gratefully acknowledge its support.

Proceedings of the British Academy, **220**, 148–166. © The British Academy 2018.

are by nature private. For example, the UK's Freedom of Information Act 2000, which provides members of the public with the right to request information, only covers public bodies. It is therefore difficult to access reliable empirical data that lends insights into how multinational enterprises are addressing forced labour in their global supply chains in practice and how effective these efforts are. One often overlooked option for researchers, however, is to work with information that companies publish either voluntarily or as a result of disclosure laws.

The chapter builds on and deepens scholarship on legal research methods and the opportunities and limitations of empirical legal research (see, for example, Cane & Kritzer 2010) in the context of business policies on forced labour, and thus makes two conceptual contributions. First, it argues that although the private nature of commercial relationships and the weakness of transparency laws constitute significant challenges for research in this area – and companies are not required to report specific or consistent information – it is nevertheless possible to gain valuable insights into business practices on CSR issues in global supply chains through the empirical legal analysis of publicly available documents. Empirical legal research can also complement research on forced labour in global supply chains in other social science disciplines. This discussion thus also contributes to debates about the further development of empirical legal research methods. Second, the chapter argues that the availability of reliable data on forced labour in global supply chains would be improved if governments made disclosure laws more stringent, by requiring companies to disclose reliable information and demonstrate the effectiveness of efforts designed to improve corporate accountability.

The chapter will begin by discussing the underlying framework of corporate transparency, and providing an overview of the data that this regulatory landscape is generating in the form of voluntary information disclosure and mandatory company publications. It will then further frame the debate about legal research methods and their potential contribution to interdisciplinary research on forced labour, before outlining the challenges of empirical legal research of business policies on forced labour in global supply chains. To demonstrate the value of these methods in practice, I will introduce two case studies: the first on how 25 FTSE 100 companies in the United Kingdom address forced labour and bribery in their supply chain, and the second on the compliance rating of the top 30 listed Germany companies. These two case studies will illustrate how research on business policies for forced labour can be conducted given these challenges. The chapter concludes with practical recommendations for researching business polices on CSR in global supply chains, as well as suggestions for how disclosure laws could improve the accountability of companies.

In terms of its jurisdictional scope, this chapter primarily focuses on English law (although many laws apply to the whole of the United Kingdom, English law and Scottish law are distinct legal systems, see Zweigert & Kötz 1998: 201–4). English law is illustrative of the situation in many other countries of a similar legal, political and socio-economic makeup that are also home to many multinational enterprises. Where appropriate, laws from other jurisdictions are referred to in order to demonstrate international legislative trends.

Whilst the two case studies originate in two different countries, it is important to note that they have not been chosen in order to compare CSR norms in these two countries, but rather as a means to illustrate how research on business policies can be conducted despite the challenges posed by private commercial relations. While the laws that constitute some of these challenges are similar, an in-depth comparison between the socio-economic, legal and political environments that companies operate in in those two countries is beyond the scope of this chapter. Rather, the chapter uses these two case studies as useful illustrations of arguments related to the possible contribution of empirical legal research to forced labour research.

The emerging field of disclosure laws on CSR issues: regulation through transparency

Tracking down accurate and reliable information about multinational enterprises' commercial relationships with supplier firms has long been a challenge for researchers. Companies are often secretive about dynamics they consider to be commercially sensitive or have the potential to damage their reputations with consumers, including information on companies they source their goods from, their conditions of purchase and manufacture, and the logistics around how the goods are transported from factory to retail. However, over the last five years or so, this situation has begun to change as companies are increasingly publishing information about their suppliers, policies and sourcing practices on their websites. Indeed, there is much information available nowadays, including sustainability and CSR reports, as well as information about the compliance practice of companies. Some of the publications accessible on companies' websites are voluntary, while others have been required by law to publish by a recent wave of transparency legislation.[2]

Disclosure is classified as a communication-based regulatory instrument intended to 'regulate behaviour by enriching the information available to the target audience' (Morgan & Yeung 2007: 96), therefore enabling the audience to make informed choices which, in turn, should lead to the promotion of the regulatory objectives, e.g. companies combating forced labour in their supply chains. The purpose of transparency is thus to increase accountability; to reduce information asymmetries between corporate executives and company stakeholders, including shareholders; to make markets work more efficiently; and to enhance trust and cooperation (Haufler 2010: 55).

---

[2] Hereafter, this chapter will use the terms 'transparency' and 'disclosure' interchangeably.

Private forms of voluntary disclosure on non-financial information by companies developed during the early 1990s in the form of environmental reports (Owen & O'Dwyer 2008: 389). In general, private governance instruments often fill the gaps left by the absence of public regulation (Bernstein & Cashore 2007: 347–71). Private labour standards in global supply chains consist of a diverse range of private actors and are of varying reach and levels of stringency (Fransen 2012). Companies adopt voluntary reporting practices to build a positive image of themselves for the public (Kurucz *et al.* 2008: 83–112), but such reporting regimes are based on corporate-led dialogue (Owen & O'Dwyer 2008: 405): companies can decide what to report or whether to report at all. In addition, there is no level playing field between companies. Researchers working with information that companies voluntarily disclose therefore face the risk of collecting patchy and unreliable data. In addition, there are risks to taking companies' voluntary reporting at face value, given their vested interest in portraying their practices in the best possible light.

With this context in mind, the public regulation of transparency may appear to be an instrument for improving reporting practices. The recent trend towards transparency legislation is not just prevalent in the United Kingdom; it is a transnational development. The transparency in supply chains clause in the UK Modern Slavery Act 2015, for example, requires companies to publish an annual statement with information about the steps the organisation has taken during the financial year to ensure that slavery and human trafficking are not taking place in their supply chain or to publicly state that it has taken no such steps (UK Modern Slavery Act 2015: s54). Statutory reporting requirements of non-financial issues in other countries, of varying stringency, include the California Transparency in Supply Chains Act 2010, the US Business Supply Chain Transparency on Trafficking and Slavery Act of 2015 and the US Dodd-Frank Act regulation of conflict minerals (see for more comprehensive overviews of the regulatory landscape: LeBaron & Rühmkorf 2017: 15–28; Phillips *et al.* 2016). At the time of writing, further developments towards more corporate transparency in other countries are under way: Australia is currently considering adopting national legislation to combat modern slavery, comparable to the UK's Modern Slavery Act 2015. While Germany has not enacted a similar piece of legislation on modern slavery, it is currently implementing the EU Directive on non-financial information disclosure. This upcoming legislation will require public-interest entities with more than 500 employees to include a non-financial statement containing information on environmental, social and employee matters, among others, in their management report. The law will be based on a 'comply or explain' approach, which means that when a company does not have a policy for the issues named in the law, it will be required to provide an explanation.

Interestingly, the existing public governance forms of reporting have received much criticism (see, for example, Villiers on the non-financial reporting requirements in the UK Companies Act 2006, 2013: 97–129). In fact, the weakness of most of these statutory reporting requirements is that they are 'soft touch' laws, with few binding requirements. For example, the UK Modern Slavery Act only requires companies to report on 'the steps' they have taken in order to combat forced labour (see for an assessment Henty & Holdsworth 2015: 11). Section 54(5) lists a number of factors that a company 'may' report on, such as its due diligence processes, but it does not require companies to report on them. The quantity and quality of reports by companies therefore vary and can be unreliable, as companies are under no obligation to publish any key indicator factors or externally verified audit reports.

The emerging trend towards transparency legislation is part of a changing regulatory landscape. Whereas, traditionally, regulation was the domain of the state, there is now a much more diversified set of standard setters (Bottomley & Bronitt 2006: 312–24). Regulation can thus be understood broadly as 'all mechanisms of social control or influence affecting behaviour from whatever source, whether intentional or not' (Black 2001: 129), and it does not need to originate from the state. It also includes other means of exercising social control or influence to affect behaviour, including 'unintentional and non-state processes' (Baldwin & Cave 1999: 2). An understanding including this range of regulatory forms – including public and private, national and international – accounts for the decline of state-based public regulation, which is a development that has occurred in many sectors over several decades (Vogel 2008: 266).

The recent wave of transparency legislation on CSR issues such as forced labour can be seen as an attempt by the home states of multinational enterprises to use public governance to fill the 'regulatory gap' (Fransen & Burgoon 2012: 236–9) in global supply chains, especially as reports about gross violations of CSR principles in global supply chains are recurrent. Some have highlighted the complementary role of the public and private forms of governance, such as Locke (2013: 177), who argues that public governance and private governance need to 'work together and build off of one another'. This public–private interaction provides many opportunities for research on, for example, how companies respond to these public governance measures. Given the unevenness of information, and given the bias introduced by using reports generated by companies, however, transparency reporting is not always and everywhere the advance for researchers that we might expect it to be.

Legal research methods and research on forced labour

Before looking at the challenges and opportunities for such research, we must first consider the role of legal research in the context of research on forced labour. Traditionally, legal research in the United Kingdom was the domain of doctrinal (often called 'black-letter') research. Doctrinal legal research is considered to be a hermeneutical discipline, as it focuses on the interpretation of texts and documents according to standard methods (van Hoecke 2011: 4). A doctrinal legal approach 'criticises, explains, corrects and directs legal doctrines' (Birks 1996: ix), and answers a concrete legal question (van Hoecke 2011: 4). According to Van Gestel and Micklitz (2011), the basis for arguments in doctrinal legal research is found in authoritative sources, such as existing rules, principles, precedents and scholarly publications. Thus, legal doctrine presents the law as a coherent system, which case decisions adhere to.

Van Hoecke (2011: 4) summarises his analysis of legal doctrine as follows:

> Legal scholars collect empirical data (statutes, cases, etc.), word hypotheses on their meaning and scope, which they test, using the classic canons of interpretation. In a next stage, they build theories . . . which they test and from which they derive new hypotheses . . . Described in this way, doctrinal legal scholarship fits perfectly with the methodology of other disciplines.

Doctrinal legal research usually concentrates on primary source materials (legislation and the leading cases). It focuses on the interpretation of 'traditional legal materials' (Cownie & Bradney 2013: 34). It has been defined as 'research which asks what the law is in a particular area' (McConville & Chui 2007: 18). Therefore, in the context of forced labour in global supply chains, traditional doctrinal legal research would focus on a critical assessment of the transparency in supply chains clause in the Modern Slavery Act 2015. Such research would, *inter alia*, assess the wording of the statutory provision, its mode of operation and its potential impact through legal interpretation. What this research does *not* do, however, is to study how companies react to this legislation, i.e. how they engage with forced labour in their supply chain, for example, through business policies. These issues could be addressed by socio-legal research, i.e. legal research that uses methods taken from disciplines in the social sciences (McConville & Chui 2007: 5). The difference between doctrinal legal research and socio-legal research is often illustrated through reference to the former as 'law in books' and to the latter as 'law in action' (McConville & Chui 2007: 5). Importantly, socio-legal research includes quantitative and qualitative research. In quantitative legal research statistical and econometric methods are applied 'in order to test whether and how legal rules matter in the real world' (Siems & Síthigh 2012: 656). An example of qualitative legal research is the interviewing of judges with the aim of studying aspects of the judicial function and practice (Jaremba & Mak 2014: 5).

Therefore, socio-legal research broadens the opportunities of legal research in the field of forced labour in global supply chains, as it enables researchers to move beyond the interpretation of statutory texts and cases. Thus, researchers employing socio-legal research methods can address research questions related to the way companies address forced labour in the legislative environment of the Modern Slavery Act in documents such as codes of conduct, terms and conditions of purchase, and CSR/sustainability reports, as a complement to doctrinal legal research of the Act itself. Moreover, it also adds to theoretical and empirical studies on the business of forced labour in global supply chains in other disciplines such as politics and management. Empirical legal studies can, for example, focus on the stringency of corporate policies on forced labour and thus make valuable contributions to research in other disciplines. In the first case study below, I discuss research that I conducted with a co-author to investigate whether the Modern Slavery Act changed companies' efforts to address forced labour in their supply chains using documentary analysis of various publicly available documents of companies. Documentary sources are considered to 'provide a rich source of data' (Webley 2010: 938). The analysis of documents is influenced by the nature of the documents. In the example here, the chosen research method of documentary analysis made it possible to assess similarities and differences among a set of 25 FTSE 100 companies. An advantage of this method, then, was to provide insight into the behaviour of a larger set of companies than would have been possible through other qualitative methods, such as a single-company case study.

It is important to note that black-letter legal research and empirical legal research are not necessarily exclusive or in contradiction. Rather, it is important to appreciate the opportunities and the limitations that each respective research method offers in any given case. When researching forced labour policies of multinational enterprises, both research methods complement each other well. Whilst doctrinal research enables the researcher to fully study and evaluate how the transparency in supply chains clause is drafted, empirical legal research allows the researcher to gain insights into the practical impact of the legislation on companies.

The challenges of conducting research on business policies

Researching business policies on forced labour in global supply chains comes with significant challenges. First of all, there is limited access to reliable data due to the private nature of contracts (Andrews 2015: 6–7). The reason for this is that the contractual documents between the buyers (i.e. the Western multinational enterprises) and their suppliers, such as purchase order forms, are not publicly available. Indeed, there is limited material available online, given that supply contracts are of a sensitive commercial nature. Companies have an interest not to share with competitors and the general public information about the quantity and quality of goods that they order, for example. Contracts are based on the agreement between the parties of the contract (Smits 2014: 41–62).

The limited availability of private commercial data can be understood in the context of the public–private divide (Cane 2011: 18). The contractual relations between buyers and suppliers are a matter of contract law and are thus part of private law. Private law is generally considered to be a residual area, i.e. the area of the law that is not public law. It is often not defined in common law systems what private law is (Hedley 2011: 89). Public law is commonly defined as being concerned with relations between the individual and the state as well as the distribution of power between public institutions and a range of non-governmental organisations (Oliver 1999: 14). The essential criterion for distinguishing between public law and private law is the function they perform. Hence, if the function is a governmental activity, then it is public law (Lord Woolf 1995: 62). Private law, in contrast, is the system that protects the private rights of private individuals or the private rights of public bodies. Hedley notes that private law would often be described as 'the law between private individuals that is contrasted with the law involving organs of the state which is public law' (2011: 89). As private law thus establishes rules that regulate private rights between private individuals, it covers areas such as contract law and tort law. The fact that the supply contracts are part of private law and are therefore on the private side of the public–private divide has important ramifications for research. As private law, these contracts are not subject to the accountability regime that exists for public law such as through judicial review mechanisms or through the Human Rights Act. This situation exacerbates the challenges that exist for anyone wanting to research in this area.

Second, and closely linked to the public–private divide, members of the public cannot make freedom of information requests about the contractual supply chain documents. The reason is that the Freedom of Information Act 2000 provides public access to information held by public authorities unless there is a good reason for it to be refused. This means all recorded information held by a public authority. There is no public access to information held by private parties. The Freedom of Information Act only covers public authorities. Anyone can make a freedom of information request (Freedom of Information Act 2000, section 1).

The purpose of the Freedom of Information Act is that the citizens should have a right to access information about the work of public authorities in order to make these accountable to the public for the work that they are doing with taxpayers' money (ICO 2015: 5). The definition of a public authority also includes companies that are wholly owned by the Crown, by the wider public sector or by both the Crown and the wider public sector (Freedom of Information Act 2000, section 6). However, this extension to publicly owned companies does not include private companies. Whilst there have been debates around the effects of the privatisation of government functions on accountability through freedom of information laws, this does not affect the situation where private companies – which are not owned by public authorities – enter into supply contracts (Bunker & Davis 1998: 464).

Third, the difficulty of accessing reliable data related to the engagement of Western multinational enterprises with forced labour prevention in their supply chain is further exacerbated by the structure of global supply chains. The global supply chain of companies often spans different levels of suppliers and sub-suppliers. This makes it difficult to assess the reality of the CSR record of multinational enterprises in their supply chains as many cases of gross violations of CSR principles, such as the use of forced labour, occur at supplier factories, at the bottom of the global supply chain in developing countries and far removed from the buyer at the top of the chain (LeBaron 2014: 245). Moreover, existing auditing regimes are often flawed. For example, the Rana Plaza building in Bangladesh which collapsed in 2013 was audited twice by Primark before it collapsed, but the audit did not include a structural survey (Jones 2014).

Fourth, as indicated above, there is a lack of quality of non-financial information disclosure (Aiyegbayo & Villiers 2011: 700). Companies tend to only describe how they are implementing their CSR principles in their supply chain and how they care about the working conditions at their supplier factories, without providing a full picture with facts, figures and externally verified reports.

Fifth, researchers can, of course, contact companies directly and ask for access to private commercial data such as purchase order forms, terms and conditions of purchase or supplier codes of conduct, but the experience of this author suggests that such endeavours have limited success.

Researching business policies on forced labour despite challenges

These challenges shape and limit researchers' access to information, but should not discourage scholars from studying company practices in relation to forced labour. There are ways around these constraints. Transparency regulation is improving the situation and prompting companies to make information public, although this creates new challenges as detailed above. In my own work, I have used company documents, including CSR reports and supplier codes of conduct, to assess company practices and the impact of recent legislation on those practices. This section of the chapter will briefly describe the methods and evidence base of two of my recent studies, in the hope of further illustrating the opportunities and challenges of this research approach. The first case study focused on research on forced labour and bribery policies of UK companies, whereas the second case study focused on research on compliance by the top 30 listed German companies.

The first case study is about a research project that assessed how the UK Modern Slavery Act and the UK Bribery Act impact on how multinational enterprises address the issues of forced labour and bribery in their global supply chains. In this research project, empirical legal research was used to examine a number of issues, including supplier codes of conduct, terms and conditions of purchase (where available) and company reports. At times, companies had posted only some of this information, so I reached out to them to secure further data. Often I didn't receive the extra documentation requested despite repeated attempts, and simply acknowledged the company's refusal to provide documentation within the methods section of my papers. In this study (LeBaron & Rühmkorf 2017: 15–28), my co-author and I used company documentation to assess the effectiveness of the Modern Slavery Act in spurring changes to company practices regarding forced labour in global supply chains, focusing in particular on sourcing practices, policies and contracts. We did so by analysing for 25 FTSE 100 companies: 1) own code of conduct; 2) supplier code of conduct; 3) terms and conditions of purchase for suppliers; 4) CSR and sustainability reports for 2015 and 2016 (the years before and after the publication of the Act); and 5) any other documentation on the website specific to forced labour policy.

Our approach was based on the recognition that companies publish a number of documents that can be utilised for research into their business practices, such as the annual CSR/sustainability report, which typically contains information on how companies approach issues like forced labour. Whilst there is an ongoing debate about the lack of quality of reporting despite the quantity of reports (Ethical Corporation 2015), these CSR documents can be a useful source for evaluating how companies approach different CSR issues. Moreover, a company's code of conduct can usually be found online. Companies with brand reputation normally publish information about CSR and their supply chain, which often includes the supplier code of conduct. Some companies also publish their terms and conditions of purchase, which can be used in legal assessments of how different CSR issues are addressed in supply contracts.

Due to the availability of these documents, the information gathering itself is not so much of a problem; the challenge is rather the process of information evaluation. For example, in this case study, we had to deal with the issue that the full contracts between the UK companies and their overseas suppliers are not in the public domain, as these are between private commercial entities. However, the fact that several companies make their terms and conditions of purchase and/or their supplier code of conduct available enabled us to study how the companies address bribery and forced labour in their supplier relations. This is an important insight as these two issues are subject to regulation at different stringency levels. We decided to use documentary analysis as a method to study the different documents about how FTSE 100 companies address forced labour and bribery in their supply chains, as this allowed us to look at a bigger sample of companies across different industries and economic sectors. That way, we hoped to be able to discover patterns of behaviour at a more general level than by conducting interviews with fewer companies. Moreover, given the reluctance of companies to share information that is not already in the public domain, it also appeared a more suitable research strategy to assess documents that were openly accessible and thus to work within the framework of available material. The purpose of this analysis was to complement the doctrinal legal analysis of the approaches to supply chain regulation taken in the Bribery Act and the Modern Slavery Act by studying the approach of business to these two areas within this legislative framework.

We first looked at the contractual quality of clauses and provisions regarding bribery and forced labour in the terms and conditions and supplier codes of conduct and applied means of legal interpretation such as wording and purpose in order to assess the stringency of, for example, clauses in terms and conditions of purchase and supplier codes of conduct. The analysis of the contractual documents was therefore influenced by traditional techniques of legal interpretation in order to have an objective standard to measure the stringency of these policies. This approach allowed us to determine the effect of these clauses in the supply contracts and to thus evaluate how these companies address forced labour and bribery in their contractual relations with their suppliers. We assessed how those clauses are drafted, how binding the wording of provisions related to bribery and forced labour are, and which obligations are imposed on suppliers. This approach allowed us to identify, for example, if the companies apply due diligence mechanisms to the issues of bribery and forced labour.

Second, we complemented this assessment of contractual documents with the documentary analysis of the 25 company CSR/sustainability reports. Here, we posed the following questions: What is the frequency of incidents of forced labour or bribery? How extensive is the reporting on these two issues? What is the content of the reporting? Once more, we applied techniques of interpretation that looked at the quantity of reporting (frequency, amount of reporting) as well as the quality of reporting, which included questions like: What language do the companies use to outline their approach to these two issues, i.e. do they write in a firm (e.g. 'anti', 'zero tolerance') or in a more aspirational manner (e.g. 'we strive to')? Are forced labour and/or bribery treated as individual sections or do they fall under a general reporting topic (e.g. human rights)?

In short, we drew together and analysed company documents into a database that shed light on how company policies and practices had evolved since the publication of the Act. We supplemented this with an in-depth case study of a single company that covered a longer timespan, to triangulate our findings and to gain a broader and clearer sense of how company policy evolved over time.

Methodologically, this documentary analysis enabled us to overcome some of the challenges described earlier in this chapter such as the limited access to reliable data due to the private nature of contracts between buyer and supplier companies and the non-availability of freedom of information requests about the contractual supply chain documents. While it may not be possible to access documents that companies choose not to share, our approach illustrates that analysing documents available online can help researchers reach important insights and detect patterns of behaviour.

We discovered that there were two very different approaches to combating bribery and forced labour. In short, bribery appeared to have become a genuine compliance issue, whereas forced labour remains one of many human rights issues that companies address with less stringency than compliance issues. This was evident not only in the contractual documents (there were often clauses that were longer and more specific on bribery), but also in reporting practices. Reporting on bribery prevention was much more frequent and prominent, and the language used regarding bribery typically included words such as 'anti' or 'zero tolerance'. Forced labour, in comparison, was an issue that was addressed in a more aspirational manner. This contrast is important as it complements the doctrinal finding that the criminal liability of companies in the Bribery Act is likely to lead to more stringent business policies – particularly the implementation of due diligence mechanisms – than the transparency regulation in the Modern Slavery Act.

Overall, the documentary analysis therefore enabled us to work within the challenges associated with accessing private commercial data from supply chains. Whilst it is not possible to entirely overcome the various challenges, it is possible to work within the existing framework and to utilise publicly available data on global supply chains in order to gain insights into business practices and, particularly, to compare approaches to different topics. This research did not assess the approach of companies before and after the enactment of the respective Acts; it nevertheless allowed us to view how policies and reporting on the two issues differ, which, in turn, complements a purely doctrinal legal assessment of the statutory provisions. The key advantage of our approach is that it provided a reliable documentary evidence base to assess how far and in what ways the Modern Slavery Act was effective in spurring corporate accountability for forced labour in supply chains.

A second example further underscores the challenges of research approaches that rely on companies to provide data, and the importance of locating data on websites and elsewhere. The second study focused on a rating that a German business magazine conducted of how transparent the DAX30[3] companies are about their compliance activities. We understand 'compliance' to mean adherence to standards, regulations and other requirements such as voluntarily adopted codes of conduct (Ghassemi-Thabir *et al.* 2016: 14). I was asked to help in developing and conducting the transparency rating. Whilst at the outset of the project the majority of the companies had stated their intention to fill in a survey, they changed their minds once they received the survey. In fact, all companies eventually declined the request and thus withdrew their support for the rating. A variety of reasons were given, including that such a rating would not be possible. The survey consisted of 30 questions on a number of compliance-related issues, such as the size of the compliance team in relation to the firm, the number of violations of the company's code of conduct in the previous year and the number of annual trainings of all staff on the provisions of the code of conduct. Although in the end the survey of companies was unsuccessful due to the companies' withdrawal from the study, our interactions with the companies were highly illuminating and gave us

---

[3] The DAX is the German stock index.

an interesting (albeit unexpected) set of insights into company policies and behaviour with regard to compliance issues. Following the companies' refusal to fill in the survey, the challenge for the evaluation of the companies' compliance systems was the absence of internal data on issues such as violations of the company code of conduct or the existence, use and effectiveness of whistle-blower systems and compliance trainings for staff. We therefore decided to shift our focus to publicly available, external data. The key issue for us was, again, to develop a research method capable of evaluating publicly available data. This constituted a particular challenge due to the absence of the important data mentioned in this section (i.e. size of compliance team; frequency of compliance trainings; number of violations of code of conduct).

We therefore decided to shift the focus of the rating to assessing the 'compliance transparency' of companies. By 'compliance transparency' we mean the way that companies are transparent about their compliance system. Assessing compliance transparency includes analysing the external assessments of the companies' compliance organisation, their recognition and administration of compliance duties and compliance risks, as well as how they present their compliance culture. We also evaluated the stringency of policies that the companies have adopted and published, such as their employee code of conduct and their supplier code of conduct. It is important to note that the prevention of the use of forced labour plays an important role in these documents. Moreover, in Germany, companies are under a statutory duty to issue a declaration of compliance with the recommendations of the German Corporate Governance Code (Aktiengesetz, section 161). Companies that do not comply with one or more recommendations have to explain why. This is therefore a further important, publicly available source of information related to compliance.

The limitation of this research method is that assessing compliance transparency might not, in every case, draw an accurate picture of how seriously companies address compliance. For example, a company that has serious human rights violations at the bottom of its supply chain may adopt the most stringent code of conduct and present its compliance system in the most detailed way. It is, however, possible to evaluate how transparent each company is. Companies that are more transparent about their compliance approach are also more likely to have a well-functioning compliance system. A lack of transparency constitutes an investment risk as, where violations of statutory duties by a company become apparent, the public will look at the quantity and quality of information that this company has made available beforehand. Given the lack of available information, we decided to call the assessment a rating rather than a ranking. A rating allows us to award levels to companies (such as triple A rating for the credit rating of countries) that appear to be operating at a similar standard. The example of this rating illustrates that, despite significant challenges due to the private nature of commercial data, it is nevertheless possible to design research that provides important insights concerning company approaches.

While these two examples are based on anecdotal evidence, they are useful for illustrating the challenges that researchers face when assessing issues related to companies' private commercial data and possible ways to overcome these challenges. The bad news is that it proves to be difficult to access information that companies choose not to make publicly available, despite these issues being of interest to a wider community of stakeholders. The good news is that as a number of governments impose transparency requirements, stakeholder groups are compiling company statements and documents into user-friendly databases that eliminate some of these challenges for researchers. TISCREPORT, for instance, at the time of writing had drawn together 45,000+ company statements published under transparency legislation in ten jurisdictions.[4]

As these case studies are based on research in two different countries, it is worth noting the different legal and political environments that companies in the two countries operate in, since these could have an impact on what information companies share with researchers and the public. While Germany is a civil-law jurisdiction, meaning that statutes are the only primary source of law, England and Wales are a common-law jurisdiction, in which both cases and statutes are primary sources of the law (Zweigert & Kötz 1998). In Germany, the ongoing emphasis on public governance can be seen by the fact that softer forms of company regulation such as the German Corporate Governance Code are often seen as lacking democratic legitimacy (Martin 2002: 59–60). This situation differs from the United Kingdom's system of regulating companies, in which softer forms of regulation are more embedded in the legal and political culture (Moore 2013: 913–56). The different approach to regulating companies in the two countries is also evident in the varieties of capitalism theory (Hall & Soskice 2001). However, despite their different approaches for regulating companies, the challenges for researching business policies are similar in both jurisdictions. Whilst there is much information published voluntarily by companies, the quality of reporting varies and companies are reluctant (as evidenced by the case studies here) to share information other than what they choose to release.

The two case studies reinforce the chapter's argument that it is possible to gain insights into corporate practices on issues such as forced labour in global supply chains despite the significant challenges outlined above. Whilst the challenges cannot be completely overcome due to the absence of freedom of information requests for private commercial contracts and the inconsistent reporting quality of companies, companies do make information available on their websites that can be utilised for research about corporate practices. This material is published online partly in response to laws on non-financial information disclosure and partly in response to pressure from the media and NGOs. Moreover, there are also some

---

[4] See https://tiscreport.org/organisations-with-statements

documents publicly available that are not primarily intended for CSR reputation management, but rather as information for current and possible future business partners such as suppliers (e.g. terms and conditions of purchase). Such material can provide valuable insights too.

Recommendations for empirical research of business policies

The main argument of this chapter is that, despite significant challenges, it is possible to gather information for research projects, as publicly available documents provide ample opportunities for research on how companies address issues of forced labour.

The first step of research based on publicly available data is to recognise what such an analysis of the data has the potential to achieve, as well as what it cannot achieve. For example, information published by companies that is not externally verified does not provide data about actual occurrences of forced labour. However, it is possible – as illustrated in the first example – to use this data for specific purposes. The different ways companies treat bribery and forced labour can be assessed irrespective of the actual prevalence of bribery and forced labour in the supply chains of companies. Working with data that is available online requires a careful web-based search. Some information, such as a company's CSR/sustainability report, is relatively straightforward to find. The same usually applies to the code of conduct of companies. The availability of additional, more specific information varies by individual company and can differ significantly. Whilst most companies publish their supplier code of conduct, fewer make the terms and conditions of purchase for their supply chain available. Also, it is important for researchers to recognise that not all of the relevant information can necessarily be found in the CSR/sustainability section of company websites. Instead, there might be separate sections intended for use by current and prospective suppliers, and these sections might contain information such as terms and conditions of purchase, self-auditing documents, etc. Anyone wishing to research the approach of companies to their supply chain might find useful information in those sections. So, whilst researchers cannot overcome the barriers of the private commercial nature of the relations between suppliers and buyers, they can access documents online that could provide interesting insights into business practices and important research opportunities. This chapter has sought to demonstrate that empirical legal research of publicly available corporate documents can not only complement traditional legal analysis of cases and statutes, but can also complement research into the business of forced labour in other disciplines.

Whilst the public–private divide limits the access to information about business practices, the present state of non-financial information reporting needs to be considerably improved. It is unfortunate that the statutory requirements of corporate transparency on issues such as forced labour are very soft and amount to little more than requiring what companies often already voluntarily disclose to the public. Meaningful disclosure laws could help fill the information gap in global supply chains, for example by requiring companies to conduct and to publish external audits of their supply chains, including information about risk-based due diligence processes. The public regulation of corporate transparency has the potential to level the playing field for companies covered by a disclosure duty. It can therefore lead to more information coherence and reliability, but it will only achieve this if it is specific and if it requires companies to provide certain facts and figures rather than leaving it largely to them to choose what information they provide. Such requirements would enable interested parties, including researchers and civil society, to engage with the conduct of companies on the basis of reliable data and thus promote accountability in the area of forced labour.

Conclusion

This chapter has shown how empirical legal research of business policies on forced labour in global supply chains can complement both traditional doctrinal legal research and research in other disciplines. There are significant challenges for researching commercial data on forced labour in global supply chains due to the private nature of buyer–supplier relationships. Freedom of information requests are not available for these private relationships, which makes it difficult for researchers to access reliable data. This chapter suggests ways in which researchers can utilise the documents that are publicly available for empirical research despite these challenges. It is argued that publicly available documents provide ample opportunities for research, but researchers need to recognise that the data only answers some research questions, such as an assessment of the stringency of corporate policies on different CSR issues. Still, research of such documents would strongly benefit from more meaningful disclosure laws, which could eliminate the information deficit resulting from the public–private divide. Existing disclosure laws, such as the transparency in supply chain clause in the Modern Slavery Act, are too vague and general and do not sufficiently require companies to publish externally verified data and facts about their supply chain. Stricter disclosure laws would therefore be an important step for future research of forced labour in global supply chains.

References

Aiyegbayo, O. & Villiers, C. (2011), 'The Enhanced Business Review: Has It Made Corporate Governance More Effective?', *Journal of Business Law*, 7: 699–724.

Andrews, N. (2015), *Contract Law*, 2nd edn (Cambridge, Cambridge University Press).

Baldwin, R. & Cave, M. (1999), *Understanding Regulation: Theory, Strategy and Practice* (Oxford, Oxford University Press).

Bernstein, S. & Cashore, B. (2007), 'Can Non-state Global Governance Be Legitimate? An Analytical Framework', *Regulation & Governance*, 1: 347.

Birks, P. (1996), 'Editor's Preface', in P. Birks (ed.), *What Are Law Schools For?* (Oxford, Oxford University Press), ix.

Black, J. (2001), 'Decentring Regulation: Understanding the Role of Regulation and Self-regulation in a Post-regulatory World', *Current Legal Problems*, 54: 103, 129.

Bottomley, S. & Bronitt, S. (2006), *Law in Context*, 3rd edn (Leichhardt, The Federation Press).

Bunker, M. & Davis, C. (1998), 'Privatized Government Functions and Freedom of Information: Public Accountability in an Age of Private Governance', *Journalism and Mass Communication Quarterly*, 75: 3.

Cane, P. (2011), *Administrative Law* (Oxford, Oxford University Press).

Cane, P. & Kritzer, H. (eds) (2010), *The Oxford Handbook of Empirical Legal Research* (Oxford, Oxford University Press).

Cownie, F. & Bradney, A. (2013), 'Socio-legal Studies: A Challenge to the Doctrinal Approach', in D. Watkins & M. Burton (eds), *Research Methods in Law* (Abingdon, Routledge), 34.

Crane, A. & LeBaron, G. (2018), 'Methodological Challenges in the Business of Forced Labour', in G. LeBaron, *Researching Forced Labour in the Global Economy* (Oxford, Oxford University Press).

Ethical Corporation (2015), '"Over-Reporting": Quality Not Quantity for CSR Reporting?', accessed 21 October 2016, http://www.ethicalcorp.com/communications-reporting/over-reporting-quality-not-quantity-csr-reporting

Fransen, L. (2012), *Corporate Social Responsibility and Global Labor Standards: Firms and Activists in the Making of Private Regulation* (Abingdon, Routledge).

Fransen, L. & Burgoon, B. (2012), 'A Market for Worker Rights: Explaining Business Support for International Private Labour Regulation', *Review of International Political Economy*, 19: 236.

Ghassemi-Thabir, N. *et al.* (eds) (2016), *Corporate Compliance: Praxisleitfaden für die Unternehmensführung* (Düsseldorf, Handelsblatt Fachmedien).

Hall, P. & Soskice, D. (2001), *Varieties of Capitalism: The Institutional Foundations of Comparative Advantage* (Oxford, Oxford University Press).

Haufler, V. (2010), 'Disclosure as Governance: The Extractive Industries Transparency Initiative and Resource Management in the Developing World', *Global Environmental Policies*, 10: 53.

Hedley, S. (2011), 'Is Private Law Meaningless?', *Current Legal Problems*, 64: 89.

Henty, P. & Holdsworth, S. (2015), 'Big Businesses and Modern Slavery: What Your Organisation Should Be Doing', *Compliance & Risk*, 4, 4: 11–13.

Information Commissioner's Office (2015), 'The Guide to Freedom of Information', https://ico.org.uk/for-organisations/guide-to-freedom-of-information/

Jaremba, U. & Mak, E. (2014), 'Interviewing Judges in the Transnational Context', *Law and Method*, 5, http://www.lawandmethod.nl/tijdschrift/lawandmethod/2014/05/RENM-D-13-00002

Jones, D. (2014), 'How the World Has Changed since Rana Plaza', *Vogue* (1 April 2014), accessed 21 October 2016, http://www.vogue.co.uk/article/bangladesh-rana-plaza-anniversary-fashion-revolution-day

Kurucz, E. C., Colbert, B. A. & Wheeler, D. (2008), 'The Business Case for Corporate Social Responsibility', in A. Crane *et al.* (eds), *Oxford Handbook of Corporate Social Responsibility* (Oxford, Oxford University Press), 83–112.

LeBaron, G. (2014), 'Subcontracting Is Not Illegal, but Is It Unethical? Business Ethics, Forced Labor, and Economic Success', *Brown Journal of World Affairs*, 20, 2: 237.

Phillips, N., LeBaron, G. & Wallin, S. (2016), *Mapping and Measuring the Effectiveness of Labour-Related Disclosure Requirements for Global Supply Chains* (Geneva, ILO).

LeBaron, G. & Rühmkorf, A. (2017), 'Steering CSR through Home State Regulation: A Comparison of the Impact of the UK Bribery Act and Modern Slavery Act on Global Supply Chain Governance', *Global Policy*, 8, S3: 15–28.

Locke, R. (2013), *The Promise and Limits of Private Power* (New York, Cambridge University Press).

Lord Woolf (1995), 'Droit Public: English Style', *Public Law*, spring: 57–71.

McConville, M. & Chui, W H. (eds) (2007), *Research Methods for Law* (Edinburgh, Edinburgh University Press).

Martin, W. (2002), 'Corporate Governance: Der Import angelsächsischer "Self-Regulation" im Widerstreit zum deutschen Parlamentsvorbehalt', *Zeitschrift für Rechtspolitik*, 7: 59.

Moore, M. (2013), 'United Kingdom', in A. Fleckner and K. Hopt (eds), *Comparative Corporate Governance: A Functional and International Analysis* (Cambridge, Cambridge University Press), 913.

Morgan, B. & Yeung, K. (2007), *An Introduction to Law and Regulation: Text and Materials* (Cambridge, Cambridge University Press).

Oliver, D. (1999), *Common Values and the Public–Private Divide* (London, Butterworths).

Owen, D. & O'Dwyer, B. (2008), 'Corporate Social Responsibility: The Reporting and Assurance Dimension', in A. Crane *et al.* (eds), *Oxford Handbook of Corporate Social Responsibility* (Oxford, Oxford University Press), 384–409.

Siems, M. & Mac Síthigh, D. (2012), 'Mapping Legal Research' *Cambridge Law Journal*, 71: 651.

Smits, J. (2014), *Contract Law: A Comparative Introduction* (Cheltenham, Edward Elgar Publishing).

UK Modern Slavery Act (2015), accessed 20 July 2018, http://www.legislation.gov.uk/ukpga/2015/30/contents/enacted

van Gestel, R. & Micklitz, H.-W. (2011), 'Revitalizing Doctrinal Legal Research in Europe: What About Methodology?', EUI Law, Working Paper, 2011/05.

van Hoecke, M. (2011), 'Legal Doctrine: Which Method(s) for What Kind of Discipline?', in M. van Hoecke (ed.), *Methodologies of Legal Research: Which Kind of Method for What Kind of Discipline?* (Haywards Heath, Hart Publishing), 4.

Villiers, C. (2013), 'Narrative Reporting and Enlightened Shareholder Value under the Companies Act 2006', in J. Loughrey (ed.), *Directors' Duties and Shareholder Litigation in the Wake of the Financial Crisis* (Cheltenham, Edward Elgar Publishing), 97.

Vogel, D. (2008), 'Private Global Business Regulation', *Annual Review of Political Science*, 11: 261.

Webley, L. (2010), 'Qualitative Approaches to Empirical Legal Research', in P. Cane & H. Kritzer (eds), *The Oxford Handbook of Empirical Legal Research* (Oxford, Oxford University Press), 938.

Zweigert, K. & Kötz, H. (1998), *An Introduction to Comparative Law*, 3rd edn (Oxford, Oxford University Press).

10

The Role of Discourse Analysis in Researching Severe Labour Exploitation

ROBERT CARUANA

Introduction: researching modern slavery

THE EARLIER CHAPTERS IN this book attest to the challenges presented to those who take severe labour exploitation as a central problem in their research. Each challenge is an outcome of the particular research trajectory that is being adopted, the nature of the questions being asked, the unit of analysis pursued, and the political dynamics involved in the production of research. Efforts to provide a clear definition of forced labour, for instance, are faced by the historical 'slipperiness' of the language used to describe it (Doezema 2000), what principal actors such definitions include, and the kinds of practices that it refers to (Quirk 2011). Similarly, attempts to measure incidences of modern slavery encounter problems of data reliability, and the credibility of claims made about its scale, distribution and frequency. Questions concerning reliability also extend into research that has prioritised the victim as the central unit of analysis. Whilst it may be possible that 'getting closer to the victim' yields better research, the continued focus on a victim perspective has marginalised the value of research into the perpetrators of extreme labour exploitation (Crane 2013). Finally, as several chapters argue, the political conditionality of data production, interpretation and implementation – such that what comes to pass as the 'truth' about modern slavery – may be influenced by organisational interests.

In light of these varied methodological challenges, the present chapter outlines the value of adopting discursive methodological approaches to researching severe labour exploitation, as one strategy to overcome some of the persistent challenges presented above. Whilst it does not claim superiority over other methods or immunity from the aforementioned challenges, it does open up an alternative research trajectory through which interested scholars might apprehend severe labour exploitation as a distinct object of research.

Discourse analysis concerns itself with the way in which language is deployed by social actors to produce knowledge about particular phenomena (e.g. modern

Proceedings of the British Academy, **220**, 167–182. © The British Academy 2018.

slavery). In this sense, when thinking about definitions for instance, discourse analysts would be interested in how certain definitions come about, why some become accepted, how others are rejected and/or marginalised, as well as how definitions shape the subjects and practices we come to associate with severe labour exploitation and how this is influenced by socio-political practices. Similarly, because discourse analysis is concerned with investigating 'texts' rather than subjective experiences or verbal accounts, it does not face the same challenges of data access, reliability and researcher ethics. However, this does not mean discourse analysis is an easy way into a difficult phenomenon. Rather, exploring written accounts, visual representations, annual reports, social media, policy documents, websites, poems, songs and even photographs can, in certain contexts, be more methodologically practicable, appropriate and revelatory than talking to the victims themselves.

In this chapter, I will be arguing that discourse analysis helps address the question of how severe labour exploitation is produced as an object of *knowledge* (Fairclough 2013), and how this shapes the *subjects* and *practices* that come to be associated with it. In this socially constructivist view, notions such as 'modern slavery' are not taken as natural, real or fixed phenomena, but as linguistic forms whose meaning is contested by social actors with respective interests in the form they adopt. Modern slavery is, accordingly, seen here as part of a 'discursive struggle' (Livesey 2001) over what severe exploitation means, who it involves and what kinds of remedial practices this articulates for actors in public discourse (Dahan & Gittens 2010). Drawing from a concise cluster of methodological literature, I will outline some of the key conceptual properties of discourse analysis that may be fruitfully mobilised. These will then be applied by drawing upon some textual excerpts from the UK Modern Slavery Act 2015 to demonstrate how different actors with vested interests – corporations, media and NGOs – attempt to construct 'modern slavery'. Through this, severe labour exploitation can be understood as a heterogeneous concept constructed around distinct sets of subjects and practices that are contingent upon actor interests. The following section will consider in more detail what discourse is, and how it might be analysed accordingly.

What is discourse analysis?

To provide a concise, capture-all definition of discourse analysis would be to go against the consensus that it constitutes a fairly wide variety of approaches, theoretical assumptions and methodological techniques (Alvesson & Karreman 2000). Moreover, it can be used in conjunction with a number of other qualitative methods such as ethnography (Covaleski *et al.* 1998), narrative analysis, content analysis, photographic analysis, conversation analysis (Wetherell & Potter 1992), interviews and other archival documentary forms of analysis. This diversity of methods is matched by the potential scope of phenomena that might become the subject of a discourse analysis. Political speech, gender, race, ethnicity, poverty, social control and exclusion, organisational change, immigration and a wide variety of organisational practices have all been subject to some form of discourse analysis. Given this variety of methods and phenomena, what are the properties that actually differentiate discourse analysis from other qualitative techniques?

Discourse analysis concerns itself with the investigation of processes of social construction (Berger & Luckmann 1966). Analysts explore the way in which knowledge of social reality is produced through the purposive use of language (Fairclough 1995). Discourse – as the purposive use of language – is not seen as a benign reflection of a hidden, 'real' social mechanism that determines the behaviour of social actors. It is inherently active in shaping the knowledge of those social actors in the first instance. Discourse analysts cannot therefore assume phenomena such as 'modern slavery' and 'forced labour' are *a priori* categories, reflective of underlying naturally occurring social mechanisms. It is more the case that notions such as 'modern slavery', 'chattel slavery' and/or 'white slavery' constitute specific linguistic representations that have distinct social functions and historical contexts:

> Discourse analysis is concerned not with specifying what sentences are possible or 'grammatical', but with specifying sociohistorically variable discursive formations (sometimes referred to as 'discourses'), systems of rules which make it possible for certain statements but not others to occur at particular times, places and institutional locations.
>
> (Fairclough 1992: 40)

This is not to say that severe forms of labour exploitation do not exist as a subjective experience of a victim, for example, but the way in which it becomes an object of knowledge – about certain kinds of subjects (victim, perpetrator) entailing specific kinds of practices (violence, deception, incarceration) – is a product of discourse.

In this chapter, I will work from the basic idea that discourse constructs knowledge ('ways of knowing') about social identities or subjectivities ('ways of being') and social practices ('ways of doing') (Caruana & Crane 2008; Parker 1992). To illustrate what I mean by this, we can consider in turn Foucault's treatise of the social categories of 'madness' and 'crime' with Joel Quirk's historical account of the anti-slavery movement. Foucault (1972) argues that the category of 'mental illness' was socially constituted in the contested discourses of psychopathology, through all the 'statements that named it, divided it up, described it, explained it' (1972: 32). Crucially, Foucault suggests that discourse produces knowledge of subjects and practices – not only connecting who subjects are with what they can *do* (Parker 1992) but also instructing what practices can be *done to them*. Thus, where the subject 'accused person' moves through the justice system into the position of 'guilty criminal', their 'body' becomes subjected to institutionalised penal practices of incarceration, punishment, isolation and rehabilitation. We can approach notions such as 'modern slavery' in a similar manner – as a category of knowledge about severe labour exploitation involving certain kinds of distinct subjects and practices. For example, whereas for subjects of human trafficking, their exploitation may be deeply connected to practices of movement, social alienation and isolation, for debt bonded labour, such practices are, conversely, associated with the lack of physical movement and the presence of deeply embedded class structures.

It is crucial to note that such subjects and practices do not just appear in or spring from discourse. Their form has context/s – emerging gradually through processes of contestation between powerful social actors. We see this in Quirk's (2011) account of the anti-slavery project in which, following the legal abolition of slavery, (now) 'free labour' was often subjected to novel coercive practices of ex-slave owners and politicians:

> Throughout the nineteenth and early twentieth century, both former slave owners and policy-makers regularly turned to other forms of coercion and compulsion to secure labor on their preferred terms . . . many strategies were developed in pursuit of these goals, including forced labor schemes, taxation in the forms of labor, draconian labor 'contracts', forced recontracting, indentured labor schemes, debt bondage [and] restrictions on movement and land ownership.
>
> (Quirk 2011: 121)

Echoing Foucault indirectly, Quirk's historical account highlights the point that severe labour exploitation has been subjected to socio-political contestation that is responsible for shaping, again, what subjects fall into 'slavery (like)' categories and, in turn, what practices can be done *by* and *to* them. The value that discourse analysis brings to this complexity, therefore, is in the investigation of processes of social construction in which forms of labour exploitation are constructed and legitimated (Wetherell & Potter 1992) and how these shape organisational and institutional responses to them. I elaborate further on this political view of discourse as the chapter unfolds and demonstrate this in relation to my research on the Modern Slavery Act 2015. In the next section we turn our attention to the mobilisation of discourse analysis.

Doing discourse analysis

I have previously stated that there is no one-size-fits-all approach to the analysis of discourse and that there is a manifest variation in approaches that reflects the nature of the research agenda, the ontological assumptions of the researcher and, not least, the object of analysis itself. In deciding upon which 'variety' of discourse (Alvesson & Karreman 2000) we might apply, it is helpful to first understand the relationship between a researcher's theoretical trajectory and the distinct properties of discourse.

Phillips and Hardy (2002) helpfully summarise the varieties of discourse analysis available along two continuums. The first continuum reflects the degree to which researchers are concerned with *processes* of social construction – i.e. how realities are assembled through discourse – as opposed to *power and ideology* – i.e. those powerful actors that shape and constrain that construction of reality. Thus we might discern between studies that focus on how slavery is communicated to consumers – via websites, adverts and product labels – to help them understand what 'fair trade' actually means (McDonagh 2002) and those studies that observe how contemporary forms of slavery are contested through discursive struggles (Livesey 2001) between NGOs and corporations, for example (Dahan & Gittens 2010). The second continuum maps the degree to which researchers are interested in the discursive dynamics within a micro 'text' – such as a single social report, advertisement or corporate website – as opposed to the broader, macro social *context* from which such texts draw their meaning.[1]

It is important to note that these are continuums and are not dichotomous in the sense that researchers focused on the construction processes in texts might also have some interest in their broader socio-political context. In this vein, Fairclough (1995) has argued extensively for a three-dimensional approach to discourse analysis in which the micro linguistics of a text should be analysed in relation to the meso and macro level socio-political practices in which they are simultaneously embedded. This is evidenced neatly in Dahan and Gittens' (2010) study of public responses to child slavery in the cocoa industry. They show that a 'responsible business' frame for addressing labour exploitation is created by vested (cocoa) industry actors as a defensive response to a 'fair trade' frame produced by NGOs that is critical of current business practices. The underlying tensions within these competing discursive frames can be summarised in terms of public calls for more extensive accountability and regulation of business and a countervailing corporate agenda of voluntary self-regulation. In this sense, how the public understands what slavery is/is not has direct implications for the subjects and practices of both NGOs and corporations in that it creates expectations for what constitute appropriate remedial actions (e.g. stricter regulation versus self-reporting). In exploring such 'discursive struggles' we are reminded again that no forms of severe labour exploitation are natural or objective phenomena – at least not to the discourse analyst – but emerge as contested categories of conditioned meaning, as will be demonstrated further below.

Before proceeding to a deeper exploration of discourse analysis as a method, it is necessary to make explicit the status of text both conceptually – as containing tissues of cultural meaning – and methodologically – as the site of data. Firstly, discourse operates in and through texts. It is in and through texts that processes of social construction occur (Phillips & Hardy 2002). Texts are linguistic, social and ideological vessels, in which ways of knowing are assembled with a particular

---

[1] See Fairclough (1992, 1995) for a discussion on 'inter-texuality' and 'inter-discursivity'.

audience in mind (Fairclough 1992). Thus texts are key sites in which knowledge about modern slavery is produced, disseminated and consumed. Moreover, a broad view of discourse makes no qualitative distinction between the value of spoken, written or visual texts. This means that a debate in the House of Commons, a legislative act or report, or even a photograph, can help discourse analysts understand how knowledge about severe labour exploitation is constructed. This is because of the property of 'inter-textuality' (Fairclough 1992), which simply means that texts are always fragments of meanings drawn from other texts, all of which channel and reify certain strands of discourse. So, for example, studying a single company's published corporate social responsibility (CSR) report before and after the UK Modern Slavery Act 2015 was passed may reveal how knowledge of modern slavery has become institutionalised within business auditing practices and whether this has shaped the subjects and practices that businesses associate with severe labour exploitation.

This conceptualisation of discourse analysis opens up a whole range of texts that might be usefully investigated as sites of data collection. Contingent upon the object of research and nature of research questions, corporate reports, NGO and activist websites, photographs, journalistic articles, political speeches, public debates, poetry, songs and even art significantly extend (and to my mind complement) existing research favouring victims' verbal accounts of severe labour exploitation. Moreover, by opening up the boundaries around the data in this way, it is possible to explore the socio-political contexts that shape and orientate knowledge of severe labour exploitation in particular ways. This will be analysed in more detail in the remainder of the chapter.

Constructing severe labour exploitation

In this next section I want to emphasise the *situated* nature of texts in understanding the construction of knowledge about severe labour exploitation. That is, the idea that what is being articulated in discourse on modern slavery is a product of who is talking/writing (text producer) and the intended audience (text consumer), coupled with the specific agent interests that may shape this process. In structuring each section, I first point to key insights from other, thematically similar discourse-based studies to elaborate the theoretical lens being used, before moving on to synthesise this in the context of severe labour exploitation. For the latter, I will draw upon some of the raw data from an ongoing discourse analysis of the UK Modern Slavery Act 2015 that I am undertaking with Andrew Crane and Claire Ingram. Specifically I will draw out some of the discursive forms – particularly *subjects* and *practices* – that the media, government and NGOs used to articulate severe forms of labour exploitation, whilst contextualising the form of discourse in each case.

Constructing subjects: media texts

The construction of subjects associated with modern slavery (e.g. slaves, victims, perpetrators, etc.) is contingent upon who is talking (or writing) about them. Moreover, those organisations constructing subjects of modern slavery (e.g. who is a 'typical victim' or 'perpetrator') tend to do so by their access to pre-existing discourses (e.g. 'sex workers' or 'criminal gangsters'). The property of 'intertextuality' (Fairclough 1995) is important here, in that subjects like modern slaves, migrants or refugees do not simply emerge from nowhere, but are rewoven into the semantic fabric of new texts, rendering novel configurations of subject-types possible. For example, Phillips and Hardy (1997) argue that the 'refugee' subject is constructed as a subject of knowledge from other discourses:

> In the case of the UK Refugee system, discourses that produce a refugee [as a subject] draw on other discourses (the UN's Universal Declaration of Human Rights, for example) and include a wide range of texts including government reports and statements, news reports, cartoons, editorials and demonstrations.
>
> (Phillips & Hardy 1997: 166)

I illustrate here how the subject 'modern slave' is, similarly, constructed from other discourses and that these constructions reflect the local con/text, in this case the socio-political leanings of the UK mainstream press. In this section I will demonstrate how different mainstream media in the UK attempted to construct the 'modern slave', as a distinct subject. In each case, it is evident that the linguistic form of each text anticipates interpretations from a specific audience, such that the common interests of the *Daily Mail* readership give form to the textuality of modern slavery in a way that is distinct from *The Guardian* readership. Whilst each media actor builds a picture of modern slavery of (attention-grabbing) interest to their audience, we can also note a tension playing out across all actors between the degree of exploitation that subjects of modern slavery face.

The passage below from *The Independent* discursively builds a picture of the victims that are normally subjects of modern slavery. The focus of the article is upon the disproportionately high number of women and children (as opposed to men), underlying the vulnerability of subjects. Moreover, the passage connects these *vulnerable subjects* to very extreme, *criminal practices* involving sexual abuse and human trafficking.

> More than 140 **children** were identified as **being trafficked for sexual abuse** last year as the numbers of people rescued from being held as slaves soared by nearly half. The **child victims** included 88 youngsters brought in to Britain from overseas, most commonly from Vietnam and Albania, and another 56 who were UK-born . . . **Sixty-four per cent were female** and 36 per cent were male, while 26 per cent were aged under 18. The increase emerged as the Home Office prepares for a major crack-down on **modern-day slavery**. Theresa May, the Home Secretary, has said she wants tough legislation in place to combat it by the time of the next election in May 2015. The

NCA disclosed that half of the women smuggled into the country **worked as prostitutes**, with smaller numbers forced into domestic servitude or labouring . . . in the **sex industry**.

(*The Independent*, 18 February 2014, emphasis added)

This passage, and others in *The Independent*, articulate modern slavery as involving highly vulnerable subjects, facing extreme (mainly sexual) exploitation. In the next sample from the *Daily Mail* we see other known-to-the-readership, criminal subjects being associated with modern slavery. Whilst the passage below echoes the metaphorical template of the previous passage in *The Independent* – that modern slaves are normally victims of sexual abuse – it extends its account to elaborate more on the subjectivity of the perpetrator:

The indictment alleges that **women and girls** were recruited from city streets or social media to join the **sex-trafficking ring**. The victims then had to deliver their earnings to **pimps** in exchange for protection, food, housing, clothing and cars. The network was run by a **gang** known as BMS, which traces its origins to San Diego's increasingly gentrified North Park neighbourhood in the early 1990s. BMS members have nicknames like 'Pimpsy', 'Stick Up' and 'Li'l Play Doh', prosecutors said.

(*Daily Mail*, 9 January 2014, emphasis added)

Here, and in other media texts (below), we start to see the invocation of organised crime in the guise of gangsters, pimps and the like. This acts as a discursive template for the audience, helping them to understand the kinds of perpetrators involved in severe labour exploitation.

When we look closer at the text, beyond gangster metaphors, we can see other linguistic devices such as normativity and moral panic. In the passage below from *The Telegraph*, the audience is initially panicked by the potential scale of the problem – 'tip of the iceberg':

The discovery of three women allegedly **held as 'slaves' for 30 years** is the '**tip of a rather large iceberg**', according to an MP in charge of reviewing evidence of slavery in Britain. Frank Field, chair of the Modern Slavery Bill evidence review, said **criminal gangs** were making '**huge sums of money**' from people being imported into the UK to work 'almost for nothing'. 'We've had this example of domestic slavery but people are being imported to work, almost for nothing, in industry', he said. 'We've got **begging gangs** being developed, with people being imported. And of course we've got the whole question of how children are being imported to work.' . . . '**It's so shocking** to just be talking to people who have been through this', the Labour MP for Birkenhead said . . . It is thought that the 30-year-old woman had been **held captive all her life**.

(*The Telegraph*, 23 November 2013, emphasis added)

Rather than pointing to 'varied types' of modern slavery subjects, the use of the term 'tip of the iceberg' highlights a very extreme example ('lifelong' incarceration) and suggests it is potentially prolific.

Finally, when we talk about how modern slavery is being defined, we can also see how these metaphorical templates (e.g. organised crime) invoke practices by other institutions (e.g. the government and/or corporations). In the example below, by referring to modern slavery as an organised crime committed by gangsters, this invites conventional remedial practices such as the seizing of assets from gangsters:

> Human trafficking **gangs** are getting away with millions of pounds in profits because the police have no incentive to **freeze their assets**, Home Secretary Theresa May is warned today. MPs warn new laws to tackle modern-day slavery do not do enough to hit gangmasters 'where it hurts' by **confiscating cash** immediately. They urge Mrs May to follow the example of **US gangster Al Capone** who was **brought down in the 1930s through his finances**.
>
> (*Daily Mail*, 4 November 2014, emphasis added)

In all of these short examples, the subjects associated with modern slavery are extreme and highly criminalised. *The Guardian* offers something of a juxtaposition to this emerging view of modern slavery as involving extreme subjects only. It, in contrast, tends to articulate to its audience modern slavery as being on a continuum of exploitation, involving a more nuanced range of subjects from the outright extreme to the more everyday:

> The committee notes that **modern slavery** in the UK **ranges** from the exploitation of adults and children in the sex industry to forced labour, domestic servitude and such forced criminal activities as cannabis farming. It says victims include British schoolchildren, children brought to the UK for benefit fraud and those who are trafficked or come to the country **legitimately and voluntarily** only to find themselves subsequently **enslaved**.
>
> (*The Guardian*, 8 April 2014, emphasis added)

The direct use of the term 'ranges' indicates a broadening view of the types of subjects that might be associated with modern slavery. There is apparent variation in the status of those who might find themselves as victims, with some travelling for legitimate and self-determining reasons (i.e. not trafficked as prostitutes). In continuing the broadening theme, *The Guardian* associates modern slavery here with potentially 'legitimate' actors and spaces (i.e. not only organised crime), such as supply chains and international corporations:

> These reports show **how businesses of all kinds are sullied by slavery** . . .
>
> The reports **pierce several myths**. Many believe that workers who knowingly migrate without papers **cannot possibly be victims**. But traffickers' force, fraud, and coercion can make them just that. Some people, conversely, assume that only undocumented migrants can be victims of human trafficking. But **many legal guest workers are put so deeply into debt by recruiters**, robbed of their autonomy and subjected to such harsh work that they become **veritable slaves**.
>
> Many people **suppose that most trafficking is for sexual exploitation** (as in Thailand's own sex trade) . . . And many executives assume that **tracing labour**

conditions in their supply chains is futile and prohibitively costly. Yet if the Guardian can do it, the **business community** surely can – and must.

(The Guardian, 27 June 2014, emphasis added)

In this extended passage, it is proffered that businesses of all kinds (not just drug or sex gangs) might be subjects potentially associated with modern slavery. Moreover, even legally recruited guest workers might be subjected to practices that are sufficiently similar (Quirk 2011) to produce 'veritable slaves'. The myth-busting narrative employed through the latter part of the passage acts as a debunking device, aimed at undermining the narrower, extreme constructions of modern slavery we saw in the earlier examples. This is most likely because *The Guardian* is championing more extensive legislation and corporate accountability in relation to this issue, which is in alignment with its support for ethical trading initiatives, corporate responsibility and sustainability – key interests of its centre-left audience. And this point is crucial to any discourse analysis of modern slavery. It is not just the subject (modern slave or refugee) that is being constructed in the text but also the organisational identities of other agents implicated in them:

> In the case of refugee discourse, it is not just refugees that are produced; so, too, are the immigration officers that admit them; the decision makers who determine their status; the members of NGOs who provide them with services; the media which report on them; the public who read about them.
>
> (Phillips & Hardy 1997: 169)

Indeed, modern slavery is not only about extremely vulnerable 'victim-subjects' who are shot, raped or sold for sexual exploitation; it can be equally associated with other subjects such as low-paid workers, governments, media and legitimate corporations such as the readership's much favoured John Lewis:

> If **John Lewis**, with its exemplary anti-slavery processes, can find exploitation in its supply chain, what hope for this modern slavery bill?
>
> Last year, 30 miles up the road from my constituency, more than 40 Hungarians were found **working for less than £2 a day** in a mattress factory in Dewsbury, and living in squalid conditions. Crammed into a two-bed flat, they were surviving on food scraps, and were threatened with violence if they complained.
>
> *(The Guardian*, 17 November 2014, emphasis added)

In the context of the previous articles, passages from *The Guardian* provide a countervailing force that seeks a wider range of subjects (both victim and perpetrator) and thus more extensive apparatus for government (legislative requirements for reporting) and corporations (supply-chain auditing) to enact in remediation.

Institutionalising practices: government texts

If the previous section highlighted the actor-contingent context for constructing modern slavery as a certain kind of subject, this next section elaborates on what it can be as a practice. However, rather than looking at practices connected to the specific subject 'modern slavery' (e.g. threats, deception, etc.) we move to a higher level of abstraction and consider the role of discourse in institutionalising certain practices (e.g. auditing, reporting, legislating). In short, this section highlights how severe labour exploitation can become constructed as an object of particular institutional arrangements. In their exploration of slavery in the cocoa industry, Dahan and Gittens (2010: 227) view labour exploitation as an 'ethical public issue' that is socially constructed through framing contests between strategising actors such as the government, firms, NGOs and the media, each actor vying to impose their preferred solution to the issue. In this excerpt from their data analysis they view NGOs' promotion of a mandatory fair trade certification scheme upon the whole cocoa industry as *the* best solution:

> This is why most involved NGOs have rather advocated an **extensive 'fair trade' certification** as the best solution. This is exemplified in this letter addressed to Mars Masterfoods: 'Through the steps outlined in the Protocol, there is no **guarantee** that **prices** will rise to sufficient levels and remain stable. Fair Trade, in comparison to the projects you are funding, is truly a "much more holistic approach".'
>
> (Dahan & Gittens 2010: 236, emphasis added)

In direct response, the industry – resistant to external governance – contests the viability of mandatory certification:

> 'Fair trade' is one of several options to consider. Ultimately, however, Fair Trade is an approach that works best with farms that have access to infrastructure such as communications and warehousing facilities. While our long-term goals include encouraging the development of farmer organizations, currently the majority of farmers in West Africa do not have access to the type of infrastructure that is needed to take part in a fair trade supply chain.
>
> (Dahan & Gittens 2010: 236)

To illustrate this in the context of severe labour exploitation, I use textual excerpts taken from government actors to demonstrate the institutionalisation of certain remedial practices. A useful starting point is to consider the prevailing interests and orientations of the incumbent party, in this case the UK Conservative Party. The period leading up to the Modern Slavery Act 2015 saw quite extensive liberalisation of labour markets under then Prime Minister David Cameron, as evidenced for instance in the proliferation of zero-hours contracts and the promotion of flexible labour practices. What we see in the discursive form of the passages below is an underlying desire not to intervene in business's dealings with labour markets, for example by extending labour legislation over corporations.

In the first passage below, we see a clear orientation to the extreme view of modern slavery that is being circulated in some of the more centre-right media (e.g. as serious, organised crime). The passage is very explicit that only the most extreme subjects are to be included in the definition of modern slavery: identifying a clear 'tipping point' at which it becomes an unequivocal criminal offence:

> I appreciate that, and that is exactly where we want to be at the end of this process: that there is a **simple-to-understand offence** for law enforcement agencies and others, which has an appropriate sentence with it. Clearly, one of the concerns is that **we don't want to end up with relatively minor offences** being brought into the definition. This is an offence that carries a life sentence. This is a **very serious offence**. You talk about the beds-and-sheds-type example and also **miracle babies**. I would be very keen, if you have any suggestions, to make sure that we can capture those offences, because, clearly, if you asked a member of the general public what they mean by modern slavery**, an offence of taking a baby** without permission would probably come within that somewhere. I think we do want to make sure—I don't just think: I know—that we are covering those offences, while keeping the Bill focused and **making sure it is the serious offences** that we are tackling here.
>
> (Karen Bradley MP, Minister for Modern Slavery and Organised Crime, Home Office, examined, emphasis added)

This extreme view of modern slavery continues in the passage below. However, I wish to emphasise more here the practices in the form of institutional responses that are being promoted. In particular, the government is underlining the importance of non-intervention in labour markets, providing an implicit distinction between corporate governance via new or extended legislation over corporations as opposed to voluntary business practices (e.g. reporting):

> I know how important it is for businesses to play their part in tackling modern slavery. I am committed to working with business to eliminate modern slavery from supply chains. That is why we have included a world-leading disclosure requirement in the Modern Slavery Bill to require all large businesses to **disclose what they have done** to ensure their supply chains and own business are slavery free. This measure will **harness consumer and investor pressure by giving them clear information** about what action businesses are taking and will drive businesses to do more to ensure that they do not unknowingly encourage these **heinous crimes**. Many businesses are already taking action to eliminate modern slavery. However, a range of NGOs, Parliamentarians and businesses have also suggested that a specific disclosure requirement focused on modern slavery would be a **nonburdensome way of increasing transparency** further and encouraging businesses to take more action. The Government has been considering these representations carefully, to determine if improvements could be made **without over-complicating existing arrangements**.
>
> (Karen Bradley, Minister for Modern Slavery and Organised Crime, emphasis added. Source: Modern Slavery Bill Factsheet: Transparency in Supply Chains)

From this we could make the argument that the discourse is working to incorporate modern slavery into existing institutional practices of both corporations and governments, rather than changing them. Corporations, for example, are required only to include modern slavery in existing reporting practices, whilst governments, for their part, are similarly attempting to accommodate modern slavery in legislative mechanisms that already exist for high-profile crimes. In the foreword to the Modern Slavery Act it is stated: 'The Bill will **consolidate the** existing slavery and human trafficking **offences into one Act** of Parliament.' In this sense we could start to assemble a more critical argument, if so inclined, for the discourse of the 'status quo' (Livesey 2001): the absorption, simplification and normalisation of something novel into pre-existing, 'known' institutional practices.

Revealing 'realities': NGO texts

Because discourse constructs 'ways of knowing' (Foucault 1972) about the kinds of subjects and practices that, in our case, constitute severe labour exploitation, studies can also consider how dominant constructions stand in for, mask over, other 'ways of knowing'. This notion connects with research that considers the powerful effects of 'representations' or 'myths' (Doezema 2000) in obscuring other potential realities. In their study of New Zealand's tourism representations, Ateljevic and Doorne (2002: 648) regard 'imagery as a political process that encodes and rein-forces the dominant ideology of tourism culture', culminating in the subversion, systematic exploitation and exclusion of Maori communities. Their study draws on a range of historical marketing texts that the tourism board has used to market the country to an international tourism audience. Representations of New Zealand successfully depict a romanticised view of the island and its rich geographic and cultural resources, whilst at the same time presenting, for example, relationships between the (colonising) Anglo-Saxon population and the indigenous Maori popu-lation as civilised and 'trouble free'. Such romanticised representations of the exotic, effectively, mask a historic reality:

> The reality of Maori as largely urbanized people suffering high levels of intergen-erational unemployment, poverty, and incarceration rates is carefully avoided by the contemporary tourism discourse.
>
> (Ateljevic & Doorne 2002: 662)

From this we can consider that as a dominant understanding of what constitutes severe labour exploitation comes to settle in public discourse as *the* view, it may well (perhaps inadvertently) mask other realities. Our research suggests that many of the NGOs are cautious about the narrow, crime-focused constructions of mod-ern slavery. As reported in the more left-oriented media outlets, there was concern from civil society actors that the 2015 Act was rather too narrowly defined to be effective:

> Without the use of indicators of modern slavery, it is **unclear how cases other than the most severe and obvious will be identified** . . . The measures in the draft Bill would be made **more effective**, with regard to both prevention and enforcement, by the **incorporation of such indicators**, either in the Bill itself or in accompanying guidance.
>
> (CORE Coalition 2014: para 4.4, emphasis added)

As distinct from the extreme view, where modern slavery is regularly depicted in the context of extreme illegitimate spaces (e.g. rape, torture, organised crime, the sex industry), NGOs often saw it potentially occurring within more legitimate ones, and involving a broad range of practices – not limited to baby theft or murder:

> In the UK food sector, research identified **at least 14 forced labour practices**, **including**: up-front fees/debt bondage, threats and bullying, disciplining through dismissal, overwork, non-/under-payment of wages, underwork/indebtedness, deductions/charges, documentation abuses, tie-ins (work permits, accommodation, money).
> (Joseph Rowntree Foundation, emphasis added)

Such passages attempt to articulate a broad scope of subjects and practices associated with modern slavery, pointing to the potentially greater scale, pervasiveness and ambiguity. This framing is far removed from the rather static, extreme view that recommends a clear and simple understanding of only the most serious offences. Consequently, by taking these broadening constructions of modern slavery, we are able to ask more critical questions about the ongoing tripartite 'discursive struggles' (Livesey 2001) between corporations, government and civil society actors, whose interests and goals shape how they attempt to construct the reality ('regime of truth') around severe labour exploitation, rendering it as a particular object of knowledge.

Conclusion

As other chapters in this book attest, investigating severe forms of labour exploitation presents a series of particular methodological challenges to researchers in the field. In this chapter I have tried to recommend an alternative trajectory for researchers pursuing a more qualitative research design, which prioritises the role of 'texts' in understanding severe labour exploitation. As discussed, this may require an ontological move on the part of the researcher who, rather than taking notions such as 'modern slavery' or 'forced labour' as *a priori* categories, instead seeks to understand the processes that socially construct the category, that bring it into being as a certain object of knowledge. Having opened the door to a discursive approach, a wide variety of discourse analysis techniques may be deployed that are more or less contingent upon the unit of analysis, object of research and, of course, the nature of the researcher's questions. Whilst these varieties of discourse analysis may convey certain methodological orientations – e.g. towards micro-linguistic processes or macro-political power structures – these are not necessarily dichotomous tendencies. In this chapter, I have suggested that researchers, if so inclined, may usefully combine different levels of analysis such that the linguistic functions of a text (e.g. metaphor, narrative, juxtapositions) can be understood in the context of interpretive effects on particular audiences, and even the macro socio-political forces that shape them. This was unfolded to an extent in considering the different configurations of subjects and practices that were used by different social actors when constructing modern slavery. Ultimately, what this chapter has tried to do for those embarking on a qualitative mode of enquiry, whether it involves interviews, ethnography and/or documentary forms of analysis, is to help them understand how severe forms of labour exploitation are variously constructed as an object of knowledge/s, and how this construction is often contingent upon a socio-political con/text.

References

Alvesson, M. & Karreman, D. (2000), 'Varieties of Discourse: On the Study of Organizations through Discourse Analysis', *Human Relations*, 53, 9: 1125–49. DOI 10.1177/0018726700539002

Ateljevic, I. & Doorne, S. (2002), 'Representing New Zealand: Tourism Imagery and Ideology', *Annals of Tourism Research*, 29, 3: 648–67. DOI 10.1016/S0160-7383(01)00077-9

Berger, P. & Luckmann, T. (1966), *The Social Construction of Reality: A Treatise in the Sociology of Knowledge* (London, Penguin).

Caruana, R. & Crane, A. (2008), 'Constructing Consumer Responsibility: Exploring the Role of Corporate Communications', *Organization Studies*, 29: 1495–519. DOI 10.1177/0170840607096387

CORE Coalition (2014), 'Submission to the Parliamentary Joint Committee on the Draft Modern Slavery Bill', accessed 24 July 2018, http://corporate-responsibility.org/wp-content/uploads/2014/07/Submission-to-Joint-Cttee-on-draft-Modern-Slavery-Bill_CORE-Coalition_10-February-2014_final-with-logos3.pdf

Covaleski, M. A., Dirsmith, M. W., Heian, J. B. & Sanjay, S. (1998), 'The Calculated and the Avowed: Techniques of Discipline and Struggles over Identity in the Big Six Public Accounting Firms', *Administrative Science Quarterly*, 43: 293–327. DOI 10.2307/2393854

Crane, A. (2013), 'Modern Slavery as a Management Practice: Exploring the Conditions and Capabilities for Human Exploitation', *Academy of Management Review*, 38: 49–69. DOI 10.5465/amr.2011.0145

Dahan, N. & Gittens, M. (2010), 'Business and the Public Affairs of Slavery: A Discursive Approach of an Ethical Public Issue', *Journal of Business Ethics*, 92, 2: 227–49. DOI 10.1007/s10551-009-0151-8

Doezema, J. (2000), 'Loose Women or Lost Women? The Re-emergence of the Myth of White Slavery in Contemporary Discourses of Trafficking in Women', *Gender Issues*, 18, 1: 38–54. DOI 10.1007/s12147-999-0021-9

Fairclough, N. (1992), *Discourse and Social Change* (Cambridge, Polity).

Fairclough, N. (1995), *Critical Discourse Analysis: The Critical Study of Language* (London, Longman).

Fairclough, N. (2013), 'Critical Discourse Analysis and Critical Policy Studies', *Critical Policy Studies*, 7, 2: 177–97. DOI 10.1080/19460171.2013.798239

Foucault, M. (1972), *The Archeology of Knowledge* (New York, Pantheon Books).

Livesey, S. (2001), 'Eco-identity as Discursive Struggle: Royal Dutch Shell, Brent Spar, and Nigeria', *Journal of Business Communication*, 38: 58–91. DOI 10.1177/002194360103800105

McDonagh, P. (2002), 'Communicative Campaigns to Effect Anti-slavery and Fair Trade', *European Journal of Marketing*, 36, 5/6: 642–66. DOI 10.1108/03090560210422925

Parker, I. (1992), *Discourse Dynamics* (London, Routledge).

Phillips, N. & Hardy, C. (1997), 'Managing Multiple Identities: Discourse Legitimacy and Resources in the UK Refugee System', *Organization*, 4, 2: 159–85. DOI 10.1177/135050849742002

Phillips, N. & Hardy, C. (2002), *Discourse Analysis: Investigating Processes of Social Construction* (London, Sage).

Quirk, J. (2011), *The Anti-slavery Project: From the Slave Trade to Human Trafficking* (Philadelphia, University of Pennsylvania Press).

Wetherell, M. & Potter, J. (1992), *Mapping the Language of Racism: Discourse and the Legitimation of Exploitation* (New York, Harvester).

11

Archival Trouble:
Researching Sex Trafficking in Early
Twentieth-Century America

JESSICA R. PLILEY

Introduction

IF HISTORY IS AN 'unending dialogue between the past and the present', then it should come as no surprise that a number of historians have taken up many of the themes suggested by movements against what is called modern day slavery and trafficking (Carr 1961: 35). The very term 'modern day slavery' invites historical analysis, as it has embedded within it a comparison to notions of pre-modern, older, historic (legal) slavery (Quirk 2011; O'Connell Davidson 2015). Historians are looking to the past to interrogate the connections, continuities and divergences between the past and current abolitionist movements; compare legal slavery regimes to other forms of forced labour; assess the role of the law and other state instruments of power in anti-slavery policy; consider the economic impact of unfree labour; and, finally, consider the experiences of exploited labourers and the ways they narrate their own experiences (Duane 2017; Swanson & Stewart 2018).

My own work examines the origins and enforcement of federal anti-white slavery (anti-trafficking) laws in the United States. In the late nineteenth and the early twentieth centuries stories of forced sexual slavery circulated throughout the transatlantic world. Descriptions of white slavery declared that urban prostitution was defined by fraud, compulsion, debt bondage and violence. When considering the history and historians' treatment of white slavery, it is important to remember the double nature of the notion of history: there is, on the one hand, the notion of history as a socio-historical process (something that happened in the past) and, on the other, the notion of history as 'knowledge of that process' (how historians tell that story). Critically, 'the boundary between the two meanings is often quite fluid' (Trouillot 1995: 3). In this chapter, I will consider both conceptions of history in order to raise some of the troubles historians face when

Proceedings of the British Academy, **220**, 183–199. © The British Academy 2018.

researching forced labour, shadow economies and trafficking (though my scope here is limited to sex trafficking, rather than other forms of trafficking).

Methodologically, historians are typically restricted to textual analysis as their subjects of study are usually no longer among the living. Cultural historians like Mark Thomas Connelly, Brian Donovan and Miki McElya offer a discursive analysis, similar to the methodology that Robert Caruana suggests in this volume, to understand the cultural work of white slavery narratives (Caruana 2018; Connelly 1980; Donovan 2006; McElya 2017). Social historians, like Timothy J. Gilfoyle, Ruth Rosen and myself, read these same sources in efforts to unravel what these sources can tell us about the practices and locations of prostitution and trafficking in working-class life, urban history and migration, and women's economic opportunities (Gilfoyle 1992; Rosen 1983; Pliley 2014).

When researching the history of sex trafficking, historians quickly encounter the numerous challenges of researching clandestine economies that have operated in the shadow of the law. They frequently contend with incomplete or sensationalising sources that erase the agency of women who sold sex and other individuals who earned a living from the US's boisterous and prosperous prostitution sector, estimated to have earned at least fifteen million dollars a year in both New Orleans and Chicago in the 1910s (Rosen 1983: 69–70). The task of researching anti-prostitution activism is far easier because many of these reformers left rich documentation of their efforts in the awareness-raising books they authored, the interviews to newspapers they gave, the correspondence they wrote, and the institutional records they kept. But anti-prostitution reformers of this period can tell us little about sex trafficking, because they faced many of the same challenges scholars currently face.

This chapter focuses mostly on the United States, though in the last 20 years historians have studied the interconnections among prostitution, migration and trafficking throughout the world. It first considers the politics of the archives that house the sources we rely upon to construct our narratives. It then looks at the challenge of generating reliable data about the numbers of women who sold sex and women who may have been trafficked. It concludes by considering the definitional problems associated with the phrase 'white slavery'.

Archival logics

My book *Policing Sexuality: The Mann Act and the Making of the FBI* (2014) examines the enforcement of the United States' first anti-sex trafficking law – the 1910 White Slave Traffic Act, more commonly known as the Mann Act. The Mann Act prohibited the transporting (or facilitating the transport) of a woman or girl over state lines for the purposes of prostitution, debauchery or 'any other immoral purpose'. Broadly speaking, I argue that anti-trafficking activism led to the building of state power through the fortification of the border control regime that sought to ritualise and rationalise border crossings (McKeown 2013), and through the expansion of federal investigative power by the Federal Bureau of Investigation (FBI). I offer a cautionary tale about the ways that anti-trafficking activism yielded statist responses that shored up law enforcement while disregarding the needs and agency of the 'victims'. To make this argument I rely on over 1,000 Mann Act investigative case files housed at the US National Archives. When I began to research, I was interested in quotidian investigations, cases that may or may not have moved beyond the investigative phase to court proceedings. Little was I aware of the extent to which the politics of the archive itself would shape my project.

Cultural theorists and historians have long noted that archives, especially state-maintained archives like the National Archives, are politicised spaces that need to be interrogated. In a lecture delivered in London in 1994, Jacques Derrida warned,

> Nothing is less reliable, nothing is less clear today than the word 'archive' . . . Nothing is more troubled and more troubling. The trouble with what is troubling here is undoubtedly what troubles and muddles our vision (as they say in French), what inhibits sight and knowledge, but also the trouble of troubled and troubling affairs (as they also say in French), the trouble of secrets, of plots, of clandestineness, of half-private, half-public conjurations, always at the unstable limit between public and private, between the family, the society, the State.

(1996: 90)

The Mann Act investigative case files capture the troubling dynamic of which Derrida speaks, that moment when the unstable boundary between public and private, state and family, is pierced. Interpreting the administrative palimpsest, the dross collected in investigations of moments when people's most private affairs become a public matter of government interest, was my goal. Consequently, my work is much more a social history of the FBI and its cultural values than it is a social history of sex trafficking in the early twentieth century. The Mann Act files capture FBI special agents' voices and concerns, while the voices of the women who sold sex or the women investigated for immorality are fragments, mediated and, often, mere whispers. As the project shifted to one about law enforcement, attending to the nature of the archives became crucial.

In the last 40 years, a critique of the neutral repository status of archives has been waged as many scholars have noted the ways in which archives themselves are sites of cultural production (Foucault 1972; Derrida 1996; Burton 2006; Chaudhuri et al. 2010; Bloin & Rosenberg 2011). Consequently, we must attend to what Ann Laura Stoler calls 'archiving-as-process rather than archiving-as-things' (Stoler 2009: 20). Also, noting the dual nature of the archive as both a place of origins and a place of political and social legitimation, Derrida calls on us to consider the multi-layered dimensions of the archive and archiving practices (Derrida 1996: 4).

Starting from these perspectives, let me offer some details about how the National Archives came to sit on well over 50,000 Mann Act cases investigated from 1910 to 1941. J. Edgar Hoover initially refused to turn any FBI records over to the National Archives when it was established in 1934. But by the 1940s the FBI was drowning in paper and Hoover ordered a review of the Mann Act files from 1910 to 1919. The FBI proposed destroying the records because there did not seem to be any current value in them and they contained 'considerable information of a very personal nature', which could place the FBI in 'an embarrassing position'. The National Archives went to Congress to oppose the destruction, arguing the records might have historic value. In response to political pressure to increase transparency in all FBI records, many of the Mann Act files from before World War II were declassified because they were seen in the post-war period as politically negligent, and the Mann Act was considered a dead-letter law. The availability of the Mann Act cases was a product of a jurisdiction squabble between the National Archives and the FBI. The tension between transparency and secrecy animated these fights but, under the intense political scrutiny the FBI faced in the wake of the revelations of the agency's many sins in the 1970s, the FBI handed over more Mann Act files, while holding back files the agency valued more highly (Theoharis 1994, 1995).

After a 1917 Supreme Court case ruled that the phrase 'any other immoral purpose' meant *any* other immoral purpose, the FBI investigated a wide range of interstate immorality cases beyond its initial mandate of combating sex trafficking. Because of the vagaries of the FBI's filing system and the inconsistent declassification of these records, I could not make any reliable quantitative claims from my research; consequently, my method consisted of reading the files for what they could qualitatively tell me – by reading along and against the archival grain (Stoler 2009).

During the 1920s and the 1930s, the FBI emerged as a stalwart defender of traditional family values that celebrated the centrality of marriage to respectability, the role of the father protector-provider, and female sexual subservience. After J. Edgar Hoover became the head of the FBI in 1924, he mandated that FBI special agents embody an idealised conservative masculinity. Due to these reforms, the bureau 'came to represent a positive, masculinised "federal" approach to crime: special agents, as they negotiated urban squad rooms, popular magazines, newspapers, and interstate investigations, articulated the State as modern; nationalizing practices as beneficial; and federal authority as legitimate and just' (Potter 1998: 33). Consequently, Hoover's modernised bureau was an intensely white, masculine, homosocial space.

The Mann Act investigations reveal special agents' and the FBI's interest in defending the idealised white American family by supporting a 'gender ideology that celebrated female sexual innocence in the young, sexual fidelity in the married, and women in traditional sex roles such as mother and homemaker', especially after the Supreme Court expanded the scope of the Mann Act to include any cases of interstate immorality (Pliley 2014: 138). Each case file included a 'Victim' and a 'Subject' of investigations and women's presumed passivity was encoded in the bureaucratic forms that special agents were required to file. Consequently, Mann Act investigations tended to follow a predetermined script that had been laid out by the administrative duties and cultural attitudes of the investigating special agents. Agents' racial reading of the Mann Act (after all, it was technically called the White Slave Traffic Act) also shaped the administrative agenda of the Act. The FBI routinely refused to investigate cases that involved African American women as victims (Pliley 2014: 99, 144–6).

These case files are narrowly purposed, capturing only the investigating agents' attitudes and reproducing findings characterised by 'fixed formats' and 'empty phrase' (Stoler 2009: 23). Yet, as legal historian Stephen Robertson reminds us, legal sources must be contextualised within the closed systems that produce them in order to be legible (Robertson 2005: 163). In these cases, the bureaucratic culture of the FBI takes precedence over the voices of people engaged in sex trafficking, because it was the FBI that was producing these narratives. What is reflected in the case files is therefore far more revelatory of the values of investigating agents than of the people being investigated. The world of unorganised and organised sex trafficking remained cloaked in the shadows and may remain so given the inherent limitations of archival research.

An old debate: contesting the numbers

Social historians are often asked to estimate the number of women selling sex within any given city in the past. These requests for quantification reflect what Sally Engle Merry calls 'the seductions of quantification' and are part of a general trend towards celebrating statistical knowledge as representing a type of objective 'truth' (2016). As historian Julia Laite reminds us: 'It is an exercise in relative futility to belabour numbers when it comes to the history of prostitution'; yet she concludes, 'One thing is for certain: the number of women selling sex and, even more so, the number of men buying it, has been very high throughout the modern period, and perhaps more consistent than has previously been allowed' (2011: 30).

Sex trafficking – called white slavery in the parlance of the time – emerged as a public concern in the English-speaking world in 1885, after W. T. Stead published his best-selling exposé 'The Maiden Tribute of Modern Babylon', which purported to uncover a miasma of child prostitution, vice and sex trafficking in London. The exposé led to demonstrations in Hyde Park, prompted Parliament to raise the age of consent, and gave a boost to the evangelical anti-prostitution movement in England (Walkowitz 1992). Significantly, publishers around the world republished the series, including the 'purest journals in the great American republic', as Stead boasted (Walkowitz 1992: 82). His story raised the profile of the anti-prostitution movement, leading to the establishment of a series of anti-vice organisations in England and the United States that sought to raise awareness about the issue through the many newsletters and magazines that constituted the 'Purity Press' (Pivar 1973; Pivar 2002, 2014: 19–23, 30–1).

The anti-vice movement was composed of a coalition of collaborating, and at times competing, interests. All of these groups – purity, feminist and social hygiene – sought to combat prostitution, venereal disease and sex trafficking through legal reform, though they frequently sparred with one another over the exact dimensions that legal reform should take (Connelly 1980; Pivar 1973; Pivar 2002; Brandt 1987; Bristow 1996; Luker 1998).

In the late nineteenth century, prostitution was generally legal or tolerated by police, depending on the particular locale. Some countries and cities regulated prostitution through the police by registering women, examining them period-ically for venereal disease, and requiring them to live in particular brothels in specific neighbourhoods. Registration emerged in Napoleonic France as a meas-ure to combat high rates of venereal disease among the military; it soon spread to other countries (Bliss 2001: 27; Limoncelli 2006a: 35; Limoncelli 2006b: 59). As European powers (and the United States and Japan) established their empires, registration of sexual labour became a key feature of colonial regimes the world over (Stoler 2010; Levine 2003; Briggs 2003; Pliley 2016). In other areas, regula-tion became a hotly contested policy. Great Britain famously introduced a highly coercive form of regulation that empowered police to detain and forcibly examine suspected prostitutes in naval ports in 1864. British women's rights and Christian activists led a pitched battle against the Contagious Disease Acts, as they were called, and got them repealed in 1888. In the United States, local municipal laws governed prostitution, and local police departments often informally regulated the sexual marketplace, though cities like St. Louis and El Paso experimented with more formal policies of regulation (Burnham 1971; Gabbert 2003).

Regulation regimes produced mountains of records about the women who came under their purview. At a minimum, age, venereal status and home town would be recorded, as would geographic distribution, but frequently registration regimes produced more detailed information about registered women's age of first sexual encounter, ethnicity or caste, religious affiliation, recruitment methods, and famil-ial and class (occupation of father) background (Walkowitz 1980: 13–31; Corbin 1990; Tambe 2009; Bernstein 1996; Legg 2016). Though the records produced by regulation can be rich in detail and certainly reveal the interests of the biopolitical state, their use is limited due to the fact that, in cities and countries that embraced a policy of regulated prostitution, the vast majority of transactional sex occurred out-side of the gaze of the state. Similarly, police and incarceration records can seem very useful, but because the police targeted the poorest women who sold sex, these records are not representative of *all* of the women who sold sex (Gilfoyle 1994).

Historian Barbara Hobson estimates that over a billion pages of ink were spilled over the issue of prostitution from 1900 and 1924 in the United States (1990: 140). By 1907, stories of exploitative prostitution and sex trafficking could be found in the mainstream media, breaking through what one historian has called the 'conspiracy of silence' surrounding prostitution (Burnham 1973). Muckraking journalists like George Kibbe Turner published widely read investigative reports about sex trafficking and its connections to political corruption to great fanfare. Reformers wrote scores of books that were peddled through magazines, reform groups and door-to-door book salesmen. Ernest Bell's *Traffic in Girls* sold over 400,000 copies. These publications were supplemented by pamphlets and social purity magazines such as *The Philanthropist* – a leading social purity publication – that saw a 50 per cent increase in circulation from 1908 to 1909 (Lagler 2000: 128–31; Brownlow 1990; Stamp 2000: 40–101).

The growing publicity about prostitution and sex trafficking revealed a general dearth of reliable data about sexual labour and prompted calls for solid social-scientific research. In the United States, non-governmental organisations like the American Purity Alliance, the Committee of Fifteen (1900–2) and the Committee of Fourteen (1905–32) in New York City conducted extensive studies, many of which were funded by corporate interests such as John D. Rockefeller's Bureau of Social Hygiene. Additionally, 43 cities organised formal sociologic statistical surveys of prostitution by sending informants into vice neighbourhoods to conduct undercover investigations. Even though these investigations yielded immense amounts of data about prostitution, urban vice and the market for commercialised sex, historians approach such materials with scepticism. Several undercover investigators noted that women who sold sex often gave investigators faulty and incomplete information. For example, investigator Benjamin Reitman claimed the pimps and women who sold sex mocked investigators by providing false information. 'They laugh when they tell me how they answered 47 questions incorrectly out of a possible 50' (1931: 239). Furthermore, as historian Ruth Rosen cautions, vice investigators frequently meddled with the data they collected to produce the outcomes they sought (1983: 138). The vice investigations, though rich in detail, varied widely in their reporting procedures and methodologies, making them particularly difficult to compare or to aggregate (Rosen 1983: 101, fn 1).

Sociologist Howard B. Woolston, writing in 1918, noted that 'complete statistics of all the prostitutes in the country [of the United States] at any time are not to be had. This is simply due to the fact that many women cannot be identified as such. There are various classes of prostitutes, which shade from apparent respectability to the well-established status of women in open brothels' (Woolston 1921: 37). Most of the vice investigators of the 1910s only interviewed sex workers they encountered in legal brothels or prostitutes who had been incarcerated. By the 1910s, various investigators predicted that between 300,000 and 1,633,050 women sold sex in America's cities. Reformers and journalists vigorously debated the accuracy of these figures at the time, and almost all estimates pose their own inter-pretive challenges. Even within a single city, estimates of the number of women who sold sex differed widely. In Chicago, the numbers veered from a low of 5,000 to a high of 68,000 (Connelly 1980: 20). Clearly, the challenges of what Nicola Phillips calls the 'dynamics of distortion' structured early twentieth-century efforts to quantify the problem of prostitution and trafficking. Activists who sought legal reform tended to inflate their estimates of women who sold sex, while city officials and police tended to offer low estimates (Phillips 2018).

The white slave hysteria in the United States expressed anxieties provoked by mass migration to the United States and, from a policy perspective, the United States interpreted sex trafficking as a problem of migration to be fought by build-ing more elaborate and effective border controls. Morality has been policed at the border of the United States since Congress passed the Page Act of 1875 to exclude Chinese prostitutes from entry into the country. Reified by the Immigration Acts of 1903, 1907, 1910 and 1917, and supplemented by the 1910 White Slave Traffic Act, by 1917 the country was engaged in sexual surveillance of women suspected of immorality who were of foreign birth. Taken together, these federal laws mor-alised the borders, making it illegal to bring a woman or girl to the United States or move a woman or girl over state, territorial, colonial and reservation borders for the purpose of prostitution, debauchery or 'any other immoral purpose'. They also outlawed the practice of prostitution by any woman of foreign birth, regardless of her citizenship status.

The US Commission on Immigration noted in 1909 'that the nature of the business precludes, of course, exact statistics regarding the extent of the traffic as to the number of women imported or the number of importers', yet it declared that trafficking to the United States constituted a threat to the country (United States Congress, US Immigration Commission 1911: 7–8). Marcus Braun, a spe-cial investigator of the Immigration Bureau, proclaimed that 50,000 women were trafficked by 10,000 traffickers, mostly of French, Dutch and Jewish extraction, to the United States, and Stanley Finch (1912), the special commissioner of the White Slave Department of the Bureau of Investigation, told the Illinois Senate that, conservatively, at least 25,000 men were involved in trafficking 250,000 women in the United States (Braun 1997; Illinois, General Assembly, Senate Vice Committee 1916: 354; *Fort Wayne Journal-Gazette* 1913).

Identifying women who sold sex at the border posed significant challenges to the Immigration Bureau. From 1910 to 1930, the agents of the Immigration Bureau barred 6,401 people suspected of engaging in commercial vice from enter-ing the country. For the same time period, 7,972 individuals connected to vice were deported. Yet, as the work of historian Martha Gardner has shown, the Immigration Bureau classified women suspected of potentially selling sex as 'likely to become public charges' (LPCs), a classification that had a much lower burden of proof than barring entry or deportation for profiting from selling sex. From 1910 to

1930, immigration officials barred 142,964 individuals from entering the United States under the designation of LPC. The majority of these women were probably suspected of prostitution (United States Department of Labor 1915: 126; United States Department of Labor 1929: 222–4; United States Department of Labor 1930: 239–44; Pliley 2017: 40–1; Gardner 2009; Luibhéid 2002).

These numbers are far lower than the estimates proposed by reformers. British suffragette Theresa Billington-Grieg undertook her own investigation into the prevalence of white slavery in 1913 and could not locate a single case of sex trafficking in England in spite of numerous newspaper stories warning of the dangers of trafficking. She concluded that the anti-vice reformers had waged a 'campaign of sedulously cultivated sexual hysterics' (Billington-Greig 1913: 443). Reformers themselves often recognised the inflated nature of the numbers they circulated. One American suffragist advised in 1912: 'Remember, ladies, it is more important to be aroused than it is to be accurate. Apathy is more of a crime than exaggeration in dealing with this subject' (Laidlaw 1912).

Like today's activists, activists of the early twentieth century were invested in framing sex trafficking and legal prostitution as a pressing concern that demanded legislative responses. And like today's activists, early twentieth-century reformers frequently operated in a 'rigor-free zone' when trying to investigate sex trafficking (Chuang 2014: 609). Those legislative responses most frequently included building the power of the state through two developments that mirrored one another. First, local laws criminalised the selling of sex and empowered local and national law enforcement to enact the new measures (Hennigan 2004; Pliley 2014). Second, because the United States conceived of white slavery as a *foreign* crime, the white slavery panic prompted lawmakers to build on earlier precedents of policing morality at the border. Anti-trafficking and anti-prostitution immigration laws contributed to the development of a more sophisticated border control regime (Hester 2017). Protecting white slaves became a pretext for the growth of the state in the early twentieth century in ways that foreshadowed how anti-trafficking discourses today are used to justify anti-migration policies under the 'migration–crime–security nexus' enshrined in the United Nations Palermo Protocol (Goodey 2008; see also Chapkis 2003; O'Connell Davidson & Anderson 2006; GAATW 2007; Jones & Brown 2014; O'Connell Davidson 2015).

Conclusion: defining the problem

In spite of the problems of reliable quantitative data, the single largest challenge for historians researching the history of sex trafficking and anti-sex trafficking policy is the definitional problem: what is white slavery? The term 'white slavery' has been utilised since the seventeenth century to refer to a wide range of exploitative labour practices, ranging from the forced indentured servitude of Irish workers in the Caribbean in the seventeenth century to the exploitation of white male wage labourers during the birth of America's Industrial Revolution (Peck 2015; Donoghue 2018; Roediger 2005; Soderlund 2013). By the 1910s, the term 'white slavery' had been feminised, yet it remained slippery.

Even when reformers agreed that the term 'white slavery' had something to do with prostitution, they differed widely in their understandings: some argued that 'white slavery' involved only forced prostitution (Billington-Greig 1913), while other reformers suggested that all prostitutes must be white slaves, because what woman would be willing to sell sex unless they were compelled to do so? The parameters of the definition of 'white slavery', like the question of what constitutes 'forced labour' today, were considerably flexible and unstable (Phillips 2018).

In the vagueness that surrounded white slavery, the distinction between the professional prostitute who chose to sell sex and the powerless sex trafficking victim collapsed. Yet, the value of the term 'white slavery' for many reformers was that it discarded the vexing problem of consent and cast all prostitutes as white slaves forced to labour for the profit of another. Anti-white slavery activist and author Clifford Roe defined white slavery as follows: 'The traffic in girls simply means the procuring of girls for immoral lives. That life of open shame, of public prostitution, is so naturally abhorrent to nearly every girl that none go into it except in one of two ways; either they gravitate into it, or they are tricked or trapped into it' (Roe 1911: 97). Though he acknowledged that some women 'gravitated' towards sex work, he argued that selling sex was attractive only because young women did not appreciate the actual exploitative conditions under which they would labour. White slavery made prostitution 'de facto nonconsensual and violent' (Haag 1999: 65).

Most reformers in the United States offered a racialised reading of white slavery, insisting that the danger posed by sex trafficking was the way that it forced white women to sexually service non-white men. This particular understanding of white slavery emphasised the *white* part of 'white slavery' and gained considerable currency in the United States, reflecting the growth of nativism during a period of intense immigration from southern and eastern Europe, on the one hand, and anxieties produced by the establishment of Jim Crow racial segregation in the South that prompted the Great Migration of African Americans to northern cities, on the other. In the United States, white slavery narratives focused on domestic sex trafficking, and most writers emphasised the vulnerabilities of native born, white girls, what one congressman called 'the blue-eyed girl' of America (United States House 1910). Sensational, and highly un-credible, stories of forced prostitution flamed the fears of racial mixing and the subjugation of white girls to men of colour (Donovan 2006).

The racialised reading of the term 'white slavery' was bolstered by the term's reliance on the political salience of the term 'slavery', especially in a country that had fought a brutal civil war over the issue. Many reformers evoked slavery and the American Civil War as part of the rhetorical framing of the problems of prostitution and sex trafficking. Reverend J. G. Shearer asserted: 'At last the great public is coming to recognise that there is a White Slave Traffic, infinitely more inhuman than the black slave traffic, for the suppression of which so much of America's best blood was willingly shed half a century ago' (Roe 1911: 19; Pliley 2014: 28–33). In this formulation, the sacrifice of America's 'best blood' would be dishonoured should another form of slavery take hold in the United States.[1]

The slavery analogy appears throughout the writing on white slavery. English reformer Alfred Dyer reported, as early as 1879, that 'English speaking girls . . . are systematically sought after, entrapped, and sold into a slavery infinitely more cruel and revolting than negro servitude, because it is slavery not for labour but for lust; and more cowardly than negro slavery, because it falls on the young and help-less of one sex only.' Comparisons like this one between forced prostitution and African American chattel slavery were quite common and are deeply problematic, contributing as they did to both the obscuring of any sexual component in under-standings of chattel slavery and the racialising of forced prostitution as a crime only when it occurred to white women (Dyer 2003: 27; Pliley 2017; Peck 2011: 224). The slavery analogy further racialised the term 'white slavery' because the comparison excluded black women as victims of sexual exploitation (Pliley 2014: 165–6; Hine 1989).

Other reformers were more reflective when they made use of the slavery anal-ogy. In 1912, Jane Addams, who tended to use the term 'social evil' in favour of white slavery, suggested that the abolitionist campaign against African chattel slavery provided a useful model of reform. Yet, she warned, 'It is always easy to overwork an analogy' (Addams 1912: 5). Nonetheless, most of the writing about sex trafficking published from the 1880s through to the 1910s uncritically employed the slavery analogy, while also offering definitions of 'white slavery' that were so capacious that they are almost useless and certainly cause all sorts of trouble for social historians seeking to uncover the actual contours of commercial sex markets of the period.

The trouble of the uncritical use of the slavery analogy and the deployment of imprecise terms continues to plague anti-trafficking activists today, especially those activists affiliated with global NGOs like Free the Slaves and Walk Free. Kevin Bales is perhaps the best-known activist who has made a cottage industry out of the use of the slavery analogy, though Bales argues that he is not addressing an analogy but rather a new set of exploitative labour practices that emerged in the second half of the twentieth century to constitute 'the new slavery' (Bales 2012). Nonetheless, Bales' influential book *Disposable People* resonates because he rhe-torically sets up 'new slavery' against the successful abolition of 'old slavery', and

---

[1] Obviously, Shearer ignored the legacy of convict leasing, prison leasing and debt bondage that was endemic to share cropping, as well as other forms of forced labour in the Jim Crow South (Blackmon 2009).

he suggests that the abolitionist struggle is not over, writing: 'We are back to those terms of the abolition campaigns of the nineteenth century: if we are going to stop slavery we must convince the world that human rights need even more protection than property rights' (Bales 2012: 249). Here, Bales echoes Addams by turning to the past for a model of reform. But his approach has generated a number of critiques (O'Connell Davidson 2015). The reliance on the rhetorical power of the term 'slavery' and attempts to distinguish between old and new slavery tend to obfuscate the continuities between transatlantic chattel slavery and other exploitative forms of forced labour (Quirk 2011: 159–63), on the one hand, and to produce an 'erasure of racial slavery', on the other (Woods & Saucier 2017). Similarly, the capaciousness of the term 'white slavery' prefigured the way that current international law about trafficking, as embodied in the Palermo Protocol, tends to be painfully imprecise in how it defines terms like 'exploitation', 'vulnerability' and 'coercion' (O'Connell Davidson & Anderson 2006). The role of consent is similarly problematic.

The resonances between anti-trafficking campaigns of the past and those of the present are striking. Many scholars of contemporary sex trafficking have looked to the past to explore the ways that views on white slavery reflected and validated circulating anxieties about women's sexuality, im/migration and sexual labour (Rubin 1975, 1984; Doezema 1999; Bernstein 2007; Berg & Boris 2014; Bromfield 2016). Shifting attention to the enforcement of anti-trafficking laws reminds us of the political utility of vague terms like 'white slavery' that can constitute a wide array of meanings to a diverse set of actors. Yet the vagaries surrounding white slavery ultimately yielded statist responses – the expansion of interlocking law enforcement and border control regimes. Though historians are uniquely positioned to shed light on these continuities, we must remain vigilant to the ways that our sources, and their institutional depositories, shape the narratives we are able to tell. The 'trouble of troubles and troubling affairs' can be multi-layered: definitional, quantitative and archivally compromising (Derrida 1996).

References

Addams, J. (1912), *A New Conscience for the Ancient Evil* (New York, Macmillan).

Bales, K. (2012), *Disposable People: New Slavery in the Global Economy* (Berkeley, University of California Press).

Berg, H. & Boris, E. (2014), 'Protecting Virtue, Erasing Labor: Historical Responses to Trafficking', in K. K. Hoang & R. S. Parrañas (eds), *Human Trafficking Reconsidered: Rethinking the Problem, Envisioning New Solutions* (New York, International Debate Education Association), 19–29.

Bernstein, L. (1996), *Sonia's Daughters: Prostitutes and Their Regulation in Imperial Russia* (Berkeley, University of California Press).

Bernstein, E. (2007), *Temporarily Yours: Intimacy, Authenticity, and the Commerce of Sex* (Chicago, IL, University of Chicago Press).

Billington-Greig, T. (1913), 'The Truth about White Slavery', *English Review*, 14: 428–46.

Blackmon, D. (2009), *Slavery by Another Name: The Re-enslavement of Black Americans from the Civil War to World War II* (New York, Anchor).

Bliss, K. (2001), *Compromised Positions: Prostitution, Public Health, and Gender Politics in Revolutionary Mexico City* (University Park, Pennsylvania State University Press).

Bloin, F. X. & Rosenberg, W. (2011), *Processing the Past: Contesting Authority in History and Archives* (New York, Oxford University Press).

Brandt, A. M. (1987), *No Magic Bullet: A Social History of Venereal Disease in the United States since 1880* (New York, Oxford University Press).

Braun to Commissioner General of Immigration, Braun US White Slavery Report, September 29, 1908 (1997), Records of the Immigration and Naturalization Service, Series A: Subject Correspondence Files, Part 5: Prostitution and 'White Slavery' roll 3, 4: 23–4. (Bethesda, MD, University Publications of America).

Briggs, L. (2003), 'Familiar Territory: Prostitution, Empires, and the Question of U.S. Imperialism in Puerto Rico, 1849–1916', in L. Haney & L. Pollard (eds), *Families of a New World: Gender Politics and State Development in a Global Context* (New York, Routledge), 40–63.

Bristow, N. K. (1996), *Making Men Moral: Social Engineering during the Great War* (New York, New York University Press).

Bromfield, N. (2016), 'Sex Slavery and Sex Trafficking of Women in the United States: Historical and Contemporary Parallels, Policies, and Perspectives in Social Work', *Affilia*, 31, 1: 129–39.

Brownlow, K. (1990), *Behind the Mask of Innocence: Sex, Violence, Crime – Films of Social Conscience in the Silent Era* (New York, Alfred A. Knopf).

Burnham, J. C. (1971), 'Medical Inspection of Prostitutes in America in the Nineteenth Century: The St. Louis Experiment and Its Sequel', *Bulletin of the History of Medicine*, 54, 3: 203–18.

Burnham, J. (1973), 'The Progressive Era Revolution in American Attitudes toward Sex', *Journal of American History*, 59, 4: 885–908.

Burton, A. (2006), *Archive Stories: Fact, Fiction, and the Writing of History* (Durham, NC, Duke University Press).

Carr, E. H. (1961), *What Is History?* (New York, Vintage Books).

Caruana, R. (2018), 'The Role of Discourse Analysis in Researching Severe Labour Expoitation', in G. LeBaron (ed.), *Researching Forced Labour in the Global Economy* (Oxford, Oxford University Press).

Chapkis, W. (2003), 'Trafficking, Migration, and the Law: Protecting Innocents, Punishing Immigrations', *Gender & Society*, 17, 6: 923–37.

Chaudhuri, N., Katz, S. J. & Perry, M. E. (2010), *Contesting the Archives: Finding Women in the Sources* (Urbana, University of Illinois Press).

Chuang, J. (2014), 'Exploitation Creep and the Unmaking of Human Trafficking Law', *American Journal of International Law*, 108, 4: 609–49.

Connelly, M. T. (1980), *The Response to Prostitution in the Progressive Era* (Chapel Hill, University of North Carolina).

Corbin, A. (1990), *Women for Hire: Prostitution and Sexuality in France after 1850* (Cambridge, MA, Harvard University Press).

Derrida, J. (1996), *Archive Fever*, trans. E. Prenowitz (Chicago, IL, University of Chicago Press).

Doezema, J. (1999), 'Loose Women or Lost Women? The Re-emergence of the Myth of White Slavery in Contemporary Discourses of Trafficking in Women', *Gender Issues*, 18, 1: 23–50.

Donoghue, J. (2018), 'Kidnappers and Subcontractors: Historical Perspectives on Human Trafficking', in E. Swanson & J. B. Stewart (eds), *Human Bondage and Abolition: New Histories of Past and Present Slaveries* (New York, Cambridge University Press), 123–53.

Donovan, B. (2006), *White Slave Crusades: Race, Gender, and Anti-vice Activism, 1887–1917* (Chicago, IL, University of Chicago Press).

Duane, A. M. (2017), *Child Slavery before and after Emancipation: An Argument for Child-Centered Slavery Studies* (New York, Cambridge University Press).

Dyer, A. (2003), 'The European Slave Trade in English Girls (1880)', in J. Jordan & I. Sharp (eds), *Josephine Butler and the Prostitution Campaigns: Diseases of the Body Politic: Vol IV Child Prostitution and the Age of Consent* (London, Routledge), 25–54.

Finch, S. W. (1912), *The White Slave Traffic*, US Senate Doc. 62nd Congress, 3rd Session, Document No. 983, Government Printing Office.

Fort Wayne Journal-Gazette (1913), 'United States in New War on White Slavery' (27 April 1913), 43.

Foucault, M. (1972), *The Archeology of Knowledge*, trans. A. S. Smith (New York, Pantheon).

GAATW (2007), *Collateral Damage: The Impact of Anti-trafficking Measures on Human Rights around the World* (Bangkok, Global Alliance against Traffic in Women).

Gabbert, A. R. (2003), 'Prostitution and Moral Reform in the Borderlands: El Paso, 1890–1920', *Journal of the History of Sexuality*, 12, 4: 575–604.

Gardner, M. (2009), *The Qualities of a Citizen: Women, Immigration, and Citizenship, 1870–1965* (Princeton, NJ, Princeton University Press).

Gilfoyle, T. J. (1992), *City of Eros: New York City, Prostitution, and the Commercialization of Sex, 1790–1920* (New York, W. W. Norton & Company).

Gilfoyle, T. J. (1994), 'Prostitutes in the Archives: Problems and Possibilities in Documenting the History of Sexuality', *American Archivist*, 57, 3: 514–27.

Goodey, J. (2008), 'Human Trafficking: Sketchy Data and Policy Responses', *Criminology & Criminal Justice*, 8, 4: 421–42.

Haag, P. (1999), *Consent: Sexual Rights and the Transformation of American Liberalism* (Ithaca, NY, Cornell University Press).

Hennigan, P. (2004), 'Property War: Prostitution, Red-Light Districts, and the Transformation of Public Nuisance Law in the Progressive Era', *Yale Journal of Law and Humanities*, 16: 123.

Hester, T. (2017), *Deportation: The Origins of US Policy* (University Park, University of Pennsylvania Press).

Hine, D. C. (1989), 'Rape and the Inner Lives of Black Women in the Middle West: Preliminary Thoughts on the Culture of Dissemblance', *Signs*, 14, 4: 912–20.

Hobson, B. (1990), *Uneasy Virtue: The Politics of Prostitution and the American Reform Tradition* (Chicago, IL, Chicago University Press).

Illinois, General Assembly, Senate Vice Committee (1916), *Report of the Senate Vice Committee: Created under the Authority of the Forty-Ninth General Assembly* (Chicago, State of Illinois Press).

Jones, J. A. M. & Brown, H. E. (2014), 'Contradictions and Complications: Trafficking Protections and Immigration Enforcement in Local Practice', in K. K. Hoang & R. S. Parrañas (eds), *Human Trafficking Reconsidered: Rethinking the Problem, Envisioning New Solutions* (New York, International Debate Education Association), 81–90.

Lagler, A. R. (2000), '"For God's Sake Do Something": White-Slavery Narratives and Moral Panic in Turn-of-the-Century American Cities', PhD thesis, Michigan State University.

Laidlaw, H. (1912), 'The A.B.C.s of the Question', 2, 3, File 77, H. B. (Harriet Burton) Laidlaw Papers, 1851–1958, Schlesinger Library, Radcliffe Institute, Harvard University, Cambridge, MA.

Laite, J. (2011), *Common Prostitutes and Ordinary Citizens: Commercial Sex in London, 1885–1960* (London, Springer).

Legg, S. (2016), 'Anti-vice Lives: Peopling the Archives of Prostitution in Interwar India', in J. R. Pliley, R. Kramm & H. Fischer-Tiné (eds), *Global Anti-vice Activism, 1890–1950: Fighting Drink, Drugs, and 'Immorality'* (Cambridge, Cambridge University Press), 246–69.

Levine, P. (2003), *Prostitution, Race, and Politics: Policing Venereal Disease in the British Empire* (New York, Routledge).

Limoncelli, S. A. (2006a), 'International Voluntary Associations, Local Social Movements and State Paths to the Abolition of Regulated Prostitution in Europe, 1875–1950', *International Sociology*, 21, 1: 31–59.

Limoncelli, S. A. (2006b), 'The Politics of Humanitarianism: States, Reformers, and the International Movement to Combat the Traffic in Women 1875–1960', PhD thesis, University of California at Los Angeles.

Luibhéid, E. (2002), *Entry Denied: Controlling Sexuality at the Border* (Minneapolis, University of Minnesota Press).

Luker, K. (1998), 'Sex, Social Hygiene, and the State: The Double-Edged Sword of Social Reform', *Theory and Society*, 27, 5, 601–34.

McElya, M. (2017), 'The White Slave: American Girlhood, Race, and Memory at the Turn of the Century', in A. M. Duane (ed.), *Child Slavery before and after Emancipation: An Argument for Child-Centered Slavery Studies* (New York, Cambridge University Press), 80–102.

McKeown, A. (2013), *Melancholy Order: Asian Migration and Globalization of Borders* (New York, Columbia University Press).

Merry, S. E. (2016), *The Seductions of Quantification: Measuring Human Rights, Gender Violence, and Sex Trafficking* (Chicago, IL, University of Chicago Press).

O'Connell Davidson, J. (2015), *Modern Slavery: The Margins of Freedom* (London, Palgrave Macmillan).

O'Connell Davidson, J. & Anderson, B. (2006), 'The Trouble with "Trafficking"', in C. L. V. D. Anker & J. Doomernik (eds), *Trafficking and Women's Rights* (New York, Palgrave Macmillan), 11–26.

Peck, G. (2011), 'Feminizing White Slavery in the United States: Marcus Braun and the Transnational Traffick in White Bodies, 1890–1910', in L. Fink (ed.), *Workers across the Americas: The Transnational Turn in Labor History* (New York, Oxford University Press), 221–44.

Peck, G. (2015), 'Trafficking Servants, White and Black: Whiteness, Anti-Slavery, and the Origins of Humanitarian Rescue, 1660–1720', paper presented at Human Trafficking: Labor Migration and Migration Control in Comparative Historical Perspective Conference, 16–17 October 2015, Chicago, IL, University of Chicago.

Phillips, N. (2018), 'The Politics of Numbers: Beyond Methodological Challenges in Research on Forced Labour', in G. LeBaron (ed.), *Researching Forced Labour in the Global Economy* (Oxford, Oxford University Press).

Pivar, D. J. (1973), *Purity Crusade: Sexual Morality and Social Control, 1868–1900* (Westport, CT, Greenwood Press).

Pivar, D. J. (2002), *Purity and Hygiene: Women, Prostitution, and the "American Plan"* (Westport, CT, Greenwood Press).

Pliley, J. R. (2014), *Policing Sexuality: The Mann Act and the Making of the FBI* (Cambridge, MA, Harvard University Press).

Pliley, J. R. (2016), 'The FBI's White Slave Division: The Creation of a National Regulatory Regime to Police Prostitutes in the United States, 1910–1918', in J. R. Pliley, R. Kramm & H. Fischer-Tiné (eds), *Global Anti-vice Activism: Fighting Drink, Drugs, & 'Imorality,' 1880–1950* (Cambridge, Cambridge University Press), 221–45.

Pliley, J. R. (2017), 'Protecting the Young and the Innocent: Age, Consent, and the Enforcement of the White Slave Traffic Act', in A. M. Duane (ed.), *Childhood Slavery Before and After Emancipation* (New York, Cambridge University Press).

Potter, C. (1998), *War on Crime: Bandits, G-Men, and the Politics of Mass Culture* (New Brunswick, NJ, Rutgers University Press).

Quirk, J. (2011), *The Anti-slavery Project: From the Slave Trade to Human Trafficking* (Philadelphia, University of Pennsylvania Press).

Reitman, B. (1931), *The Second Oldest Profession* (New York, Vanguard).

Robertson, S. (2005), 'What's Law Got to Do With It? Legal Records and Sexual Histories', *Journal of the History of Sexuality*, 14, 1/2: 161–85.

Roe, C. G. (1911), *The Horrors of the White Slave Trade: The Mighty Crusade to Protect the Purity of Our Homes* (Chicago, Clifford G. Roe and B. S. Steadwell).

Roediger, D. (2005), *The Wages of Whiteness: Race and the Making of the American Working Class* (New York, Verso Books).

Rosen, R. (1983), *The Lost Sisterhood: Prostitution in America, 1900–1918* (Baltimore, MD, Johns Hopkins Press).

Rubin, G. (1975), 'The Traffic in Women: On the "Political Economy" of Sex', in R. Reiter (ed.), *Toward an Anthropology of Women* (New York, Monthly Review Press), 157–210.

Rubin, G. (1984), 'Thinking Sex: Notes for a Radical Theory of the Politics of Sexuality', in C. S. Vance (ed.), *Pleasure and Danger: Exploring Female Sexuality* (Boston, MA, Routledge and Kegan Paul), 267–319.

Soderlund, G. (2013), *Sex Trafficking, Scandal, and the Transformation of Journalism, 1885–1917* (Chicago, IL, Chicago University Press).

Stamp, S. (2000), *Movie-Struck Girls: Women and Motion Picture Culture after the Nickelodeon* (Princeton, NJ, Princeton University Press).

Stoler, A. L. (2009), *Along the Archival Grain: Epistemic Anxieties and Colonial Common Sense* (Princeton, NJ, Princeton University Press).

Stoler, A. L. (2010), *Carnal Knowledge and Imperial Power: Race and the Intimate in Colonial Rule* (Durham, NC, Duke University Press).

Swanson, E. & Stewart, J. B. (2018), *Human Bondage and Abolition: New Histories of Past and Present Slaveries* (New York, Cambridge University Press).

Tambe, A. (2009), *Codes of Misconduct: Regulating Prostitution in Late Colonial Bombay* (Minneapolis-St. Paul, University of Minnesota Press).

Theoharis, A. (1994), *The FBI: An Annotated Bibliography and Research Guide* (New York, Garland Publishing).

Theoharis, A. (1995), *J. Edgar Hoover, Sex, and Crime: An Historical Anecdote* (Chicago, IL, Ivan R. Dee).

Trouillot, M.-R. (1995), *Silencing the Past: Power and the Production of History* (Boston, MA, Beacon).

United States Congress, US Immigration Commission, 1907–1910 (1911), 'Importation and Harboring of Women for Immoral Purpose', in *Reports of the Immigration Commission* (Washington, DC, Government Printing Office).

United States Department of Labor (1915), *Annual Reports of the Commissioner General of Immigration to the Secretary of Labor* (Washington, DC, Government Printing Office).

United States Department of Labor (1929), *Annual Report of the Commissioner General of Immigration to the Secretary of Labor* (Washington, DC, Government Printing Office).

United States Department of Labor (1930), *Annual Report of the Commissioner General of Immigration to the Secretary of Labor* (Washington, DC, Government Printing Office).

United States House (1910), Congressional Record (19 January 1910), 45, 811 (Washington, DC, Government Printing Office).

Walkowitz, J. (1980), *Prostitution and Victorian Society: Women, Class, and the State* (Cambridge, Cambridge University Press).

Walkowitz, J. R. (1992), *City of Dreadful Delight: Narratives of Sexual Danger in Late-Victorian London* (Chicago, IL, University of Chicago).

Woods, T. P. & Saucier, P. K. (2017), 'The Sadism of Anti-Trafficking and the Erasure of Racial Slavery', *openDemocracy: Beyond Trafficking and Slavery*, https://www.opendemocracy.net/beyondslavery/tryon-p-woods-p-khalil-saucier/sadism-of-anti-trafficking-and-erasure-of-racial-slaver

Woolston, H. B. (1921), *Prostitution in the United States* (New York, The Century Company).

Index